SCENARIOS FOR

SUCCESS

SCENARIOS FOR
SUCCESS

Turning Insights into Action

Edited by

Bill Sharpe
and
Kees Van der Heijden

John Wiley & Sons, Ltd

Other Wiley Editorial Offices

John Wiley & Sons Inc., 111 River Street, Hoboken, NJ 07030, USA

Jossey-Bass, 989 Market Street, San Francisco, CA 94103-1741, USA

Wiley-VCH Verlag GmbH, Boschstr. 12, D-69469 Weinheim, Germany

John Wiley & Sons Australia Ltd, 42 McDougall Street, Milton, Queensland 4064, Australia

John Wiley & Sons (Asia) Pte Ltd, 2 Clementi Loop #02-01, Jin Xing Distripark, Singapore
129809

John Wiley & Sons Canada Ltd, 6045 Freemont Blvd, Mississauga, ONT, L5R 4J3, Canada

Wiley also publishes its books in a variety of electronic formats. Some content that appears in
print may not be available in electronic books.

Anniversary Logo Design: Richard J. Pacifico

British Library Cataloguing in Publication Data

A catalogue record for this book is available from the British Library

ISBN 978-0-470-51298-2 (HB)

Typeset in 11.5/15pt Bembo by Integra Software Services Pvt. Ltd, Pondicherry, India
Printed and bound in Great Britain by TJ International Ltd, Padstow, Cornwall, UK
This book is printed on acid-free paper responsibly manufactured from sustainable forestry in
which at least two trees are planted for each one used for paper production.

CONTENTS

LIST OF CONTRIBUTORS

Bill Sharpe

Independent researcher in future studies of technology. Prior to 1999 he was a research director at Hewlett Packard Laboratories researching everyday applications of computing. He then co-founded his innovation and consulting company, the Appliance Studio, and has since specialized in long-range technology studies for business and public policy foresight. He now works independently and as an Associate with several other organizations in the futures field.

Associate www.normannpartners.com
Associate www.martininstitute.ox.ac.uk
Member www.internationalfuturesforum.org
Email: bill.sharpe@appliancestudio.com

Professor Cornelius (Kees) A.J.M. Van der Heijden

Kees is currently an Associate Fellow at the Said Business School, University of Oxford, UK. He is an emeritus professor of General and Strategic Management at the University of Strathclyde, Glasgow. He is the author of *Scenarios: The Art of Strategic Conversation*, and the lead author of *The Sixth Sense*. Prior to 1991, he headed the business environment division of Group Planning at Royal Dutch/Shell, responsible for monitoring and analysing the business environment, scenario planning and communicating with top management on strategic implications. Previously, he headed Shell's internal strategic consultancy group.

Global Business Network co-founder
Email: Kees.Vanderheijden@templeton.ox.ac.uk

Ronald Michael Bradfield

Director, University of Strathclyde Business School UAE
Strathclyde Business School, International Division, Sir William Duncan Bldg., 199 Cathedral Street, Glasgow, G4 0GE
Email: ron@gsb.strath.ac.uk

Andrew Curry

Director, Henley Centre HeadlightVision
Henley Centre HeadlightVision, 6 More London Place, Tooley Street, London, SE1 2QY
Email: andrew.curry@hchlv.com / andrew.nextwave@googlemail.com

Alexander Fink

Founder and Member of Executive Board, ScMI Scenario Management International AG
ScMI Scenario Management International, Klingenderstr. 10–14, 33100 Paderborn, Germany
Email: fink@scmi.de

Phil Hadridge

Co-founder, idenk Ltd
+44 (0)7867 538 184
Email: Phil.hadridge@idenk.com

Don Heathfield

President, The Future Map
The Future Map, 111 Trowbridge Street, Unit 9, Cambridge, Massachusetts, 02138 USA
Email: dh@thefuturemap.com

Anthony Hodgson

Founder, Director, Decision Integrity Ltd
Email: tony@decisionintegrity.com

Karim Medjad

Associate Professor of Law, HEC PARIS
GREGHEC, unité CNRS (UMR 2959)
Email: medjad@hec.fr

Lennart Nordfors

PhD political science; deputy CEO Gullers Group
Gullers Grupp, Box 7004, 103 86 Stockholm
Email: lennart.nordfors@gullers.se

Rafael Ramírez

Professor of Management, www.hec.rf
Fellow in Strategic Management, www.sbs.ox.ac.uk and www.templeton.ox.ac.uk
Associate Fellow, www.martininstitute.ox.ac.uk
Director, Oxford Scenarios Masters Class, www.sbs.oxford.edu/scenariomasters

Gill Ringland

CEO & Fellow, SAMI Consulting
Sami Consulting, 152 Tachbrook Street, London SW1V 2EN
Email: gill.ringland@samiconsulting.co.uk

Paul De Ruijter

Director, De Ruijter Strategy bv
De Ruijter Strategy, Amsterdamseweg 423, 1181 BP Amstelveen, The
    Netherlands
Tel. +31-20-6250214
Email: info@deruijter.net web: www.deruijter.net

Cynthia Selin

Assistant Research Faculty
Center for Nanotechnology in Society (CNS) & Consortia for
    Science, Policy and Outcomes (CSPO), Arizona State University
    Tempe, AZ USA
Email: Cynthia.Selin@asu.edu

James Tansey

Chair in Business Ethics
Associate Fellow, James Martin Institute for Science and Civilization
Sauder School of Business and the W. Maurice Young Centre for
    Applied Ethics, University of British Columbia, 6356 Agricultural
    Road, Vancouver, BC, V6T 1Z2, Canada
Email: james.tansey@sauder.ubc.ca

Jan Verloop

Founding Director, Causa Innovatie
Jozef Israëlslaan 30, 2596 AR The Hague, The Netherlands

PREFACE

Scenarios have been used in companies for over three decades and even longer by military planners and policy makers. In business, Shell's successful use of them to anticipate oil crises gave them prominence in the private sector. The Lexis–Nexis press database identifies over 400 papers annually on the topic, and about 450 academic papers are cited each year on the subject of scenarios in social science journals. Thus scenarios have now become part of the landscape in business strategy and public policy.

The year 2005 marked the 40th anniversary of two important events in the history of scenario practice. The first was the production of the initial scenarios (on French energy) by Pierre Wack. He is credited with having been the first individual to institutionalize scenarios in a corporate context (within Royal Dutch/Shell), and everyone who worked with him remembers him as a remarkable individual. He has passed away, but remembering his work and utilizing its insights in the future is regarded as essential by leading practitioners. The second event, coincidentally also 40 years ago, was the publication of Emery and Trist's seminal paper 'The causal texture of organizational environments' in *Human Relations*, which provided the first theoretical underpinning of what scenario thinking and planning is about.

To mark this anniversary John Selsky of the University of South Florida and Rafael Ramírez and Kees Van der Heijden of Oxford University convened the 'Oxford Futures Forum' (www.oxfordfuturesforum.org) at Templeton College, Oxford University, in November 2005 to further the understanding of scenario practice and thinking. The overarching theme was: 'What have we learnt in the last 40 years?' At the same time they worked with Napier Collyns and Jaap Leemhuis to arrange for Templeton College to accept and take care of Pierre Wack's library and personal papers. The library was formally opened at the 2005 Forum.

The conveners invited to the Forum academics and practitioners interested in scenario thinking and practice, or research into turbulent environments. Seventy participants came to the Forum for which the ticket to participate was: a brief written contribution to the 'strategic conversation'; and an openness to deliberate on the issues assembled with other participants.

Over the course of two days the participants self-organized into an intensive series of conversations, sharing both their learning from practice and new theoretical insights. The participant abstracts and notes from the meeting are available on the Forum website.

The convenors felt the dialogue at the Forum was so rich that it needed to be placed before a wider audience. They invited participants to contribute chapter-length papers for possible publications that would build on the work of the Forum. Going through the submissions, the organizers found a logical cluster around the topic of scenarios and strategy. It became clear that in those contributions many insights were 'leading edge', never published before, and the material justified being collected in a book for wider distribution. The book is built on first-hand experience, and authors agreed to include detailed reflection on actual case studies wherever possible. This volume is the result of these efforts.

ACKNOWLEDGEMENTS

The editors would like to acknowledge here the help of several individuals who agreed to be interviewed for these chapters or provided important input: Philip Idenburg, former corporate strategist at Rabobank for his cooperation in writing the Rabobank case; Angela Wilkinson for her input to the chapter on scenarios and innovation; and Chris Metcalfe, among many others. We would like to thank those who provided detailed case studies but chose to remain anonymous to retain confidentiality.

Particular thanks are due to Peter Schwartz and Napier Collyns for their interviews which were so helpful in framing the key issues explored in this book.

Finally, we are pleased to thank Templeton College for hosting the 2005 Oxford Futures Forum and Andromache Athanasopoulou for her organizing talent and dedication.

OVERVIEW

How can organizations survive and thrive in a world of growing complexity and rapid, unpredictable change? What degree of influence do leaders have and what insights do they need to develop? What tools can leaders use to guide decisions that may have far-reaching impact for success, and even survival, when they must look far beyond the familiar and knowable conditions of their current daily business? Decisions that shape the future of an organization beyond its current activities are the domain of strategy making, and over the last 30 years many organizations have used the practice of scenario thinking to help them to explore strategic questions of future direction and policy design.

Scenario thinking has stood the test of time as an approach to organizing thinking about the future in ways that can be built up into a repeatable practice and applied to any domain of strategy making, from long-range global public policy to the business plan of an entrepreneurial start-up. From its early days in the 1960s a generation of practitioners has taken the core of the approach and built it into a wide range of methods. In the process they have produced a powerful body of work, seen in organizations that have found effective action in the face of major change. This strength can be attributed to the way that scenario thinking, viewed as a cognitive skill, helps us to hold in creative tension many opposing ways of future thinking, and integrates them into one overall methodology – reducing unmanageable confusion to a more structured uncertainty. Practising these skills has proved to be a major step forward in the quality of long-range thinking.

However, there has been a growing realization that even the best scenario practice does not always result in entirely satisfied strategists. Specifically, the connection between the analysis of the business environment and firm conclusions for strategic action by the organization has sometimes been weak, producing a 'so what' response from the very people it is intended to inform. Against many scenario projects that have helped a senior team to navigate a major change, there are others where the scenario builders are bewailing that they cannot bring the results of their work through to the needed strategic decision making, that their organization failed to act in time to grasp an opportunity, or did not prepare for major changes to the environment that their scenarios had revealed.

Leading practice, as reported in this book, reveals three key requirements for the effective use of scenarios in strategy, relating to the context in which they are used, their content, and the process by which managers are engaged in using them.

- *A proactive, innovative context for use.* The primary purpose of using scenarios is to prepare for strategic change. By strategic change we mean initiatives that bring new relationships, value chains and constellations into existence. The day-to-day operation of any business rests on the stability of a wide set of relationships which do things in repeatable ways. Within these relationships there may be continuous innovation to maintain a competitive position, and many changes of individual relationships as individual players in the system are replaced by others; but the overall pattern of who does what will be evolving in fairly gradual and incremental ways. The game will manifest discontinuous change when, through internal initiative or changes in the broader context, these relationships must be significantly reconfigured. The first requirement for effective use is therefore a willingness on the part of decision makers to open up their thinking to the possibility of strategic change in their organization.

- *A focus on prototyping the future.* In order to support strategic change, scenarios must be developed in ways that explore specific systemic possibilities for the organization in terms of how it relates to other players. It is not enough just to explore the overall context as a set of challenges to business as usual. Frequently, scenarios are used first to challenge the status quo, and then simply to 'test' or 'wind-tunnel' strategies against such challenges, leaving all the work of actually generating alternative strategies to some undefined process. The true power of scenario-building lies in helping to generate and develop these new strategic possibilities in ways that relate to the unique position and capabilities of the organization, without being locked in 'business-as-usual' thinking. Effective practice helps decision makers to explore the delicate and shifting boundary between what they can control and what they cannot. The second requirement for effective use of scenarios is therefore to use them to create specific models of the organization linked to the imagined futures; seeing this as essentially a design task, the requirement is to support a highly interactive, and iterative, business prototyping process.

- *An embedded learning process.* The power of scenario methods lies in the way they enable leaders to break out of their commitment to their embedded view of the future – the current pattern of success – and systematically explore the ways the future could be different from a straightforward development of the present; and what new roles might open up for the organization to play as a result. Strategic scenario practice will fail unless the people who make decisions are deeply engaged with it as a continuing process of entrepreneurial learning and adaptation, using the scenario insights to develop their appreciation of the environment around them, and, through this, of their own organization. Scenario thinking is a cognitive skill that must be developed as a learning process, linked to the perceptions and knowledge of the decision makers.

Game-changing decisions are effective only if they are executed. This requires active involvement at every level in the organization; the powerful built-in reinforcement of the current patterns by which things get done in the present must be overcome. But many observers have become sceptical about the ability of most organizations to execute strategies that deviate significantly from their dominant model. They argue that most intended strategies get sidetracked, and are replaced with what the organization as a whole considers to be sensible and useful action in the real world. It is suggested that most strategies are not rationally developed but reflect a retroactive interpretation of actions already taken in line with the accepted majority view. In the literature this is called 'emergent strategy'.

In this book we argue that, while much strategy is emergent, many decision makers do manage to bring their organization to execute intended innovative strategies; they take the dominant view as their starting point, and from there use available levers for change, such as organizational design and the conception of innovation projects. But before these management tools are used, decision makers need to engage in 'strategic conversation' with their organization (and possibly beyond) to understand and affect the dominant view on the logic for change, so that all resources can be mobilized for the creation of relevant strategies. This is the *embedded* learning process in which scenarios play a key role in bringing new potential for strategic action to light. It is a coherent and consistent effort; as a practice it lives between the view that strategy is emergent and the view that strategy is the execution of a preconceived plan.

As we turn our attention to exactly *how* the people in an organization can create new strategies, we come up against a profound question: How can any process be set up to produce original insight? Every technique and process that is advocated for helping us to do better in business or policy in the end depends on the sagacity of the people who use it. It is easy to lose sight of this essential requirement: you can take the horse to the water, but you can't make it drink; and you can take people to the scenarios process but you can't make them think. Effective practice of scenarios demands an understanding of how people think, individually, in groups and in organizations, and the relationship between tools, techniques, facilitation, and the essentially unpredictable nature of insight; Napier Collyns (see Chapter 1) refers to this as a form of 'magic' that can only flow from deep engagement with the situation. In this book we aim to illuminate this deep relationship between technique and insight on which successful strategic practice relies.

While these criteria for success in the strategic use of scenarios were implicit in the earliest practice, they have been clarified and developed by leading practitioners over the last 30 years. There has been steady progress; but having a professional community of people interested in futures work can be a drawback: the work can sometimes get trapped in the 'strategy group' of an organization, or delegated to an outside consultancy, and thereby lack the deep engagement of the decision makers in their organizational setting that is critical to its effective influence in strategic choice. In this book we explore the process of the 'strategic conversation', which links insights resulting from the scenarios to 'strategic action', choosing and implementing changes in what we do up and down the organization, which together creates insightful strategy.

The overall content of the book is summarized in Figure 1.

On the left we have the organization faced with a strategic situation, and requiring a linking set of cognitive tools; this is known as 'thinking in the world of business' (WOB). On the right we bring to attention how the organization really works through the coordination of the people within and beyond it, which is known as 'thinking in the world of management'. While in the world of

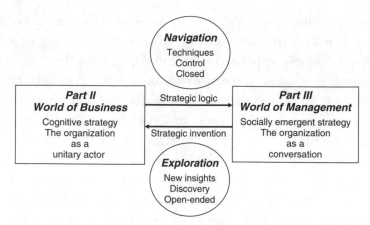

Figure 1   The shape of the book

business we construe the organization as one unitary actor on the playing field, interacting with competitors, customers, stakeholders, etc.; in the world of management the organization is considered as a collection of many individuals, each with their own agenda, trying to harmonize many separate actions that will, it is hoped, cohere as a way to ensure survival and success. Good strategy requires superior skills in both thinking domains. While the world of business is the arbiter of its success and failure, the original invention of strategy by individuals flows from the world of management. And while techniques can inform our understanding of logic, and support our processes of navigation, we eventually rely on the open-ended nature of exploration and insight to invent and create truly distinctive strategy.

The book is organized in three parts, each of which has an introduction from one of the editors.

- **Part I: Origins: Navigating with Invisible Islands** sets the scene for the whole book by discussing the evolution of the field with two of its leading practitioners – Peter Schwartz and Napier Collyns – and by going deeper into the essential tension between technique and insight with a review of the practice of Pierre Wack and his seminal work at Shell.

- **Part II: Scenarios in the World of Business** shows how the power of scenario planning is derived from the manner in which it integrates many different ways of thinking about the future into a coherent practice, and how the methods are being developed and extended into such areas as the exploration and evaluation of new strategic options.

- **Part III: Scenarios in the World of Management** explores scenarios as an embedded learning and decision-making process, and how processes can create the setting for insight to emerge. It looks at the different ways that have been developed to take the core methods of multi-future thinking and turn them into a range of effective techniques for engaging the entire organization in the creation of strategies and commitment to action.

The contributors to this book have in sum many decades of scenario practice gained in helping organizations to face the full breadth and complexity of present day challenges and to invent original strategic initiatives. Many examples of that experience will be found throughout the book, both successes and failures. What the writers present here is the result of their critical reflections on that experience, to distil the essence of scenario practice for generating unique insights, and for turning those insights into effective action.

ORIGINS: NAVIGATING WITH INVISIBLE ISLANDS

INTRODUCTION

> In the end success derives from being different. It requires orig-
> inal invention. Management can contribute by creating favourable
> conditions for inventions to emerge.
>
> Blending invention into the logical language of strategy is an art, the
> art of strategic conversation.
>
> Kees Van der Heijden

How do you write a good book, compose a song, design a
good product, invent a competitive business strategy, research a
breakthrough technology, or anticipate the future?

To produce a book is easy. There are lots of standard plot lines.
Ideas are cheap. The publishers will tell you what the market is
looking for and what they will promote. Sit down with your coffee
and just do it. How hard can it be? Finding it a bit difficult? Go
to a creative writing class and you can polish up your storytelling
technique and learn the craft – the tricks of the trade. Still no
success – perhaps this is a bit harder than I thought. Who can
tell me how to produce a really *good* book? That's easy too – as

Scenarios for Success: Turning Insights into Action   Edited by Bill Sharpe and Kees Van der Heijden
© 2007 John Wiley & Sons, Ltd

Ursula LeGuin says, just set up a possible world and let the arc of the imagination spark. Presented with the right conditions the imagination cannot help but respond; what it produces is unique, but will it be any good? It is a making, and making is mysterious. We can practise our technique, but in the end we do not control the arc of imagination. I will never write a story that is as good as one of LeGuin's. But perhaps a lifelong passion for storytelling will pay off, at least I can write some stories that fill a few pages in the local magazine.

Yes, but that's just art. We know that's different. Knowledge work and business strategy are altogether different things. It may be hard to work out what to do, but that's because the world is a really complicated place and you don't control anything except what you do yourself. A business that has failed might have been a really good idea – in fact it might have been beaten by something not as good that just seems to have been the right thing in the right place at the right time. Succeeding in business is all about developing the craft, knowing the tools, and having the guts to get on with it however tough the challenges. If we fail, we should be able to do better next time – Silicon Valley values the knowledge of the entrepreneur who has been through a few failures and has developed a feel for what works. So, there's nothing really special about any business, and any of them could have been created by anybody skilled in the art. Is the success of GE, Apple, Ikea, Tetrapak, Amazon, IBM, or Microsoft just due to good management? Not so.

As any venture capitalist will tell you, about a third of any pool of investments will fail, a third will just return their investment, and a third will do well enough to make up for the failures. However, one of the pool will become the sort of success that makes a big return and establishes a new leader in its industry, perhaps creating a whole new sector around it. If you look into big companies and the success of public policy you will find similar sorts of numbers. A huge number of attempts to move forward into new products, businesses and policies are like the run-of-the-mill novel; they don't completely fail, but they don't particularly succeed. So the business section shelves at the bookshop groan with the weight of advice on how to do better, and we would do well to read those books and develop our craft to the point that we might at least be able to hold a business together and achieve modest success. But creating a really *good* business is no easier than writing a really good book. To stand out from the ordinary is to be original, to have a quality of insight that cannot be reduced to formula, because, if it could, then everyone would be doing it. It's easy to see what any of those successful companies does, but it is very hard to do it.

Even those successful businesses have had their fair share of failures and disasters. IBM seemed on the verge of disintegration and failure in the 1990s, and who still remembers GEC that came to grief in the technology bubble? Apple has had plenty of flops, and Microsoft has not managed to extend the dominance of PCs into markets such as mobile phones. Shell, having managed so well through the oil shocks, then had a very troubled time. A business may have a unique insight and yet fail to thrive. Artists may not be recognized in their lifetime, and only later be appreciated for the quality of their vision and creativity, but you have never heard of business people who were unrecognized in their lifetime. A failed business does not have this second chance – it is what it is while it exists; success in the conditions of the time is of the essence. So business, and any organization that aims to sustain activity in society and has some notion of success in its mission, is bound irrevocably to the flow of events, like white water rafters navigating a river. Just staying afloat requires constant attention to the conditions of success, and takes the practice of all our skill.

So business and organizational strategy is demanding on two fronts. On the one hand it is deeply embedded in the flow of events that are mostly uncontrolled, and, on the other, true success flows from a unique vision and the ability to bring an idea to reality.

We can now see that the essential property of strategic insight is a systemic appreciation of the environment in which we must act. It rests on deep, informed perception of the forces at play, and how we can bring our own contribution into alignment with them. Like the teams competing in a sailing boat race, we must sense all the forces simultaneously and by using all our seacraft choose a unique path that makes the best use of them to outpace the competition. As sailors we can always use more knowledge, and we will want every instrument we can get; but we also need to develop and understand our unique capabilities and use them perceptively to align the things we control with those we don't in every moment. We need essentially an *entrepreneurial* mind that will make choices based on insight as events flow towards us.

An entrepreneurial commitment is one that is based on a judge-ment on how things will turn out, for which past information is only a partial and incomplete guide. By the time things are certain it will be too late to seize the advantage. It is the person who acts who must reach this commitment because of the inherent risk, and because the decision must be constantly remade and adapted to evolving circumstances. Important decisions of this sort are arrived at rather than made – a moment comes when the course of action you must take stands before the mental eye with complete clarity, with a sense that one can carry it forward in a still uncertain world.

We can pursue the sailing metaphor a little further to understand the nature of future thinking and strategic insight. In a remarkable account of the sailors of Polynesia, Hutchins (1995) describes the traditional skills used to navigate between small islands in the Pacific Ocean. When these islands lie out of sight from each other separated by hundreds of miles of ocean, this is a very demanding task. One method of navigation relies on using intermediate islands that help to maintain a sense of course. There is nothing surprising in this, until you learn that sometimes the intermediate islands are themselves out of sight over the horizon to one side of the course or another, and that if there is no such convenient island they might make one up. Just how did it become easier to find your way by reference to a non-existent and invisible island? The answer as explained by Hutchins is the way that the sailors must combine many sources of complex information about the wind, the currents, the stars and so on. By using these imagined reference points they can bring all these factors and forces into their minds in more effective and powerful ways. This capability is deeply developed in their culture, and the use of specific reference points is built up and passed on through the generations.

Scenarios are tools for future thinking that act rather like invisible islands. They don't have to really be there in order to bring the critical information together in ways that allow us to see, understand, and act in tune with the forces at play to reach a real future.

We have now introduced several ideas that need to be expanded. First, technique and process in strategic decision making can never be a substitute for insight. They are critical for success, and we must keep developing our craft, because only the greatest skill will give us a chance of navigating turbulent events, but success will always demand something more. Our strategic processes must create the conditions for such insight to emerge. Secondly, the nature of the insight particular to organizational strategy is inherently *systemic* — it is concerned with the alignment of what we can do with what is going on in the world to create a logic of success and growth embedded in the flow of events. Thirdly, insight and action must be brought together in the individual and organizational mind; insight only counts in organizational life if it creates the readiness for action in the actual flow of events: we must be ready to commit to action in the face of unfolding uncertainty. Finally, the development of systemic insight is hard, and needs support from cultural tools. Scenarios are a way to harness the power of systemic insight into the continuous unfolding of strategic action.

Before expanding these ideas we must leave our sailing metaphor behind and say more about the systemic nature of the world of societies, economies, and the organizational fields within which we act. In the world of human affairs we live within systems that are produced, and reproduced, by our own actions. Anticipating and responding to change is only so important and difficult because it stands in opposition to the stability that is needed for anything to get done in the world from day to day. At any one time there have to be myriad agreements, tacit and explicit, on how we will keep our societal world going round, so that we can all get up, go to work, and get something useful done. Our own contribution must mesh with those of the people and organizations around us in well understood and relatively stable ways. We use stability as the context for the unique – even the artist making a new and unique contribution needs the infrastructure of the cultural world to be seen or heard.

One way to think about this is the concept of a value system that 'locks in', i.e. a pattern of behaviour that becomes adopted across many individuals and organizations and is then sustained over time. This is illustrated in a simplified way in Figure I.1.

This shows three types of actors – Governments, Businesses, and People acting both as citizens and in the market. These three interact in the arenas of regulation, standards (*de facto* or *de jure*) and consumer market choice. The diagram illustrates the idea that through action in these arenas a value system, shown by the loop which encircles the diagram, can be established and then lock in and be maintained over time. This phenomenon is particularly powerful in technology industries where the ability to control the momentum of technology development can create positions of extraordinary market dominance. For example, in the computer industry, the players in the PC sector referred over many years to the 'Wintel' platform to express the combined leadership of Microsoft and Intel that appropriated most of the profits of the sector. This concept

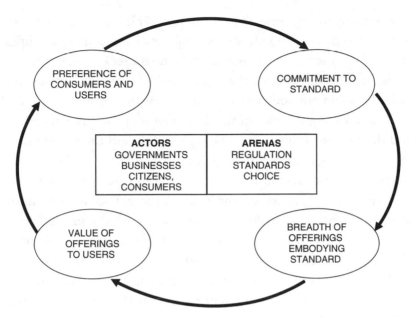

Figure I.1   Value systems lock–in

of value systems locking in gives us the idea of a 'dominant loop' which, at any one time, is the one that is most important in our area of interest. Although there have been many other systems of value creation in the PC business over the last two decades, the Wintel system has dominated and exerted the most influence over all the other players.

We have used technology examples to illustrate this idea, because the incremental development of technology creates particularly powerful momentum effects, and can confer huge strategic advantage to those organizations that can use this to capture the position of a prime mover. However, in order for anything to get done from day to day, the fundamental point, that there must be some stable, dominant pattern of activity, can be used to discuss any area of societal activity, not just technology markets; and this fact gives us a very powerful tool for strategy work.

Viewed in this way, the flow of events can be seen as the movement from one dominant loop to another; and the essence of strategic decision is to anticipate, and perhaps drive, such changes, and certainly to align oneself in the best possible way with whatever is going to emerge as dominant. We can now see that there are three types of knowledge and insight that we might seek in our strategic decisions. The first two are the familiar predetermined elements and critical uncertainties of scenario-building. As the section below will explain, by using the idea of the dominant loop we can strengthen and sharpen our insights into these elements with the system idea, so that we begin to feel them with a force that a scenario story might otherwise lack: in the simplicity of a single system loop lies its power; we begin to see and feel a logic unfolding. The third type of insight is essentially *entrepreneurial* in the way this has been described earlier: holding in our minds these imagined systems of the future we must choose and commit to a path for ourselves. Only with a clear conviction that we understand the forces at play can we take action in the present to align with and harness those forces, and perhaps even shape them to our advantage.

In this book we aim to illuminate both the technique and magic of insight – how the one supports, but cannot be a substitute for, the other. This was discussed in the book's Overview and is illustrated again in Figure I.2.

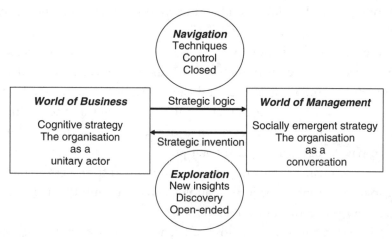

Figure I.2   Navigation and exploration

On the top we have the strategy process conceived as the application of technique and the craft of better decision making; on the bottom we view strategic decisions as inherently entrepreneurial and dependent on unique, systemic insight. The tension between these two approaches is played out as we 'think in the world of business' to explore the nature of the decisions in themselves; and as we 'think in the world of management' to understand how organizations really function with respect to reaching and implementing decisions.

The second and third parts of the book separate out these two worlds, but of course in practice they are two aspects of one lived reality. While the separation of WOB and WOM makes for presentational convenience, Part I of this book emphasizes how one cannot exist without the other. The two chapters in Part I consider the field as a whole, looking back to its development in order to illuminate current practice. In the first chapter we interview two of the founders of modern practice – Peter Schwartz and Napier Collyns – who particularly illuminate the contrast between process and practice. In the second chapter, Cynthia Selin provides a detailed discussion of the practice of Pierre Wack who led the original Shell work and can be considered as the originator of the deep, practice-based approaches.

CHAPTER 1

CONVERSATIONS WITH PETER SCHWARTZ AND NAPIER COLLYNS

Bill Sharpe

Any account of the rise of scenario planning in strategy is bound to recognize the importance of the pioneering work of Pierre Wack and his colleagues at Shell which enabled them to anticipate the oil crises of the 1970s. From that team came three of the founders of Global Business Network – Peter Schwartz, Napier Collyns, and Kees Van der Heijden – who have done much to bring scenario planning into widespread use. Following the Oxford Futures Forum, Peter and Napier, in a series of individual interviews, reflected on their experience of key elements of scenario planning in its original and current practice. The interviews are combined here under the main questions they addressed.

How do you describe strategy?

PS: Strategy is that pattern of actions that intervenes in the ongoing development of the organization to make desirable outcomes

---

Scenarios for Success: Turning Insights into Action   Edited by Bill Sharpe and Kees Van der Heijden
© 2007 John Wiley & Sons, Ltd

more likely. Strategy is always in motion; unless you are a start-up, where you are focused on one big bet, you always have something in motion.

NC: It's making decisions about what to do next. It's very often about survival: it is commonplace that CEOs change every few years, and if a company or CEO wants to survive, they need to think strategically; without deep thought they will be swept away. Strategy is also often about options, which are given validity by scenarios.

Why do you think scenario practice has endured so well?

PS: I think the answer to that is simple and not at all profound. There are three reasons.

First is the reality of uncertainty. People just keep getting surprised. There are not a lot of organizations for which the world is a certain, predictable place. That case does not have to be made any more, especially after 9/11.

Secondly, this is really easy operationally and conceptually. The basic idea of telling a small number of consistent, yet divergent stories about the future, and building them based on driving forces is straightforward by comparison with many techniques. For instance, 'Real Options' is a powerful approach and we have worked on using it with organizations, but it's just too hard to do – most people don't get it.

Thirdly, storytelling is what people do; it is how their brains work. Even if we didn't invent the scenario approach, people would sit around having ideas and telling stories about the future. Since time began people have done this, and scenarios simply build on that innate capacity.

What are the conditions for effective use of scenarios in strategy?

PS: It's not one thing, but several conditions, in varying degrees and combinations, that make scenarios most effective.

The first requirement is that significant people in the organization who are involved in making important decisions must want to find a better way to think about their decisions. If they don't feel that need, it is going to be very hard to make scenarios work. For instance, the Chief Technology Officer says, 'If I look around the world I really wonder where the next great technological leadership is going to come from and so where should I be thinking about establishing my future labs?' That is an interesting scenario question and may lead him to look at several scenarios for national science strategy in China, India, and so on. So that is number one: people who are engaged in making meaningful strategic decisions are feeling the need to think better about their choices.

Secondly, the decision makers must be prepared to engage in new ways of thinking. That they feel the need doesn't mean they actually will do it. When confronted with the reality of what's involved, even though it's operationally easy, they may fall back on old ways of doing things. That is a very common response; the easier strategy is denial of uncertainty and convincing yourself that you really understand what's going on. Then it's a roll of the dice: you may get lucky, you may not, but it's gambling, not good decision making, at that point. Scenario planning is about avoiding gambling with the company. So, that's the second point: being willing to actually face the uncertainty and take a different approach.

Third is time. To do scenario planning well – to do it thoughtfully, to absorb the ideas, to make better decisions – all of this takes time. It takes time to do homework, to think together, to communicate, to develop options. It takes time to *absorb* new possibilities, and I think this is the most critical aspect of all. If you are really going to give somebody a new view of the world, then it requires letting go and re-absorption. That rarely happens. Even in a great 'Aha!' moment you may see a new possibility, but have you internalized it sufficiently to act upon it? And this is one of the ways scenarios often fail. People come up with a set of scenarios and say, 'Well we can now make a better decision; let's meet tomorrow and make our choice.' But then their colleagues say, 'Well, you know...I'm not sure I take that scenario seriously...and that scenario seriously', and so on, because they haven't *really* absorbed the new realities. It's not two days and it doesn't have to be six months; but you need enough time for people to get comfortable with what the scenarios mean.

There is a demand for methods that are quicker, and cheaper to implement – where have you gone on that?

NC: When we formed Global Business Network (GBN) we worked with four or five large companies for several years, such as AT&T, Nissan, and PG&E, much as we did with Shell. AT&T, for example, gave us 150 people to work with, 12–15 of them full time, on a twenty-first-century scenario project in the late 1980s. I acted in a coaching role on these projects and I assumed that the companies would have the same experience we had in Shell. As time has gone on, and GBN has done more and more projects, there has been the need to find fast turnaround methods that might help the client in just a few days. I can't imagine anything more different from Pierre [Wack] looking at a stone for 17 days in order to perceive a new reality!

PS: I go both ways on this. You are right that people are feeling incredible time pressure. And organizations have slimmed down. When I was in Shell I had 50 people on my staff; the current incumbent has 5. Big difference! If you want to conduct original research, run a two-year-long, in-depth process, and engage 100 people around the company and you have the team I had, you could do so easily. I had a budget of several million pounds and in those days that was a lot of money. I could do a great job because Shell gave me great resources.

And there was already a great process; when I arrived I was standing on the very tall shoulders of Pierre Wack. So for me it was relatively easy.

On the one hand, being able to do things in great depth is very important in many situations, and you wish you could do it in many more. But unfortunately the reality is that many organizations do not have the time or the resources in terms of people. And they don't have the intellectual stamina, frankly; in a lot of organizations people are not used to thinking long and hard in complicated ways. So do you say, 'Well, if you can't do it in the way I think is best, we are not going to help you; we are not going to give you any better tools than you already have; there is no way you can possibly improve the quality of your decision making without doing everything we recommend'? Well, that is not a helpful attitude, particularly because my experience tells me that starting at a more modest level is often a first step towards doing things in greater depth. People tend to find scenario thinking interesting and useful, and realize that, by delving even more deeply, they could get even more value. We've had that experience again and again in companies. So one way to think about so-called 'light' approaches is that they are opportunities to learn, to get comfortable, and to begin the process.

Moreover, in our experience, people are still better off even if they have not gone as far as we think they ought to go, particularly when dealing with really big decisions. I am appalled sometimes at the scale of decisions that people make with so little thought. Having said that, we know from experience that we can actually improve the quality of decision making with less in-depth, lengthy approaches. And in the end the objective is a higher quality strategic conversation that enables decision makers to be more thoughtful and more adept at dealing with the risks and the opportunities, the options and the alternatives. So, my view is a very pragmatic one. If I was the strategic planner in Shell with abundant resources, as I was many years ago, I wouldn't think twice about the depth of research and engagement. But as a person trying to get the scenario methodology used in many places and contexts, to teach it, to engage people and move them forward, I am quite prepared to begin where they are rather than where I wish they were.

Andrew Curry (one of the authors in this book) describes this as 'Getting more meaning in the room.'

PS: I like that a lot – a very nice phrase.

NC: It is a profound experience for a human being to have their certainty undermined by uncertainty. This is how skilled facilitators like Peter perform – in an afternoon he can make them feel and behave differently. It's a lifetime's practice to facilitate teams in this way.

Looking at the framework for scenario planning introduced in this book (Part I, Introduction), which elements of the practice do you think survive this transition into 'any better thinking is better thinking'?

PS: I like the framework of dimensions; there are a variety of ways to cut this and your approach is helpful and an accurate and appropriate reflection of people's real experiences. I think complexity is harder to get across the transition. If you really want to unpack complexity, it's not all that obvious, otherwise it wouldn't be complex – it would be simple! So, that often takes both time and subtle thinking. There are people and companies and organizations that are comfortable with complexity and others that are not. The other frameworks all translate well.

How do you relate this problem of reaching a deep understanding of complexity to the original emphasis in scenario practice on understanding the logic of underlying systems and predetermined elements?

PS: This is a wonderful intersection between Peter Senge and Peter Schwartz. Senge's systems-thinking tools are sufficiently widespread that people are often comfortable using some of them in the context of scenario planning. If the culture is already comfortable with some of the better systems-thinking tools to deal with complexity, you can deal with the pre-determined elements. When people are not familiar with these tools it's much harder.

NC: It is really important that you have described this as an enquiry into *practice*. The pressures to have repeatable processes can lead to scenario planning being seen as a sequence of standard steps, as if deep understanding can be achieved by a routine approach. This is anathema to Wack's practice, and as a historian, I approach it like Pierre.

Scenarios are doing history forward; doing history is always a new way of looking at the past, and scenarios are a way to understand the future in new ways. Scenarios have to have a logic to have validity as something that can plausibly happen. And so, there is a heavy emphasis on *systems thinking*. It is able to reveal when a system doesn't work, or is running into conditions that will cause profound change. The whole point of scenarios is that you can't see the future, but in a sense with predetermined elements and the guru practice you *can* see certain key elements and how they might unfold in the midst of the uncertainty. Many scenario practitioners don't really know about predetermined elements; Pierre used this phrase to indicate something very different from factors we were still unsure about. Excessive snow in the mountains predictably 'had to' result in floods in the valleys. It didn't mean the whole future was predictable; it meant that we could foresee how certain trends or developments might emerge in an overall uncertain future.

I sometimes use the word 'premonition' when talking about these predetermined elements. This is not prediction. Nor is it filling up the quadrants of a scenario uncertainty matrix. Rather it is out-of-the-box thinking that foresees a key aspect of the future when no one else can. We had a feeling of premonition when, after Pierre's rigorous contemplation of driving forces, we felt that something was certain and no longer 'a critical uncertainty'. Not the whole future of the world but a particular key issue, such as the oil price rises of 1973 and 1979, and in Peter's case the greening of Russia and the decline of oil prices in 1986. My memory of doing this work is of feeling ill half the time because you are hit in your gut about things you hadn't thought of before and the impact they might have.

In my experience, scenario planning is an interpretive practice – it's really closer to magic than technique. That is the technical essence of what Pierre did and the impact it had on the people around him. Pierre's approach was based on his experience with Gurdjieff and his own guru, although this is not something he talked about a lot. Selin's chapter in this book goes into this background and is the result of us revisiting the archive of Pierre's papers that is now at Templeton College.

A lightweight practice that has been criticized as ineffective is where people just go for the uncertainties and draw up four scenarios in a two-by-two grid without addressing the predetermined elements. Have you seen that?

PS: I, too, see that. Unfortunately, the issue is subtle. It is less about time and more about people's discomfort with simultaneously holding two apparently contradictory ideas: 'You mean there are trends that are inevitable and others that are uncertain? If things are uncertain, isn't everything uncertain? And if there are things that are inevitable, isn't everything inevitable?' The difficulty with such simultaneity of thought is evident with scenarios that embody both predetermined and uncertain elements. I just went through this recently with a set of scenarios on Latin America in which we were dealing with the impact of certain resource commodity prices on Latin American countries. It was a real struggle to convey the idea that actually there *was* something predetermined as well as something uncertain at the same time.

NC: The scenario two-by-two grid of uncertainties has become a sort of shorthand for scenario planning, yet it is really thinking 'in the box' – the grid box!

You just cannot pretend that the creation of predetermined elements is easy; you cannot get it in a quarter of an hour – it's nonsense. So we just have to distinguish between the useful ways to free up people to investigate possibilities from the sort of insight you can only reach if you spend three months on it. It's not something you do in a hurry. It's done after several dreams. You suddenly know what you are going to do next. Brainstorming is not a substitute for magic. Look long enough, hard enough, and the pieces will fall into place. Magic is a very difficult thing – most people spend their whole life cutting magic out.

Turning to the impact of scenario planning, it happens that people do scenarios, and then they say 'yes, but what does this mean?' The process can fail to address the development of strategic options, and they are left with a set of contextual uncertainties that are just too different, too challenging, and just don't seem to connect. Is that a failure mode you see?

NC: There is no point in doing scenarios unless they make a change in your thinking and a change in your doing. So the key is to get decision makers to expand their point of view and mental maps. There is a lot more to this than just seeing a new possibility, or even recognizing that more than one future might unfold; it's a completely new way to understand what's at play, and what the available information might mean. As a result, when they ask for research on a decision they ask different questions in different contexts.

Once, at the end of a scenario session I heard a couple of managers on the way out saying 'Let's get back to work', as if the session belonged to a different world. To address this, the first psychological technique was to interview the people making the decisions to find out *their* hopes and fears – to get to a different sort of being than the *rational* being. I don't know that these factors have been adequately brought out – I almost daren't say this – that's why there is so much attention on technique rather than magic. Pierre said that unless you have strong short-term knowledge of the business environment they won't trust you to talk about the long term.

PS: I think this sort of failure has mainly to do with decision-making structure and rules: for example, who gets to play and under what conditions. Let's take a hypothetical example of a company that is looking at a portfolio of products, and wants to make some decisions about new markets – whether to do more of this and less of that. So the marketing organization commissions some consultants to do a set of scenarios to look at the future of these product lines. There may be *no* connection between the marketing organization, the scenarios, and the people in the end who actually make the choices about which products to go with and which not to pursue. The actual decision makers can accept or reject the choices for one reason or another – 'I don't like that product, that's in my home town, or that has good or bad politics behind it.' The decision makers are not directly connected to the set of scenarios: it is not theirs; it is somebody else's. This is a very common situation and the cause of many failed scenario efforts.

For me, this was *exactly* the situation that pertained to Exploration and Production in Shell until 1984. E&P said they didn't need to use scenarios; they told Pierre that, and they told me that when I presented my first set of scenarios. It was, in fact, the mindset of the organization and how they saw their decision rights versus Group Planning and anybody else. It was half politics and half the engineering mindset of the person who ran E&P at the time. But he left, and someone else came in – a great strategic thinker, who ultimately became chairman of the company. He was looking at the reality of the world and said he was worried and that we had better introduce some scenario-thinking into our leadership quickly. We did and completely transformed E&P in about two years. *But* it was because we had a change in mindset at the top.

Is it your experience that where the ownership is right, and the right people are in the room, the development of strategic options informed by the scenarios just flows quite naturally?

PS: Precisely right. Texaco's experience of scenario planning is an example from the early days that has been well documented. We started out working on natural gas and then migrated to corporate. It was a classic case of a fairly light beginning, and then doing much deeper scenarios internally and having a huge impact that was perceived by corporate. After the first scenario project they said, 'Gee, that was interesting, let's now look at a really important set of issues and do a deep dive.' We had the CEO of natural gas in the room and he was deeply engaged; he often said that one of the reasons he became so successful in the company was his experience doing scenarios. He was quite prepared to develop and think through the options, to make decisions, and to act; and so it worked. Because we had all the right conditions, we had no problem developing the options, testing, weighing, and working our way through them, dealing with the politics. In fact, we had many of the important players in the room so that the politics were in some sense embedded in the scenario options already.

How do you view the challenge of getting senior managers to think strategically while being embedded in operational demands – do they have to think in two different ways?

NC: There is a difference between being a scenario practitioner and being educated in scenario methods. We are not trying to enable everyone to create scenarios but to understand the importance of scenario-thinking; they have to understand how these things impinge on the way they behave. My work has always been in a coaching role, influencing people.

It's a bit like maths – if you are coached you can bring it into your daily life. Scenarios are similar. Once you have taken the step and recognized that one future is not as good as thinking about uncertain futures – that is the essence – then that is the point from which you can develop preparedness. It's not easy to be a good manager unless you think scenarically, though of course some do it naturally. If Napoleon had not had scenaric capability he would not have been at the top.

PS: I see it as understanding how the manager thinks and adapts. I served three chairmen in Shell; they were all very different and I want to contrast two of them metaphorically. One thought like a long-range strategic bomber pilot. He was interested in the important targets that would really reshape the landscape over the long run. He was quite capable of thinking about the array of forces we needed to bring to bear on the targets, what the lead flight would be going forward, and so on; you had no difficulty doing good scenario thinking with him.

But I worked for a second chairman who was in some ways even better: really brilliant, a fighter pilot rather than a strategic bomber pilot. He was the most aggressive fighter out there in the world, taking on every battle every day. So what kind of scenarios could you do for him that would be useful? His question was: What kind of plane do you need to fight tomorrow's battles? If your enemy is learning from how you fight and what kind of planes you've got, you had better be developing some new planes. He understood that analysis of the situation perfectly: 'Future competition . . . what are the dimensions, how do I play, what kind of capabilities do I need to develop, what are the challenges to my existing game?' He knew he needed

to develop new competitive competences in the face of a continually learning and adapting environment. He was very good
at tactical scenarios, at how you play the game in a given situation; yet, you talked to him in completely different terms than
you did to the other chairman.

While you're flying that plane you are not thinking about building the
next one, so do you need different discussions and to construct occasions very
deliberately to get people out of flying and into designing the jet?

PS: He accepted that you needed a well-structured process that,
every once in a while, forced you to stop and ask, 'What are
we learning, what do we need to do that's new and different,
what do we need to stop doing?' He was pretty tough-minded
about it.

What have you learned about how to keep that process alive when there isn't
a strategic-planning group like there was in Shell and you are supporting it
from outside the organization?

PS: First, having an ongoing champion who will be engaged, and
finds it helpful, and is willing to stick with it. That's what
happened in Texaco: they stuck with it for over a decade and
had a great impact as a result; one of the real success cases,
I think, of good scenario planning. That is critically important.

On the other hand, precisely the opposite can happen when
you have too much success and challenge, and people shut you
down because it's too challenging. The *worst* case of scenario
planning that we experienced was a mining company looking
at the future price of their commodity. The CEO was betting
the ranch on the price going higher. The Board was worried
and one of the members had done scenarios before and brought
us in. So we did a range of scenarios that showed a very low
likelihood that, in the appropriate time frame, the price would
rise to where he thought it would go. There was also a pretty
broad consensus among the senior leadership that the balance

of probabilities was on the price being lower. So he fired seven members of the executive committee after the workshop. Basically he used it as a way of smoking out difference and killing it. We fired him as a client and gave him back his money. Using scenario planning as a way to suppress dissent can happen and kills scenarios.

In contrast at Texaco, where we had one success after another. We did great projects, which made a difference, the company learned a lot, the scenario planning was highly valued, and it just kept going.

The third factor is that the environment continues to present new challenges. In a world where the important variables for a business may be stabilizing or not perceived as high risk – demand, or price or competition – people say 'why bother?' And there are such situations – not everybody faces massive uncertainty. If you are doing the capital budgeting for a mass transit system in the Bay Area, nothing much is going to change in the next 10–15 years. So the question is: How quickly do I have to replace my rolling stock, the rails, and so on? There may be an uncertainty that something really tragic could happen, like a terrorist incident, to prepare for, but the organization's basic strategy and development are pretty fixed. So there are many organizations for which scenario planning is less relevant.

And at the other end are many start-ups, where you very often have to bet the ranch on *a* view that this product or market, is going to take off. You may be right, and DVDs go gangbusters, and you are in business. Or 8-tracks disappear and you're out of business.

So for incremental change they don't have much to say, you can handle that with other tools and other methods; scenarios function strategically when there is something game-changing to explore, when...

PS: that's right.

CHAPTER 2

PROFESSIONAL DREAMERS: THE FUTURE IN THE PAST OF SCENARIO PLANNING

Cynthia Selin

Most managerial practices are plagued by fleeting popularity only to be overruled by the new-fangled, sexy cure-all introduced by the freshest management guru. Every half year or so, a hyped technique is miraculously drawn from the ever-expanding toolbox and managers and consultants scramble to develop yet another new competence. One of the few management practices that stands apart from this tool-of-the-moment phenomenon is scenario planning, a prospective practice that has evolved from the late 1960s and survives today with continued, if not increased, relevance.

Scenario planning is part of a toolbox to help organizations to examine their business, as well as their expectations and beliefs, in order to adapt to emerging conditions. Scenarios are typically defined as stories describing different but equally plausible futures

Scenarios for Success: Turning Insights into Action   Edited by Bill Sharpe and Kees Van der Heijden
© 2007 John Wiley & Sons, Ltd

that are developed using methods that systematically gather perceptions about certainties and uncertainties. Scenario planning is a means to analyse and make sense of reality when 'the speed of the business environment is faster than your own ability to react' (Wack, 1995). Such proactive intelligence – or prospective research in action – is more critical than ever in the knowledge era characterized by volatility, rambunctious markets and emerging technologies.

Despite the relentless invention of new management tools, memory and a sense of history can offer lessons for revitalizing existing management practices. Remembrance is critical because lessons learned in the 1970s and 1980s are still plaguing practitioners and managers alike. The same problems arise: struggling with uncertainty, making scenarios relevant for decision makers, how to evoke fresh perspectives and perceive novel developments; these are all ongoing challenges. As a case in point, Mankins (2004) conducted a study of 187 companies which revealed that valuable managerial time is squandered due to a lack of focus and discipline around agenda setting, too little attention paid to strategy, and unstructured management meetings. Each of these dilemmas suggests that scenario exercises – time for mediated, systematic, focused discussions about strategic decisions well integrated into managerial practice – are still an urgent, but overlooked, necessity.

This chapter remembers the history of scenario planning from the point of view of early corporate planners, with the aim of learning anew and deepening our understanding of an enduring management practice. Although scenario planning emerged from a number of different arenas and professional practices in the 1960s and 1970s, this historical gaze focuses on one particular repertoire of practice – *The Gentle Art of Re-perceiving* (Wack, 1984a) developed during Pierre Wack's tenure at Royal Dutch/Shell. While SRI and Shell both began to use scenarios in the 1970s – both inspired by Herman Kahn's scenario thinking – Wack is considered to be the founding father of corporate scenario planning, and his intellectual contributions, along with the culture that formed at Shell, serve as historical roots for many of today's scenario practitioners.

In the light of recent excavations in the Pierre Wack Memorial Library (PWML) and extensive ethnographic study, Wack is reconsidered here in the context of modern dilemmas of decision making amidst uncertainty. In order to dig deeper into Wack's work and life, investigations were made into the hundreds of files documenting his different scenario projects, writings, and sources of inspiration. Among other books, journals, magazines and private diaries at the PWML, were multiple drafts of his famous *Harvard Business Review* articles. Also of importance were notes from interviews conducted with Wack as well as transcripts of speeches and a video of a scenario methodology seminar given in 1995. In addition to ethnographic fieldwork at scenario consultancy firms and foresight conferences, this research is informed by multiple formal and informal interviews with key actors within the scenario-planning community who worked with or were influenced by Wack. The cataloguing of PWML, fieldwork, and interview data is complemented by a thorough, interdisciplinary literature review of scenario planning.

Drawing on new sources and a noteworthy revitalized interest in Pierre Wack's repertoire of practice, the question is: How applicable are his methods in dealing with today's organizational challenges? Wack's legacy is rediscovered to understand the source of the methods of scenarios planning, including how he worked, what his intentions were, and how his methods evolved. The reasoning behind the methods and the context of use are as critical as the process itself.

After three decades of work with scenarios, Wack died in 1997. His colleague, Ian Wilson, remembers him as a man who practised scenario planning in a way that 'reached both backwards to change our way of thinking about the future and our approach to uncertainty, and forwards to expand our range of options and influence our strategic actions' (Wilson, 1998a). While Wack remains an admired mentor, innovative thinker and strategist, many contemporary practitioners are forced to skip over the depth of Wack's practice and instead focus on short-cuts to revelation: abbreviated methods geared towards changing managerial perspective and developing strategic options.

Clearly, new temporal pressures, including an emphasis on immediacy and a chronic shortage of time for reflection, problematize both the deep reflective seeing and the depth of research and knowingness that Wack practised. Wack's seductive means of developing strategic options involved grappling with discontinuity in an untraditional and time-consuming way that included vigilant attention to managerial blind spots. How fragile is Wack's method when adapted to different conditions of practice? This question, coupled with the broader investigation of what is lost and gained with today's methods of scenario planning, is best initiated with a remembrance of Wack's repertoire developed through his experiences at Shell.

As we shall see in the section below, Wack considered the persuasion of managers as a highly nuanced, iterative art developed in a specific institutional setting that was able to evolve with him over the years. The second part of the chapter then traces two lines of thought evident in the repertoire by delving more deeply into Wack's repertoire of knowing and seeing. Finally, we question how the business context and conditions for practice have changed, and discuss the rationale for the continued relevance of Wack's repertoires.

THE PRACTICE OF SCENARIO PLANNING

In his seminal work, *The Gentle Art of Re-perceiving*, Wack contends, 'In our times of rapid change and discontinuity, these crises of perception – the inability to see a novel reality emerging by being locked inside obsolete assumptions – have become the main cause of strategic failures' (1984a). Since decisions are born from one's assumed certainties and uncertainties, the key is to unlock those fixed views and *re-perceive*. Wack saw two purposes of scenarios: to avoid regret and 'to see new strategic options that you were not previously aware of' (1984a). Recognizing the uncertainties attendant to the decision at hand is a fundamental goal of the practice. More plainly, one of the definitive and lasting elements of scenario planning involves the sorting of certain and uncertain elements.

Wack believed that the future comprises some predetermined or inevitable elements and some critical uncertainties. The trick, as Wack understood it, is to separate the *predetermined*, inevitable elements from the critical uncertainties and work to create pictures that shift the variables to get a sense of change over time. Predetermined elements are 'those events that have already occurred (or that almost certainly will occur) but whose consequences have not yet unfolded' (Wack, 1984b). Wack's predetermined items were forces that were:

- in the pipeline and obvious
- interrelated, or 'system predetermineds'
- slowly changing
- impossible.

(Wack, 1995)

How each predetermined plays out in the future is understood through systematic reasoning. The obvious predetermineds are important to recognize and to develop managerial consensus around. However, the system predetermineds are the most interesting, and are not immediately obvious but rather are uncovered through the careful articulation of exploratory scenarios. Only with deep reflection and study of the possible actions of each key actor can some of the important predetermineds emerge. Slowly changing predetermineds are often so slow as not to register and thus require careful rendering. Impossible predetermineds are critical because, on first glance, they may be considered likely and reliable, but upon further inspection cannot endure. Each type of predetermined element is critical in that 'by already existing, [they] constrain or determine the future in important ways' (Tibbs, 1998).

The deciphering and categorizing of certainties and uncertainties is a key element of the practice, but there are also unlikely or non-determined events, sometimes delineated as surprises. Such accidental but significant happenings highlight how the certainties and uncertainties are subject to a near incomprehensible interaction of unpredictable forces, actions and ideas. It is the emergent discontinuities that must be elaborated upon in the process.

The legacy of the past

Scenarios were introduced to Shell to cope with problems arising from uncertainty (which made traditional planning unreliable), and to address the growing concerns over oil shortages and maintaining competitive advantage. For the Shell planners, the early 1970s marked a period where the impacts of globalization and accelerating advances in technology began to restructure the business environment and alert them to new temporal and structural dynamics. Wack saw volatility in the environment and said that the tenets of their existing planning strategies were 'a dangerous substitute for real thinking in times of uncertainty and potential discontinuity' (Wack, 1984a). Shell's professional planners and analysts began to seek out new methods to cope with the newly perceived complexity, and they viewed scenarios as a promising technique for the job.

When the Shell planning team presented the first round of scenarios to managers, they received little response and saw that the stories did not elicit any change in behaviour or strategy. Napier Collyns, who joined the team in 1972, recalls, 'I was reminded over and over of the myth of Cassandra. Like her, we were telling the truth about the future – but no one was willing to believe us' (Kleiner, 1990).

> **Box 2.1   First-Generation Scenarios at Shell**
>
> The planners created scenarios that illustrated the likely uncertainty and several responses to it, to introduce Shell managers to the scenario process. They presented an A-family of scenarios that put forth a main discontinuity but questioned the timing and nature of it. While this A-family represented the best research hypotheses developed by the planners, it was at odds with the 'worldview' or mindset of the Shell managers. The group, therefore, made a B-family set of scenarios that assumed *business as usual* and served an educational role in demonstrating that it would take certain miracles or counter-intuitive developments to occur in order for the scenario to appear credible. In other words, the worldview common to the Shell managers was proved unrealistic as 'the B-family of scenarios destroyed the ground any of them may have chosen to stand on' (Wack, 1984b).

The managers' response to the scenarios was little more than intellectual interest but had no real effects. Wack likened the impact to water rolling off a stone, and referred to a Japanese saying regarding existential effectiveness: 'When there is no break, not even in the thickness of a hair, between a man's vision and his action' (Wack, 1984b). So, while the Shell managers were amused, they were not acting or deciding any differently as a result of their exposure to the issues through scenarios. The scenarios lacked persuasion.

Mental models and microcosms

This led Wack to seek what could and would affect the decision maker's mind to such an extent that action would follow. Wack came to make a distinction between the microcosm (an individual's worldview) and the macrocosm (the operating environment). This distinction led Wack and his team to reconsider completely their task at hand: to lead decision makers to question their inner model of reality. Wack's revelation was that without changing the microcosm of the decision maker there was no hope of communicating the messages the scenarios had to offer concerning the macrocosm. Wack remembers, 'Our initial aim had been to produce scenarios that we would not be ashamed of when subsequently confronted with reality.' The emphasis then shifted to create scenarios that would 'lead our decision makers to question their inner model of reality and change it as necessary in order to take action that *they* would not be ashamed of later' (1984a). The scenarios themselves needed to be designed to create a change of behaviour through instigating a change in mind frame or mental model.

Mental model is a key concept for scenario planning and refers to the way a person sees the world. Mental models serve as the perceptual and conceptual structures that dictate how one interprets, reacts, and acts in the world. An individual's worldview is the composite of experiences, values, knowledge and dispositions that formulate the content and co-construct the reality map. This understanding maintains that an individual's view of the world is formulated within his or her unique perceptual system, which serves to filter experience and information into awareness, conceptualization, or an image of reality.

Re-perception

From his new understanding, Wack began to see many management problems as a 'crisis of perception', and he championed a perceptual approach to planning. In stable environments, he maintained, one's mental model might serve well and inform the decision-making process successfully, but new frontiers require new ways of thinking:

> ... in times of rapid change and increased complexity ... the manager's mental model becomes a dangerously mixed bag: enormously rich detail and deep understanding that can coexist with dubious assumptions, selective inattention to alternative ways of interpreting evidence, and illusionary projections. In these times, the scenario approach has leverage to make a difference.
>
> (Wack, 1984c)

The Shell managers' thinking – their mental models – did not change, because the scenarios were too easily dismissed or embraced depending on the prejudices of the managers. Such prejudices had to do with the corporate culture at Shell which was accustomed to predicting with a sense of certainty the future of oil prices and energy demands, thereby assuming the inevitability of their continuing prosperity. Wack's scenarios presented unstable oil prices and, as such, the future the scenarios presented was too foreign for the managers to accept. Since mental models can be such a 'dangerously mixed bag' with blind spots and simplified references to larger, more complex forces, Wack's goal was not to convince the Shell managers of something, but rather to open their minds to enable them to approach a problem or a strategy from a fresh perspective, without the narrow, myopic gaze informed by their worldview.

Wack thus came to characterize scenario planning as a discipline to *re-perceive strategic openings*, orchestrated through a shift in mental model. Scenario planning became a means to break down existing mental models and rebuild another view of reality. In the case of the 1972 scenarios, the B-family scenarios served a destructive function where the existing worldview was dismantled. However, as scenarios are meant to have a productive function, something must be built back in the place of the archaic world-view. Wack found that 'the easy part would be to destroy their existing view of the world' but 'reconstructing the new inner model of reality would be the task of decision makers themselves' (1984a). While the burden of building new architectures of reality lies with the individuals, scenario exercises are meant to structure the process and provide some conceptual frameworks for possible futures.

New realities: scenarios and decision making

Reconstructing realities is aided by the use of different kinds of scenarios. For Wack, each scenario had a special purpose in this process. The way that he helped decision makers to question their own mental model was to use *learning scenarios* which began with a 'surprise-free' scenario built on the 'implicit views of the future shared by most managers' that serves as their entry, or 'bridge', into the future and builds acceptance around the process (Wack, 1984b). The construction of a 'surprise-free' scenario, or a 'consensus forecast' gathers expectations, articulates them and puts them on the table for critique. 'Without the surprise-free scenario, all possibilities may appear alien to the managers and they may reject the process out-of-hand' (Wack, 1984a). Creating such a fit with expectations is a necessary step towards the acceptance of more startling scenarios that may have more heuristic value.

The surprise-free scenario is coupled with other learning scenarios that aim to map out future contexts and present raw uncertainties. Wack (1984a) also called these learning scenarios 'first-generation scenarios' or 'global scenarios'. He explained, their

> purpose is not action, but to gain understanding and insight . . . The aim is to perceive more clearly the connections between various forces and events driving the system, and this understanding of the

interrelatedness of the system shows that some apparent 'uncertainties' are really 'predetermined'.

However, if only raw uncertainties are presented, the manager has no way to use the scenarios. In order to interact and engage with the scenarios, the manager must be offered hooks – known frames of reference – from which to pass judgement.

The next phase is to make decision scenarios, which are 'focused scenarios', tailor-made around a focal or strategic issue. Perhaps one of Wack's most valuable contributions is making scenarios that matter. By linking the scenarios with the microcosm of the manager, he provides an opportunity for re-perceiving. If successful, the consequential revelations will have a direct impact on strategy and decision making. Scenarios are thus part of a larger dialogue that aims to respond to changing terrains and help decision makers to become smartly assertive.

It is important to note that helping managers to become wiser was possible for Wack, in part, due to his integration within Shell. Compared to many of today's external practitioners, Wack had a professional position that afforded him extra legitimacy and knowledge of context, enabling him to successfully orchestrate organizational change. Without institutional support and legitimization from executive management, the value of scenarios would have been harder to establish. Wack was – and modern practitioners are – careful to note that scenario planning is a method to be incorporated into a larger process of strategy making, negotiation and action.

As we have seen, a whole host of intellectual processes must occur to enable enlightened decision making. Wack orchestrated scenarios to measure regret, highlight discontinuity and show consensus, and also created recovery scenarios to help managers to think through recuperation after the impact of a major discontinuity. Each round of scenarios helped managers to gently and gradually re-perceive their problematic situation.

KNOWING AND SEEING

Digging deeper into Wack's repertoire of practice, his focus on perception and mental models brings to light an interesting dynamic in scenario planning. One of the goals of scenario planning, as Wack explains, is to make a 'sound analysis of reality' (Wack, 1984a) and 'to see things as they really are' (Wack, 1993). Reality is contemplated in terms of driving forces or structural patterns *out there* for one to observe, reveal or discover. If one can approach the world with the right state of mind and the right analytic tools, the driving forces can be accurately accounted for. In this sense, the world is an object composed of driving forces, certainties and uncertainties that exists despite one's ability to perceive it. This view is indebted to realism.

At the same time, Wack's repertoire gives primacy to mental models, the inner landscapes that formulate perception. Here we see that knowledge is dynamic, changing and contingent upon boundaries of space, time and perspective. There is no objective world outside perception, or outside interpretation. Worlds are then constructed by sensing specific things through a selection process that is informed by history, beliefs, specific contexts and mental models. It is interaction with the world that causes knowing, albeit in subjective ways. This frame is more akin to a constructivist approach, as it is one that acknowledges that knowing will always be partial and thwarted by limited sight and perspective. Under the guidance of mental models, whether that guidance is correct or erroneous, knowing is an *interpretation* of the world and a consequence of unique constructions, orderings and weightings.

The practice of scenario planning is characterized here as populated by *professional dreamers*, capturing both the rational and esoteric elements of the practice. Wack's focus on perceiving *and* knowing reality is an interesting conflation of epistemologies or, in other words, a way of knowing that has two distinct meanings where the boundaries between the two are not clear: Wack's practice balances ambiguously two seemingly contradictory understandings of the world. The world is something to be understood both subjectively *vis-à-vis* maps and objectively *vis-à-vis* forces. Both elements are crucial, given Wack's focus on managerial perception and the problem of persuading managers to face new realities. This balance of knowing and seeing is positioned as the hallmark of Wack's repertoire and the frame within which modern relevance is questioned.

Dreaming

As we learned from the early experience of Shell, the focus on perception was born from the absence of 'existential effectiveness' of the first-generation scenarios. However, Wack's attention to perception extended beyond the psychology of decision making. He had a well-known interest in esoteric subjects and seriously studied the 'gentle art of re-perceiving'. Wack travelled extensively for personal and professional enrichment, and drew on many sources of inspiration that shaped his unique approach to planning and opened up the concept of perception in his work and life. Wack (1993) speaks of a lesson he learned from a man in Bengal:

> It is not common to see, to see things as they really are. Usually we see with our mind. With inferences, with comparisons, with expectations, with all our past experience. To see, and I mean not to see in the narrow sense to see with one's eyes, to perceive totally, to see through, to see is a function of pure consciousness. It is a wonder of what is, because it is so. Is describes it; it is a shock when you really perceive it. The word 'wise man' in Sanskrit is 'rishi' and 'rishi' means a seer. This, by the way, is the best definition of a scenario builder I know.

Whether as a rigorous researcher, or a wise man, or a seer, Wack was committed to the task of right vision, where perceptive prowess and intuition are primary assets.

The intensity of inquiry was also a matter of style for Wack. He is remembered to have rendered everyone intelligent by his questioning and refusal to give ready-made answers. He did not advise, but rather helped the inquirer to question. His modus was to ask, reflect, research and then reiterate the process again and again until an original insight occurred. He saw learning as a process of discovery where new knowledge was worthwhile when it gave a sense of delight and bestowed the gift of intellectual travel.

This right vision came to be a spiritual practice for Wack such that he viewed constructing and communicating scenarios as his personal yoga. In particular, his view of predetermined elements sets him apart from his colleagues. It is commonly held that one cannot predict events and happenings, but an understanding of the drivers and the structures of change will shed some light on particular certainties, or predetermined elements. However, Wack departed from this party-line of strategy and futurism and instead thought that the future was not unknowable, but rather had to be approached with the right gaze.

While Wack was very discreet about his esoteric knowledge, his devotion to Sufi mysticism and later to a sort of Zen Buddhism led him to believe that sensing predetermined elements was an art of meditation. The discipline of meditation allowed him to intuit through the noise in order to reveal the essence of a dilemma. Such deep reflection led to unique insight and the creation of new distinctions that enabled novel strategy development. Given his attention towards coaching managerial perceptual shifts, Wack was the managers' guru.

Professionals

Alongside Wack's mysticism, penchant for eclectic religions and focus on intuition, there lay a hard-core, professional economist. This professionalism was not only an attitude, but also an approach apparent in the rigorous research and serious analysis put into the scenarios themselves. Beginning with inclusive, in-depth interviews, research coupled with reflection is a hallmark feature running through the entire process. Wack attempted to get others to question their preconceptions armed with heavily researched evidence of coming discontinuities.

Scenarios made by Wack and his colleagues were renowned as the result of hard labour, including the intensive collection and interpretation of hoards of complicated data and information. The Shell scenarios were created from quantified predetermineds generated through long hours, expensive resources and expert knowledge. Shell scenarios of 1972 were fully quantified in terms of volumes, prices and their impacts on individual oil-producing and oil-consuming countries as well as on inter-fuel competition in different markets. In addition, the scenario projects that Wack did for Anglo American in South Africa on diamonds and gold, as well as his work in Japan, were based on a notable depth of research.

In addition to the sources used to create the predetermineds, scenarios were regularly packaged in a larger report containing historical and geopolitical data as well as large amounts of hard facts that served as background information or context for the stories. Graphs, statistics, economic indicators, demographics, models and other calculations fortified the narratives.

The depth of the analysis and background research had not only to do with the precision of the content of the scenarios – and hence the quality of the work – but it was also linked to a methodological dimension, a process that Wack called 'rooting'. Rooting occurs when the predetermineds have entered the minds of the decision makers, thus creating a joint point of departure. Wack maintained, 'you must go back in time far enough to provide for a common interpretation to events and data' (1984a). Telling far-out future stories may be entertaining or amusing, but if the purpose of doing the exercise is to enable decision makers to think with scenarios, then the futuristic stories must be grounded in a reality to which the decision maker can relate. Illustrating facts and analysing the predetermineds tethers the scenarios. Here, a mix of numbers and narratives, fact and fiction, serve to enhance credibility and legitimacy.

Wack seemed to be comfortable amidst such contradiction and with both standpoints. His wife, Eve, remembers Pierre as 'tolerant and rigid, curious and discreet, introvert and open to all experiences. What fascinated me with Pierre is that he was everything and the opposite' (Wack, 1998). Hardin Tibbs, scenario practitioner, remembers Wack as combining 'sensitivity to expanded perception with his own highly rational and logical style of thinking' (Tibbs, 1998). Wack's spiritual life, his dreaming, is important because it influenced the epistemological perspectives that became ingrained in the practice. Sensing, intuiting and reflection are foundational points of the practice that incorporate the more fleeting, emotive and tacit forms of knowledge in hard, positivist analyses.

Knowing and seeing today

The uniqueness of Wack's contribution – that of knowing and seeing – is fortunately continued by many inspired practitioners that are developing their own repertoire of practice. While some of Wack's lessons were transient, important traces of Wack's legacy exist in the practice today while others, unfortunately, are forgotten. Wack's repertoire of mental models, discontinuities, predetermineds, rooting, intuitive logics and re-perceiving still have currency, though sometimes cloaked in other terms.

However, much current practice hardly resembles Wack's. As we will see in the next section, his methodology is but a skeleton and inspiration. Was it the mix of deep research and reflection that allowed discontinuities to be realized? Do the specifics of Wack's method – the embracing of knowing and seeing – enable radical re-perception and successful organizational change? If knowing and seeing is by-passed in favour of more abbreviated methods, what is truly lost?

REFLECTING FORWARD: THE FUTURE OF SCENARIO PLANNING

The times since Wack have changed for scenario practitioners and managers. Not only can we speak of increased global volatility, but also of entangled human, material and institutional actors that are difficult to resolve. Further, the extreme specialization (and consequent compartmentalizing of knowledge) within firms makes grasping complexity an even more daunting task. Making strategic sense is made none the easier with the deluge of information available. Instead, coupled with the urgency of contemporary competition, the searching and filtering of signals has become overwhelmingly time-consuming. Researching creatively and intelligently, and finding the right balance of sources, is arguably made more complicated by the growing number of options and increased accessibility of data.

The paradox is that, with higher uncertainty and increased volatility, there is a greater need for complex, often time-intensive, tools to look at complex problems. Many managers insist that they have neither the time nor the intellectual resources to think in such a holistic manner. Organizations are too busy and projects are moving too fast to stop and think. The irony is that constant change creates more demand for deep thought so that a company can continually rework competencies and strategies.

It is clear that modern practitioners are pressed for time and resources in a way that Wack did not experience. Wack and his team of smart researchers and diverse colleagues were able to devote months to projects and delve deeply into content. And Wack's methods require this time and investment. Today, practitioners are working on shorter time horizons that simply don't allow the systematic study of context and rigorous under-standing of clients that Wack enjoyed. Quite the reverse, the time intensiveness of scenario planning disables many smaller firms from engaging in the practice and, in troubled economic times, many larger firms regret not being able to luxuriate in reflection.

Atomized methods

This resource crunch has led many practitioners today to do quick 'stunt scenarios', and write about creating a 'scenario in a day' and develop other means to abbreviate the process. One solution to meet the resource challenges of managers is to atomize the tools to deal with emerging complexities. We see the methods for scenario planning becoming abbreviated, fractioned and simplified while nonetheless still promising results similar to those Wack and the planners at Shell achieved.

Under the pressure to deliver quick approaches – and solutions – consultants often reduce scenarios to simple steps, and have to go into companies without the time, resources or experience to get to know the decision makers or the industry. As one practitioner reports, 'consultants should not be expected to tell clients about their industry. The division of research labor should generally be that the consultant looks at the external environment while the client is responsible for researching issues in their own industry' (Ertel, 1998). The jury is still out about the best division of labour, but it is important to note that the acclaimed successes at Shell were linked to the devotion and immersion of Wack in the energy industry.

Nonetheless, one thing is clear: the implications of the resource crunch and such a delegation of responsibility is that today's practice often skims over a deep analysis necessary for articulating prede-termineds. There are ample examples of scenario projects where uncertainties and certainties are short-handed as driving forces that are quickly sorted into critical uncertainties. Any presumption that it is possible to know the certainties can easily be lost to a mood of wallowing in uncertainty and explaining how chaotic and volatile the scene is. The focus is on the tumultuous, uncertain, unknowable world of today, and few are confident to say what is evidently certain.

This diverges from Wack's careful study of discontinuities and predetermineds where elucidation of 'future implications of something that has already happened' is often not obvious. Wack would contend that predetermineds reside in our periphery and are not given ample attention. The point is then not just to be imaginative and reflective, but also to use scenario planning to become well educated about new competitors, future customers, likely conflicts and opportunities. Wack's practice shows that with careful study some emerging trends – or predetermineds – become apparent. Only upon sustained inspection can such dynamics be sensed and then incorporated into the strategic outlook.

Another deviation from Wack's practice is that many modern practices of scenario planning develop scenarios in isolation, with scant input from the decision makers or the people who should respond to the scenarios. Time spent researching and understanding individual managerial mental models has diminished, and instead, scenario planning has shifted focus to collaborative group discussions or, in more extreme deviations, consultant-created scenarios that lack grounding in organizational particularities. Group brainstorming often falls prey to 'group think' and could thus provide a partial explanation for the superficial reflections often evident in scenarios. Other schools of scenario planning opt for quick, abbreviated methods that completely erase stakeholder involvement in favour of scenarios created from extensive desk research. These modes of scenario planning are costly in terms of loss of diversity and legitimacy.

Re-perceiving is a deep art that must be grounded in an organizational context that renders the expectations of managers in a new light. Wack's practice differs from modern scenario-planning consultancy, which is instead characterized by methods that quickly address key uncertainties and have limited engagement with managerial thinking and local knowledge. With superficial coverage of the company and industry, one cannot expect the traditional value of scenarios to be reaped. In order to anticipate properly, respond, and develop contingency plans that affect stakeholders, scenarios must not only be recognizable to managers and properly researched, but also be well integrated into the corporate culture. Without attention on the managers and their environment, how should re-perceiving take place?

Wack's work was well integrated in Shell, fortressed with in-depth research and supported by Shell management. Multi-generational scenarios tailored to redressing the particular problematic situation informed decision making. Strategy was an iterative cycle of scenarios, research and reflection. These cycles are contrary to the kind of incremental, compartmentalized procedure of scenario planning that is viewed in isolation of, or in addition to, other management procedures.

Such integrated reflection should lead to a cogent grasp of the dynamics shaping the industrial terrain, knowledge of the key players, and an enlightened understanding of how elements interact over time. Such an integrated style of inquiry takes commitment and involves not only accessing new and unlikely information, but also time for reflection and making sense of the findings. Breaking down archaic thoughts and replacing them with a new architecture of reality takes time, understanding and even empathy and patience. Or as Leonard and Swap (2004) suggest, accessing and transferring an individual's deepest knowledge can only happen 'slowly, patiently and systematically'.

Short and fast or deep and long?

Whether the absorptive reflection and intense research that Wack championed can occur within rushed contexts is nonetheless up for debate. While the abbreviated methods are obviously a corrosion of Wack's work, what is left in place is notwithstanding an enduring practice. We must ask how scenarios, and particularly Wack's ways of knowing, are relevant under these conditions. With superficial research, a lack of contextual grounding, and without a deep understanding of managerial perspective, what is left of value in the process? How fragile is the method if sliced up, adapted to other contexts (without research) and applied in unfavourable conditions of practice (time and resource constraints)? Since scenario planning is a tool of management, it is important to consider if the methods have, in effect, forgotten the managers and their understandings of their business and environments.

However, there are some advantages to short, cursory methods. Aside from recognizing that they might be necessary, a less expensive and quicker process can sometimes yield noteworthy results. Small, abbreviated methods can offer inspirational thinking that can unleash creative potential in a company making scenarios a novel addition to existing problem-solving and decision-making techniques. Experimenting successfully with scenarios can lead to a simple and clearly outlined vision of the business, which corresponds to tactics that can be adjusted as new dynamics emerge.

Employing futures-oriented methods highlights that the future is malleable and provides a good starting place for assertive business practices. Also, the atomized methods can serve to articulate existing, institutionalized, anticipatory knowledge and expectations. Scenarios can thus be developed quickly and superficially as a means to experiment with and elucidate existing organizational expectations. This articulation of expectations, however superficial, is a good start to clarifying strategic missions. Instead of becoming an insincere ritual that has no heart, cursory scenario planning can be an apt communication tool that begins a dialogue with a forward stance.

The strength of the atomized method relies on the idea that the main leverage in decision making amidst uncertainty lies with an organization's ability to learn. Scenarios ask managers to go on an adventure of discovery in the hope of gaining fresh perspectives relevant to everyday decision making. While this leaves behind the hallmark of Wack's repertoire, abbreviated methods are nonetheless a way for organizations to experiment loosely with managerial thinking and begin to integrate new learning.

Overcoming blind spots is a matter of attention where a *glance* – rather than a deep stare – may be fruitful in its own right in some cases, but dangerous in others. Short scenario exercises may inspire managers to take a look around – to notice the periphery – which may, in certain cases, be an improvement to a sharply focused orientation. Developing peripheral vision through the use of scenarios enables managers to look at the edges and the outliers in order to catch a glimpse of the non-obvious.

This suggests that instead of the large-scale bi-annual scenario projects of Wack's day, an alternative for today's organizations involves frequent processes of reflection, iteration and sketching of more compact stories. Such a tactic approximates Wack's repertoire of knowing and seeing, where a continuous articulation of the business vision is juxtaposed with the business environment, and managerial perception of it. Many small stories, or vignettes, can be created in shorthand and distributed widely. The medium of 'story' is an apt vehicle for condensing a complicated picture into an easily memorable and portable reference for emerging conditions.

Since, unlike the centralized planning apparatus of Wack's time, most of today's organizations are decentralized or networked in a way that precludes top-down transmission of new information, such probing stories must be distributed widely in order to be well integrated into organizational cultures. Legitimacy may, in this way, be garnered in a more grassroots style. The organization can have many discreet parts sensing environmental changes, relating them to the stories and reporting on an ongoing basis from the bottom-up.

With an appreciative system like this built into organizations as small, fast glances solidified into stories that can become part of the organizational learning, some of the benefits of scenario planning are maintained, even amidst dramatically changed circumstances.

CONCLUSIONS: THE ENDURANCE OF WACK

Scenario planning is more than a tool, it is also a practice laden with community norms, rules and rituals. In this chapter we have re-examined the source of its durability by a return to its intellectual foundations. The repertoire of predetermined driving forces, uncertainties, deep reflection, overcoming blind spots, is an early contribution to strategic thinking whose relevance continues today. However, this founding repertoire, characterized as embracing ambiguously both *knowing* and *seeing*, has been, for better and worse, subjugated to selective memory.

The practice of scenario planning, this gentle art of re-perceiving, is not a lost art, but is just mildly forgotten in these tumultuous, volatile times. This chapter helps us to remember one influential character in the practice, and to reflect upon how memory can aid future work. As the practice ages, it is transformed and adapted from its origins by innovations of contemporary scenario planners, yet origins still provide a frame of reference and an identity, which set the stage with success stories and accomplishments.

Wack helped to formulate a repertoire of practice by importing ideas that remain its conceptual building blocks and inform the foundation of the scenario-planning method. Wack is the 'reflective practitioner' – one who mixes highly rational processes of discovery with interconnected areas of research in a thoughtful synthesis. Wack's repertoire is, on the one hand, a constructivist's view of maps, perception and interpretation – *dreaming*; and on the other, forces, certainties, patterns and a reality that can be known – *professing*. Seeing and knowing present dichotomies as evidenced in Table 2.1.

Table 2.1 Seeing and knowing Dichotomies

Seeing	Knowing
Maps	Forces
Process	Content
Subjective	Objective
Constructivist	Positivist
Perceptions	Facts
In there – 'inner space'	Out there – 'outer space'
Art	Science
Fictions	Facts
Open	Closed

Seeing involves both an immediate knowledge, situated in perspective, and a deeper gaze. Knowing refers to a factual intelligence, or justified believing based on a reasoned context. The dualities that he introduced have been structured into the method. Understanding uncertainty and managerial mental models, as well as re-perceiving the strategic outlook, are guiding features, still crucial elements of any scenario practice – whether Wack's style or the modern incarnations.

If the future of scenario planning involves a continual foray into quick-storied representations of incremental change, the abbreviated version of scenario planning may very well be good enough to engage both *seeing* and *knowing*. However, despite the advantages and possible necessity of an abbreviated method, vision is still not only about breadth and periphery, but also depth and reflection. Novel developments are not always obvious, but can be partially revealed through careful study and questionning. Though inquiring glances around may often suffice, we might just have to gaze intensely into the forces affecting business to really grasp the fleeting change that creates the ripples and signifies the larger swell of a predetermined.

While Shell beginnings deserve accolades, the complexity and depth of prospective research has not been carried through into modern abbreviated methods. This may or may not be a problem. It is all about *purpose*. If an organization needs to sort through a complex environment and make tough decisions with significant consequences, the heavy method may be most relevant. If the aim is to disrupt groupthink and build teams through creative exercises, the simplified methods will do just fine. A quick method may suffice for shaking things up, having a look at current or near term conditions, and grasping incremental change. Yet the further the time horizon extends, the greater the need to seek out sustainable options amidst radical change. Authentic reflection takes time. Simple solutions work for simple problems; more complex dilemmas often require more rigorous, thoughtful and time-intensive methods. Put another way, in order to achieve radical re-perceiving, diligence is required.

We should strive to develop this decades – old practice and take it to the next level, keeping in mind the old lessons that need to be relearned. The main tenets of the 'gentle art' remind us to take the time to reflect and to look around, not only at the periphery, but also into the depths of change. When and how to use a deep, broad penetrating stare or a cursory glance will continue to be a challenge for the practice of scenario planning if the benefits are to be realized. The future of scenario planning relies upon the development of evolving, experimental and heuristic processes that enable a strong knowledge of context to be embedded within the organizational mind. The art and science of scenario planning, trying on different systematic ways of knowing to gain novel insight, continues to be a practice that enables organizational flexibility and endurance.

SCENARIOS IN THE WORLD OF BUSINESS

INTRODUCTION

As we discussed in the overall introduction to this book, good strategy requires skilful thinking in both the world of business (WOB) and the world of management (WOM). The WOB needs the personal contributions of many individuals in the WOM, and the WOM needs the underlying logic of rational strategic thinking that results from thinking in the WOB. Both are necessary and one cannot be done without the other. However, in a discussion of tools available to enhance our thinking skills the WOB/WOM distinction is convenient to clarify and emphasize the purpose of a particular thinking process being discussed. Part II concerns a discussion of strategic thinking in the WOB. In Part III the emphasis moves to WOM.

WOB thinking involves seeing the organization as a unitary actor in the world, in interaction with other players such as customers, competitors, the government and other stakeholders, and engaging in a thinking process to decide what optimal strategy to follow to ensure its future in its playing field. Most people find this anthropomorphic view an intuitively comfortable perspective. It is the normal way in which the world likes to talk about strategy. We read in the newspapers how Shell has managed its relationships in Nigeria, we read about Microsoft's slow response to the internet,

Scenarios for Success: Turning Insights into Action   Edited by Bill Sharpe and Kees Van der Heijden
© 2007 John Wiley & Sons, Ltd

Airbus' attempt to enhance its cost position, UNICEF's activities in Africa, Greenpeace's successes, and so on. Whenever we feel the need to attach a personal face to the abstract notion of the organization's strategy we move towards visualizing the role of the manager or the CEO as the individual who has the ultimate power of decision and therefore stands for this activity. Alternatively, we think in terms of a more abstract 'decision maker' who needs to do all this thinking in order to reach a valid conclusion, or we talk about 'we' and 'us', imagining ourselves in the shoes of the organizational decision-maker or thinking on that person's behalf. We accept that others may be delegated to think about the organization's strategy – for example, a strategic planning department – but always on the basis of the assumption that this thinking is done on behalf of the organization as a whole, and we implicitly suppose that strategists are objective and able to separate their professional thinking from any personal interests or perspectives.

There are many aspects to strategizing that make this WOB type of thinking crucially important. First of all, there is the concrete reality of the situation in which the organization finds itself. Its environment is configured by objectively determinable conditions, many of which can be analysed, as taught in executive courses such as the MBA. There are the laws of economics and the laws of the marketplace. There is the logic of technological development and the imperatives of the political and cultural realities faced by the organization. There is the major issue of relative productivity and the relation between cost and income. And so on. No organization can ignore any of this if it wants to survive and prosper. And since most organizations are subject to competition they need constantly to increase their skill in evaluating these issues to stay ahead in the game. One of the key tools that CEOs and strategists can use today to distinguish themselves is scenario thinking. While many management planning and decision-making tools have come and gone, scenarios have become firmly established in strategy making and policy work across the world. In this introduction we look at some of the reasons for this endurance and provide a framework for understanding the core of what scenario methods do in the WOB, and how these core ideas are being developed into a wide range of tools for different circumstances.

To understand the power of scenario methods we must first of all clarify what is meant by strategy – just what sort of question or problem is it that scenario thinking can help us with? So we will start with two simple definitions of strategy and scenarios, and will then analyse them together, showing how a wide range of specific WOB problems in strategy making can be tackled by the disciplines of scenario thinking:

- **Strategy** is a statement about how to enhance an organization's chances of survival and success under conditions of uncertainty in the environment.
- A **scenario** is a self-consistent account of one plausible way in which uncertain future events may play out with a bearing on the future of an organization and its ability to fulfil its purpose. Scenarios always come in sets, reflecting future uncertainty.

Scenario planning is the term in common use for scenarios in strategy. This draws attention to the ultimate outcome of business strategy – which is some organizational plan of action – but it tends to obscure the point that the goal of using scenarios is to improve the organizational capacity to think about the future, and to be more alert and responsive to change. A plan is one particular way of organizing our actions, and tends to make us think of laying out a sequence of steps that must all be executed to reach a destination, like a route plan for our holiday. Strategic plans of this sort are, rightly, not much in favour, because the world is constantly changing and we value the ability to adapt our plans as we receive new information. So, we are looking at the relationship between scenario *thinking*, and strategy, allowing us to have a broader view of both.

We can now explore the power of scenarios for strategy making in terms of the range of challenges presented by the strategic situation of an organization, and the way that scenario planning integrates different thinking approaches towards understanding and acting on them. This is shown diagrammatically in Figure II.1. Above each double-ended arrow is shown an aspect of the strategic situation. At each end of the arrow is shown a response represented as a particular thinking approach that we might make to it. Each arrow contrasts two approaches that appear to be opposites, and will seem paradoxical if we attempt to practise them together. Here we have a dilemma: a conflict between two choices, each of which is valuable, but where each excludes the other. Below the line is the technique that scenario planning uses to resolve this dilemma, allowing us to use aspects of the two contrasting thinking approaches in a constructive way.

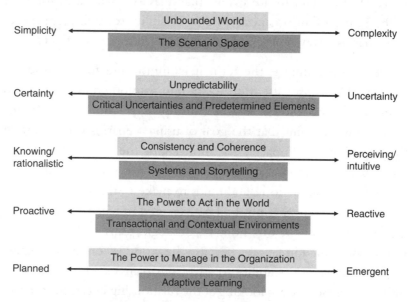

Figure II.1 Five aspects of the strategic situation and how they relate to scenario planning

So, we can take a quick tour through the power of scenario planning before taking each of these elements in more detail.

At the outset, strategy making must deal with the boundless and ever-shifting complexity of the world, and yet must reduce it to some choices that are simple enough to understand, communicate and implement. There is no limit to what we might legitimately bring within the scope of our analysis, but first we must find a way to bring this unbounded world within the reach of our finite minds. We must respect the complexity, but avoid collapsing into a blinkered simplicity. Scenarios do this, not by forecasting a single simple future, but by giving us a small set of self-consistent pictures of the future that cut this complexity down to a manageable size.

As we bring the world within the scope of our minds we must preserve the essential uncertainty of the future, which is the setting for the exercise of judgement. Holding uncertainty in mind creates an open stance to information that allows us to examine each event for its significance. Good scenarios help us to sort out uncertainty into those differences in outcome that will have the greatest impact on us. They also provide a way to develop specific premonitions of how events might unfold, and to see in what respects they are more or less predetermined or contingent.

We cannot reach deep insight into alternative futures without enquiring into the underlying coherence and pattern around which particular events will unfold. On the one hand, we can look towards deep 'lawful' models and, on the other, we need to remain open to the infinite possibilities of human action in the world; we must harness both the strongest logic and the deepest intuition. This lies at the very heart of scenario planning, and is the centre of the discussion concerning technique and insight that runs through this book.

As we start the move from understanding to action, we must frame judgements about the extent of our influence and power to act in the world. We must hold the ground between being purely passive and reactive to events on the one hand, and overestimating our ability to shape outcomes on the other. Scenario planning gives us the language of the contextual and planning environments to support a principled investigation of our field of action.

Finally, as we move our thinking into the world of management (which is addressed in more detail in Part III), we use scenarios to raise the performance of the entire organization to the level of adaptive learning, where strategic action is the result of individual actions by many different people, each engaging in constant, vigilant interpretation of the environment; each making different judgements on the best course of action; and all, therefore, having to engage in a process of accommodation and consensus building to build an organizational action pattern that is coherent and effective towards the outside world.

In the following analysis we expand on each of these core elements of scenario thinking and introduce the following Part II chapters which show how leading practitioners are using and extending them to meet the demands of modern strategy making.

SIMPLICITY VS COMPLEXITY: THE SCENARIO SPACE

The most important role performed by scenario methods is that they free us from being captured by all the assumptions on which our business-as-usual rests, and open our minds to question those assumptions. To help us to break free of one model of the future, scenarios are constructed to give us one or more convincing alternatives that provoke us to think more effectively about what the future environment could be and its effects on us. It is very hard to think about all the sources of uncertainty we are faced with in all their complexity, so we often resolve the dilemma by collapsing back into our dominant future story, and a vague, unstructured sense of everything else. By bringing the future into focus with a specific, self-consistent account, we can start down the path of reducing confusion to more structured uncertainty.

The introduction of multi-future thinking is a key step in developing the organizational culture towards a more flexible and adaptive approach to the future. The dominance of the official future may be maintained by inherent conservatism, and scenarios are then a way to start opening up the organization to a more innovative attitude. On the other hand, highly innovative organizations may also be locked into their own interpretation of the world; leaders are often valued and value themselves for presenting a clear view of the future and their organizational purpose. This can act as a very strong filter on the organizational perception, and scenario methods can be used to create a way for the organization to make the key step towards an open and exploratory understanding.

Verloop (Chapter 3) lays out the basic distinction between business as usual and game-changing strategy as a fundamental distinction that goes across many descriptions of strategy and innovation. He shows how scenarios can play a central role in opening up this exploration. Ringland (Chapter 6) describes the wide variety of tools that are available for understanding the environment, and shows how scenario planning methods relate to them and can be used to integrate them. Nordfors (Chapter 8) makes the case for scenario methods having the power to cope with the full complexity of current day geopolitical complexity.

CERTAINTY VS UNCERTAINTY: CRITICAL UNCERTAINTIES AND PREDETERMINED ELEMENTS

Information is a difference that makes a difference!

Bateson

Scenarios are not forecasts, they are not meant to be individually right or wrong, but to call up in our mind alternative possible futures. They are intended to move our minds into creating 'memories of the future' in which we visualize some future situation, and in so doing create a mental memory that will allow us to encounter unfolding events with a sense of recognition. The principle here is: what we have thought about we will be more ready to respond to. The job of scenario making is therefore to explore the relationship between possible futures and the potential success or failure of the organization in ways that are specific and relevant, but without supposing that we can have a complete picture. By building broad accounts of the future we are able to give significance to individual events, even those that would otherwise pass us by. Anyone who has been on a scenario project will report the effect of seeing items in the news over the next few days and weeks that jump out as being relevant to the scenarios on which they are working – an effect known as 'cognitive priming'. These instances are referred to in scenario practice as 'pockets of the future in the present'. It comes as a surprise to realize how much information about the future is around us if we know how to look for it.

The power of scenarios as a thinking tool is that they hold certainty and uncertainty about the future in creative tension. We do not have the time or the inclination to question everything in the world on which we rely and which could, in principle, change; some possibilities just have to be left to one side. If *everything* changed, then we would probably not be worrying about the continuity of our organization; we do strategy because we aim to operate in a way that is relevant to a range of possibilities in the world. To be useful, strategic thinking must therefore be seen as close enough to the official future to be relevant, and different enough to be challenging to our assumptions. This is reflected in scenario methods by careful attention to both predetermined elements and critical uncertainties. The predetermined elements create the underlying movement that we choose to regard as 'assumed given', against which we can explore critical uncertainties that might affect us. For example, over the last three decades scenario projects in the

IT industry have generally considered the convergence of computing, communications and content to be a long-term predetermined trend, riding on fundamental progress in the underlying digital technologies. Critical uncertainties have related to such things as timing and intensity of change, and how the power structure of the industry would shift.

Finding relevant structure in future uncertainty is the central task of scenario building and, as was discussed in Part I, reaching real insight can never be easy. Each of the chapters in this part demonstrates the very exploratory process needed to develop the critical uncertainties. They show how this needs to flow from an active prototyping which brings the issues of relevance to the decision makers into the process from the start. A particular approach to structuring the uncertainties is put forward in Hodgson and Sharpe (Chapter 5) which focuses on the idea of a single 'dominant loop' in the underlying dynamics and how it varies between scenarios.

KNOWING VS PERCEIVING: SYSTEMS AND STORYTELLING

> Scenarios can be successful ... only when (1) they are based on a sound analysis of reality, and (2) they change the decision-maker's assumptions about how the world works and compel him to change his image of reality.
>
> Pierre Wack (1984a)

The power of scenario methods comes from their ability to render an infinitely complex world accessible to our limited imaginations and decision-making skills. Their resilience as a management tool owes a lot to the flexibility of the central idea of using scenario *stories* to capture meaning. Stories are infinitely flexible; in telling a story we can move along a spectrum from the realistic and analytical to the free flow of creative imagination. The task of scenario thinking is to move from an apparent disconnection between the world as currently known and imaginative views of a very different future, to seeing dramatic challenges and possibilities as part of the fabric of the world as it will, or might be made, to unfold.

To harness the perceptual power of our imaginations, scenarios not only can, but *must* bring together the grounded logical understanding of the world, with our imaginative perception of possibilities. Unlike settling down with a novel for pure enjoyment, the job of strategic thinking is to bring radical change into sharp focus as a threat or opportunity to the organization's own future. It is therefore core to successful scenario work in support of strategy making that it connects deeply to the decision maker's own understanding of how the world works and the way structural change might happen. To be useful, scenarios must analyse the whole pattern of relationships within which the organization acts and evolves, and must be rooted in a system's understanding of the world. The systemic grounding of the narrative scenarios is achieved in scenario building by the key requirement of internal consistency.

Two chapters particularly develop this element of scenarios. Hodgson and Sharpe (Chapter 5) develop the systems approach to deepening scenario structure and exploring structural transitions over time. Nordfors (Chapter 8) makes the case for the power of narrative, and looks to the practice of historians for the most powerful methods of storytelling appropriate to scenarios.

PROACTIVE VS REACTIVE: TRANSACTIONAL AND CONTEXTUAL ENVIRONMENTS

If the first job of strategic thinking is to make us explore our conventional assumptions, then the second and more important task is to shape our actions – having thought about future possibilities, we must decide what we want to do, and what we can do, and then carry it out. This is not just a deductive process, it is in essence a creative and entrepreneurial act, where we see a way to create a successful organization and then commit resources to implement it. Developing a successful new strategy requires a keen sense of the things we can or might control – and which therefore create possibilities for proactive shaping – and those that are controlled by others, and to which we must therefore be able to react. Scenario thinking gives us the language of the 'transactional' and 'contextual' environments to make the distinction between our field of action, where we believe we have some influence, and the remoter world which is considered primarily as 'given'.

An example of reactive strategy is contingency planning or defensive plans whose intent is to anticipate disasters or attacks and ensure that we have ways to preserve our organization against them. Entrepreneurial organizations are entirely proactive – they are trying to carve out a new position in the market for themselves, establishing a pattern of relationships in their transactional environment within the constraints of their contextual environment. For most organizations strategic thinking will lie between these two extremes.

Strategies ultimately express themselves in the transactional environment; we must envisage in specific and precise ways how we and other actors might relate in the future, and what potential for action we have. Many of the most significant changes in the business landscape flow from shifts between contextual and transactional spaces, such as the way digital media technology is reshaping whole industries. Truly great strategies are always based on new and innovative insights about the context in which our strategic decisions are enacted. At their most effective, scenario methods allow us to bring within view the broadest context beyond our control, and link this with our own field of action.

Every chapter in Part II is concerned in one way or another with this central dimension of strategy making. Verloop (Chapter 3) argues that scenarios enable managers to explore the 'new game' and how they might want to play it. This is examined in depth by Ramírez and Van der Heijden (Chapter 4), who present their approach of 'staging' as a systematic exploration of strategy options by redefining the boundary between transactional and contextual spaces. Medjad and Ramírez (Chapter 7) draw attention to the underdeveloped potential to include legal reasoning in strategy exploration. Fink *et al.* (Chapter 6) bring the multitude of specific business decision tools into a framework which integrates them with scenario planning. Nordfors (Chapter 8) discusses how stories act as 'springboards' for strategy exploration.

PLANNED VS EMERGENT STRATEGY: ADAPTIVE LEARNING

> From the moment of acknowledgement of uncertainty, the key to success moves from the idea of one-time development of 'best strategy' to the most effective ongoing strategy process.
>
> Van der Heijden, *The Art of Strategic Conversation*

As we watch a tennis match between top players we hear the commentator pass judgement on a shot played well or badly on which the match might turn, and then reflect on whether one or other of the players needs to rethink his or her whole game plan if he or she is to have a chance of success. Effective action requires us to keep moving between fluent action in the flow of events and deliberation on our whole approach; the world does not allow us to rest on either side of the dilemma for long. Are our challenges to be met by a more imaginative and effective execution of our plan, or must we rethink, reorganize and radically change what we are doing? This is the fundamental dilemma of strategy when thought of as pursuing organizational success under conditions of uncertainty. To survive we must be constantly adapting and learning. In this process the very purpose of the organization must be in play – organizational strategy is not about fulfilling a given mission, it is about exploring and redefining our purpose in a changing world.

The previous sections have shown how scenario methods make two contributions to resolving this dilemma: they free us from our dominant model of the future so that we are more alert to the significance of change, and allow us to explore the full complexity of the unfolding world in ways that are within the reach of our minds. The third way to resolve the dilemma is for the practice of multi-future thinking to become established as a continuing organizational event. This means that the significance of daily events can be framed as business as usual that can be met by our normal organizational planning, or as signalling the need for strategic renewal.

In this part of the book we are primarily concerned with thinking in the world of business, and therefore showing how scenario tools bring adaptive strategic options to light. The full discussion of how this can be embedded in organizational life is found in Part III, where we turn to thinking in the world of management.

APPRECIATIVE SYSTEMS

Strategy making can be summed up as the need to make three sorts of judgement. The first judgement is outward looking, to inform our mind about the world in which we will be operating in the future, with a particular concern for those things that are uncertain and beyond our control but which might have significant impact on us. The second judgement concerns our response to what we see out in the world, and whether our value system stimulates us to try to do something about it. The third judgement concerns our potential for action in the anticipated future world: to make up our mind about what our levers for action are, including who we can align with, or cause to align with us.

A key figure in developing the understanding of these three forms of strategic judgement is Sir Geoffrey Vickers who developed the idea of the *appreciative system*. This is a qualitative view of a system that is inseparable from human perception and understanding. Vickers distinguishes three aspects of appreciative systems, all of which are forms of human judgement; these aspects have mental and emotional skills associated with each of them. *Reality judgement* is the ability to represent to oneself a total state of affairs around a policy issue in a comprehensive and balanced way. *Instrumental judgement* is the ability to see and understand one's ability to operate and to design possible actions. *Value judgement* is the prioritizing of options. The combination of all three forms of judgement will determine the integrity of the appreciative system. Integrity implies an integration of fact and value. The three modes together combine fact and value in an act of decision.

CHAPTER OVERVIEW

Chapter 3 – Innovation and Scenarios, by Jan Verloop

The fundamental question all decision makers face when thinking in the WOB is whether they can go on operating on their business-as-usual model, or whether they face the opportunity or imperative for change. We start Part II with a discussion of this central question, which, as shown by Verloop, unites many discussions of strategy in the literature around a basic distinction between 'inside-the-box' and 'outside-the-box' innovation. Innovation and scenarios are linked through change – anticipated or created. Scenarios are used to explore alternative outcomes resulting from trends that could lead to a disruptive change in the business environment. Scenarios are thus most useful in the context of game-changing, out-of-the-box innovation; the context for incremental innovation is the business-as-usual. The critical question in game-changing innovation is whether the company wants to play the new game. Scenarios provide the best backdrop to make that assessment, provided that the scenarios are specific; generic scenarios are seldom relevant.

Besides this 'obvious' use of scenarios for assessing radical innovation projects, there is a deeper and more pervasive advantage for a company to use scenarios. This advantage stems from the similarity between innovation and change processes and the creation of scenarios. All three processes pass through three similar stages: an open, creative stage with drivers and external input; an analytical phase in which assumptions are tested and choices made; and a final implementation stage, in which the commitments have to be made. Scenarios steer the creative effort as well as handling the structural uncertainty in game-changing innovation.

Anticipating the WOM discussions in Part III, Verloop also discusses how scenarios provide a rich communication platform for shaping outside-the-box innovation. In radical innovation there needs to be a balance between top-down and bottom-up initiatives. Communicating the strategic intent of the innovation effort with the company strategy is an option, but including the background scenarios makes the message more effective, because it leaves space for outside-the-box opportunities.

Chapter 4 – Scenarios to Develop Strategic Options: A New Interactive Role for Scenarios in Strategy, by Rafael Ramírez and Kees Van der Heijden

As Verloop has shown, scenarios come into their own when strategic change in the WOB must be explored. Chapter 4 proposes ways to strengthen the role of scenarios in that exploration. The traditional use of scenarios in strategy formulation has often been to 'testbed' or 'wind tunnel' options that have already been arrived at, exploring the options in the transactional environment against 'given' drivers of change in the contextual environment. However, under the modern conditions of market complexity and rapid change, methods are needed that tackle the generation of new strategy options directly, and bring the boundary between transactional and contextual environments into play. In particular there is a need for ways to generate options that will change the whole pattern of value-creating relationships within which the organization works, while relating them to the organization's capabilities.

In this chapter the potential for scenarios to be used in this proactive, entrepreneurial way is explored further, building on the way scenarios integrate a contextual and transactional view of the environment: the authors propose using scenario planning to create options that reposition the boundary between the more immediate transaction ('task' or 'business') environment in which organizations operate and the broader contextual environment in which they are placed.

Four case studies are presented that illustrate both the potential power of this approach in revealing strategic options, and the scale and speed of change which organizations are experiencing that can overtake their strategy making. The challenge of bringing these processes into the organizational processes in ways that can deal with the pace of change is developed further in Part III.

Chapter 5 – Deepening Futures with System Structure, by Tony Hodgson and Bill Sharpe

The previous two chapters have established the way scenarios support the exploration of systemic relationships between the organization and its environment, and the generation of entrepreneurial options for action. In this chapter the nature of systems concepts is developed further, showing how they can help us to reach deeper insights with our scenarios. As discussed in the Introduction to Part I, from a systems perspective the organization is always viewed as part of a field of relationships that all support each other, so the growth of the organization fits into a larger pattern of behaviour maintained and reinforced by many other actors. This system can be characterized as a self-reinforcing 'dominant loop' in which the business-as-usual of the organization is embedded. Alternative scenarios of the future can then be described as different dominant loops which provide a context for strategic change in the business idea of the organization. A new dominant loop provides a new growth logic for the organizations that capitalize on it, and at the heart of entrepreneurial insight is the anticipation of such possible new configurations of value creation. Thus, the use of the dominant loop serves to bring out the essential underlying structure of the scenario space in ways that relate directly to the strategic issue of concern – what does it mean for the organization?

The second part of the chapter introduces a new approach to discussing the nature of transitions between systems. It describes the dynamics of change in terms of three different orientations to the future that are found in the present. This is the three-horizons method: the first horizon is described by the current dominant loop; the second horizon is the emerging field of disruptive innova tion; and the third horizon is concerned with fundamental changes to the values of the existing systems. The three-horizon method helps to bring out many different dynamics in the contests between existing systems and new ones that underlie the development of scenarios.

Chapter 6 – From Signals to Decisions, by Alexander Fink, Philip Hadridge and Gill Ringland

The next two chapters turn from the general to the specific in their discussions of scenarios in the World of Business. In the Oxford Futures Forum that was the origin of this book there was a discussion among strategy practitioners about how scenario planning fits within the wider field of strategy- and decision-making tools that are designed to deal with specific business issues. For example, long-range technology planning is relevant to R&D intensive organizations, whereas retail businesses have different issues to worry about. To understand this relationship between scenarios and other tools, they felt it necessary to look at the whole process: from the ability of an organization to detect and sort signals from outside their organization; from inside; and from the future through to the decision-making processes. They asked the question: What approach and tool should be used in what circumstances?

The result is this chapter, which positions scenario planning alongside the broad set of tools and techniques that have earned their place in the repertoire of strategy and decision making. It defines an idealized six-step process from signals to decisions, describing the tools appropriate for each step and how they fit into the approach to scenario thinking that is developed in this book.

Chapter 7 – When Strangers Meet: Scenarios and the Legal Profession, by Karim Medjad and Rafael Ramírez

This chapter opens up a previously underdeveloped aspect of scenario planning by proposing that scenario thinking and legal thinking have not had the conversation they might have had, and that such a conversation would strengthen them both. The authors find the roots of this disconnect in the very different cultures of the two traditions: the scenario culture is concerned with uncertainty and future orientation in which legal considerations are traditionally confined to mere environmental (contextual or transactional) variables; the legal culture deals with rules and the removal of uncertainty even when the laws have a forward-looking dimension. As far as the legal profession is concerned, scenario thinking is very occasionally – and exclusively – used for the purposes of creating common values among stakeholders or for making sense of complex environments which have changed so much that they need to be reassessed by a central actor.

The authors claim that there is room for a more strategic use of scenarios in the legal domain to sort out and test legal options before choosing one, and even to generate new ones. Taking as an example the area of international corporate social responsibility from the point of view of a hypothetical NGO eager to increase the obligations of Multinational Corporations, they show how neither 'pure' legal reasoning, nor scenario reasoning that lacks sufficient attention to legal considerations, is adequate: each will generate predictions plagued with expensive strategic blind spots.

They conclude with practical considerations of how scenarios could be developed for, and by, the legal profession. Scenario thinking might itself be rendered more robust, and certainly more relevant to an influential population of decision makers, if it were to lend itself to this profession. The chapter is offered as an initial exploration of this relationship, in the hope that it will inspire initiatives to make these two conceptual worlds meet and help each other.

Chapter 8 – The Power of Narrative, by Lennart Nordfors

Finally, we return to the heart of scenario methods: the use of stories to capture complexity and render it in ways that bring it within the reach of our minds. In this chapter Nordfors makes the case that this foundation in narrative form allows scenarios to maintain their role as interpretive tools in the face of the full complexity of modern geopolitics, and discusses how this role can be strengthened. For the most powerful methods of storytelling appropriate to scenarios he looks to the practice of professional historians who must deal with the infinite diversity of human affairs, and for whom narrative is a core research method. He also reviews the use of storytelling as a method for innovation in organizations.

Nordfors makes two claims. The first is that the efficiency with which narrative describes complex matters and processes carries more weight in our minds than attempts to build an argument through long or complex chains of causal reasoning. The narrative depicts both complexity and causality more efficiently than formal modelling, enhancing intuitive understanding. Secondly, narrative has a special capacity to initiate and guide action in organizations. He shows how well-told scenarios are powerful tools for engaging people creatively in organizational innovation and change. In doing so he makes a bridge to Part III of the book in which we explore the organizational side of strategy making.

CHAPTER 3

SCENARIOS AND INNOVATION

Jan Verloop

In a certain way innovation is similar to happiness. It seems easy when it just happens, but it is difficult to achieve in a planned and structured way. Planning and managing may not be the best way to achieve happiness, but that is the only way to achieve continuous success with innovation. Innovation is too important to be left to serendipity and spontaneous creativity. Managers, politicians, academics all agree that innovation is the key to success in today's continuously changing environment, but there is less agreement on how to do it successfully. Business and political leaders often attempt to push innovation by increasing research budgets assuming that with more knowledge, more creative ideas will be generated for bringing more exciting innovations to the market. But this is not the way the innovation process works.

Scenarios for Success: Turning Insights into Action   Edited by Bill Sharpe and Kees Van der Heijden
© 2007 John Wiley & Sons, Ltd

Innovation is bringing an insightful idea successfully to the market. Insight is the key to success in innovation. Insight is required to understand how a customer need can be met in a novel way. Innovation typically starts with identifying a new combination between a customer need and the capabilities to which one has access. Schumpeter was the first to identify the creation of 'Neue Kombinationen' as the essence of innovation. Intrinsic in his thinking as an economist also was the concept that the new combination between technology and market would only become an innovation if it created value. Innovation is not a single, one-off activity or a flash of genius, it is a process; it is the arduous process that is required before value can be created out of a novel idea. This process from idea to customer always goes through three main stages: the creative, the development and the entrepreneurial. The innovation process is often modelled as the passage through the 'innovation funnel' with the three stages. At each subsequent stage the number of ideas reduces because they appear to be unattractive or are monetized in a different way.

With happiness, pushing harder is not always the best way forward. Similarly for innovation, simply pushing more ideas into the funnel increases the resistance in the funnel, but not necessarily the flow of innovations into the market. Innovation is rarely hampered by a lack of ideas. The effective way to increase the rate of innovation is to remove the obstacles in the funnel, reduce the risks in the process and create an incentive pull at the end of it. This sounds simple and evident, but practice proves otherwise.

To be effective, innovation requires an efficient business process with the right people and resources at the right stage, where decisions are made at the right point in time and the assessment starts with the right questions: Is there demand for the new idea and does it have potential for creating value? Managing innovation requires understanding of the nature of the innovation process and the sources of resistance in the funnel. For the former issue it is important to recognize that different types of innovation need to be managed differently, and, for the latter, one has to appreciate that innovation leads to change and change creates resistance.

TWO MODES OF INNOVATION

It may appear that there are many types of innovation as the literature is littered with different descriptors for innovation, such as: game changing, radical, break-through, disruptive, strategic, revolutionary, adaptive, incremental, evolutionary, competitive. Each descriptor refers to a specific characteristic of the type of innovation under discussion and the specific message that the author wants to convey. All these descriptors refer to the type of innovation, but from a managerial perspective only two types of innovation need to be distinguished (Table 3.1). The different descriptors can be grouped into two clusters: Inside-the-Box (ItB) and Outside-the-Box (OtB).

Table 3.1 Two classes of innovation

Inside-the-Box	Outside-the-Box
Incremental	Game-changing, radical
Evolutionary	Breakthrough, revolutionary
Competitive	Disruptive
Adaptive	Strategic

The fundamental difference in innovation is whether it creates a new product (or service) with a new value constellation, or whether it only improves an existing product in an existing value system. In *Insight in Innovation* (Verloop, 2004), the distinction inside-the-box and outside-the-box was introduced because the terminology is neutral, and from a management perspective that distinction captures the essential difference. With ItB innovation the game is played on familiar territory, whereas for OtB innovation one has to play on new, uncharted grounds with unknown scope and scale of challenges. The distinction between ItB and OtB innovation is fundamental and affects all aspects of the innovation process, as illustrated in Table 3.2.

Table 3.2   Characteristics of the two modes of innovation

Inside-the-Box	Outside-the-Box
• Improving existing value systems	• Creating new value systems
• Operates at product strategy level	• Operates at company strategy level
• A 'must-do' activity	• Optional activity (strategic choice)
• Significant, but identifiable risks	• High and unknown risks
• Done for growth and profit	• Done for robustness and continuity
• In-house development	• Developed with partners

Consequently, the two modes of innovation need to be managed differently in line with their own specific requirements. However, few companies have different business processes for the two types of innovation. The quote from Christensen and Raynor (2003) that *Disruptive innovations occur so intermittently that no company has a routine process for handling them* is a clear illustration. However, in a fast-changing competitive environment few companies can survive without game-changing innovation and thus will need two business processes for the two modes of innovation.

Process wise, the distinction between ItB and OtB innovation overlaps to a large extent with the differentiation 'closed innovation' and 'open innovation' introduced by Chesbrough (2003). Both approaches argue from the competitive position of the company in the global knowledge pool. OtB innovation needs to be open innovation because the territory is unknown to the company, and ItB innovation tends to be closed innovation because the company should have a know-how advantage in its own product domain.

The issues to be addressed by the decision makers are completely different for the two types of innovation. For ItB innovation the key factors for success are known and the innovation process is geared to providing the data required for supporting a considered decision. Such data include customer response, competitive position, costs, margins, sales volume, market share, etc., and the techniques to create these data are known. In OtB innovation the end-point – the final product and customers – is not known at the start and only becomes clear and defined during the process. As a result, the issues and data requirements change during the process. Typical questions are: Who will be the customers? Which channels to market are appropriate? Where in the value system will value be created? Where can it be extracted? Will there be a first mover advantage, and if so, will it be defendable?

The essential question for managers in game-changing innovation is: '*Will we like to play this new game?*' Will we be in a position to play it and can we do it better than the competition? These are strategic questions, and not just marketing or research issues. Disruptive innovation is a strategic issue that affects the business idea of a company. Incremental innovation brings 'more of the same', only better or cheaper, whereas OtB innovation brings change, potentially radical change.

And it is here that scenarios can kick in: providing the right backdrop for assessing game-changing innovation. Scenarios can improve decision making by creating the right framework in the minds of the managers for answering the question whether they would like to play the new game in the future.

INNOVATION AND CHANGE

The world is changing continuously and in order to remain competitive in this fast-changing world one has to be innovative. This permanent state of change is the result of an ongoing flow of innovations that enter the markets. The process of change is a circular process where change is created by the need for ever more innovations and where each innovation creates change, and the more radical the innovation the deeper the change.

Whereas the basic reason for ItB innovation is the need to improve, for OtB innovation it is the need to change. OtB innovation can be a proactive strategic initiative by the company to create a step-change in its competitive position, or it can be a reactive strategy forced upon the company by external reasons because the business environment has changed so much that the company has to reinvent itself.

A company that aims to be successful in innovation also needs to be able to manage change. Each innovation process is accompanied by simultaneous transformation processes in the market and in the organization. An external process is needed to align the customer to the new value system, and an internal one to change the business idea of the company and reinvent the business processes that are required for the new value constellation. The unavoidable, but often unexpected, side effect of OtB innovation is that it changes the existing business idea and the way of doing business. The new product or service not only creates new business, but it will compete with existing products and change the customer interface and expectations. These side effects are often not part of the original objectives, but the truism remains: '*If you don't want change, don't innovate.*'

Another, very important side effect of radical innovation is that it makes a company more aware of and resilient to external changes. In today's world radical innovation needs to be 'open innovation', and that means close contacts with external parties, such as customers and partners in development. A shift from closed to open innovation will induce a change in the culture of a company and an ability to recognize and accept change. Openness to the world outside and readiness to change are important factors for continuity in a business. In the words of Darwin: 'It's not the strongest who survive, but those most responsive to change.'

And it is here that scenarios can kick in: sensitising for change. The intrinsic link between OtB innovation and change makes scenarios such a useful tool in radical innovation. Innovation scenarios can trigger in the minds of managers and innovators a readiness for the necessary changes.

SCENARIOS

Scenarios are alternative stories of how the future may unfold. They are not predictions or forecasts, but credible, consistent and challenging stories that help to focus on the critical uncertainties and to understand the balance of forces that will shape the future. Scenarios can have different shapes and formats ranging from an eloquent unfolding of possible dramatic events to a clinical analysis of the forces of change.

Scenarios are usually created to support the development of the company strategy and subsequently to test its robustness. Scenarios appear not to be a very important part of the decision–making process. Most managers tend to minimize the impact of the scenarios on their ultimate decisions. And that is correct: the essential role of scenarios is not to shape decisions, but to alert the manager and open his or her mind for possible changes in the business environment. Pierre Wack, one of the great scenario raconteurs, called scenario planning *the gentle art of re-perceiving.* Scenario planning is about preparing the mind of the manager for changes and disconnecting his perception from the established 'business as usual' view. Scenarios shift perception towards emerging events and sensitize people to change and the impact it can have on the business. They can prepare a company for the occurrence of potential events so that it can respond faster and better; and they can help in identifying successful strategic options for the company and assessing the risks involved in long-term investments or commitments.

Innovation scenarios

Change is the object for both innovation and scenarios; for innovation it is creating change and for scenarios it is preparing for change. That makes scenarios the tool of choice for innovation. Scenarios are very useful for understanding the events that can transform the business or for appreciating the conditions for success in innovation. Managers involved in closed innovation make the decisions within the embedded values of the company, and need to be able to step out of that value constellation to assess the new, OtB value constellation. But the scenarios need to be 'fit for purpose'. Generic scenarios may not be very useful for creating the right reference framework in the manager's mind to judge which innovative games he or she would like to play. Generic scenarios are general purpose scenarios that address potential developments in the business environment at large for use in decision processes for a variety of business issues. The best support for innovation will come from purpose-made scenarios that create images of alternative playgrounds in which the game-changing innovation may have to be played competitively. Such 'innovation scenarios' can help to identify the best innovation options. Innovation scenarios should be derived from, and be consistent with, the scenarios used to develop the company strategy. But the shaping forces and the stakeholders are different in the two types of scenarios. Whereas the strategy scenarios may include geopolitical and socioeconomic developments, and competitive position, the innovation scenarios will focus on future customer markets and trends in technological developments.

It is useful if one of the innovation scenarios is based on a 'business-as-usual' future, in which the balance of shaping forces stays as it is or changes only gradually. Business-as-usual is the arena in which the ItB innovation game is played. This scenario should be familiar terrain for the decision maker and will provide a sound reference point for the alternative scenarios. Whereas a company strategy has to be robust in 'all' the developed strategy scenarios, it is the advantage of an innovation strategy that it can develop different innovation portfolios for different futures. The article by Gosselink (2002) provides a real-life example of distinct innovation responses for three different energy futures: one based on solar energy, one with hydrogen as dominant energy carrier and one based on clean fossil fuels.

Innovation scenarios have a role to play in each stage of the innovation funnel that takes an idea from a speculative possibility to an implemented business offering. In the first stage, company management has to define the 'competitive arenas' for which ideas should be generated. In the second stage of the funnel the new rules of the game have to be developed, and in the final stage management has to commit the company to the rules of the new game. These questions have to be addressed without the comprehensive range of quantitative data available for ItB innovation, and scenarios can help to put the questions in a relevant context. The importance of using the proper tools for assessment in the innovation process is readily illustrated in the first stage of OtB innovation and it is here that the use of familiar ItB tools can do most harm. In OtB innovation the first stage of the process is mainly conceptual, to identify how value can be created for potential customers. For ItB innovation the answers to these issues can be addressed in a quantitative way, but if the same level of quantification is required for an OtB idea, the assessment will be made in the wrong context: tackling OtB ideas with ItB tools will lead to mistakes. This is largely because the level of uncertainty in a sound OtB innovative concept is intrinsically much greater than in an ItB one. Uncertainty is indeed the key element in OtB innovation that needs to be managed with great care. Many managers want to have too much certainty too early in the process, preferably the same as in ItB innovation, and as a result many good ideas die prematurely. Alternatively, if the risks associated with the uncertainties intrinsic to innovation are not properly managed, the innovation effort may turn out to be expensive and unrewarding. OtB innovation is risky; most radical innovations fail.

Scenarios provide a good tool for supporting decision making in innovation. The overarching issues in the assessment process in OtB innovation are achieving alignment between the innovation effort and company strategy, and safeguarding that the new value constellation under design or construction in the innovation process will fit into the future company business. Scenarios also help to identify risk and to structure uncertainty when quantified data are lacking or unreliable. They provide an effective communication platform to discuss and assess these complex issues with all stakeholders in a consistent way, and ensure continuity as the innovation project passes through its various stages involving different players and decision makers.

STRATEGIC INNOVATION

OtB innovation is a strategic effort and scenarios are a strategic tool. Van der Heijden (1997) calls them *the art of strategic conversation*, emphasizing the point that scenarios allow management to discuss the future of the company in a structured way. And if the future of the company includes the need for drastic change, then OtB innovation can play a role. Scenarios create a structured platform to discuss change in an open format from a variety of perspectives. Slightly modifying Van der Heijden's words to emphasize the link between scenarios, strategy and change, we can say that scenarios are instruments to develop '*the art of conversation about strategic change*'.

Iansiti and Levien (2004) argue that stand-alone strategies do not work, because 'a company's success depends on the collective health of the organizations that influence the creation and delivery of its products'. A healthy company needs healthy customers, suppliers, partners and competitors. It needs to be part of a healthy value constellation. Its strategy has to be based on understanding the totality of its business environment, and it has to aim to keep not only the company, but also the 'ecosystem of the company', healthy. Scenarios are a perfect tool for scanning and mapping that ecosystem, and this links scenarios to innovation in a number of ways.

In their most recent book, Seeing What's Next, Christensen *et al.* (2004) explore the potential for using innovation techniques to predict industry change. Although a scenario builder will never use the word 'predict', effectively the method that Christensen *et al.* suggest is equivalent to using innovation techniques for building innovation scenarios. Searching for innovation opportunities includes analysing the signals for change, and this is part and parcel of scenario building.

The use of scenarios in innovation can have a wider benefit than supporting the decision makers and providing them with the right tools. It can be a communication tool to involve the whole company in the innovation effort. An important issue in OtB innovation is the communication between the 'top' and the 'bottom' in the company. OtB innovation is a strategic effort and needs to be initiated and steered from the top, but the grassroots effort is needed to mobilize the creative powers in the company. Innovation scenarios are excellent tools for communicating the strategic intent and defining the domains for innovation. Scenarios provide the right balance between giving direction and allowing sufficient freedom for generating game-changing ideas.

But scenarios cannot only be used to advantage inside the company. Modern OtB innovation tends to be open innovation, where importing ideas and capabilities from outside the company form an integral part of the effort. A valuable source of ideas can be the existing or potential partners or customers, and innovation scenarios can be the communication link between partners, customers and company in a joint effort to co-generate value.

However, there is a hidden danger in the use of innovation scenarios. There is an innate temptation when developing them to create 'ideal futures' that provide the perfect environment in which to implement the company strategy and the innovative ideas. But scenarios should result from the interplay between external trends and forces of change, and not describe preferred developments. Creating idealized scenarios usually occurs with the best of intentions with the aim of making a better, more sustainable world, but it misdirects the innovation effort away from customer needs to 'internal' preferences. This is a 'scenario push' approach to innovation, similar to 'technology push', and it reduces the chances of success in the same way.

Given that a certain objectivity is necessary, should decision makers be involved in developing the innovation scenarios? On the one hand, their involvenent ensures that they can relate to the issues and understand the language (as is the case with so many management tools, the process is at least as important as the product); on the other hand, their involvement may lead to focusing on desired change rather than emerging change.

Idealized scenarios are used in 'backcasting' efforts to design development paths backwards from a desired image of the future. The ideal futures are then used to develop alternative transition paths and associated changes in the system. Idealized scenarios can be useful to structure discussion around 'system innovation' and can be appropriate if there is a reasonable degree of control over how to achieve the desired future. This may be the case for governments under certain conditions, but it is typically not the case for companies. System innovation needs a 'closed' environment, but the open global economy is not conducive for successful system innovation.

SCENARIOS, INNOVATION AND STRATEGIC CHANGE

Scenarios are the instruments of choice for supporting game-changing innovation efforts. They can provide the context and backdrop for management to decide whether they would like to play the new game. Other techniques can also provide this, but not with the richness scenarios can give. The use of scenarios in strategic innovation has a number of key advantages.

- Scenarios provide a sound platform on which to discuss complex issues in a neutral way from a variety of perspectives with stakeholders from both inside and outside the company. This is a significant advantage since game-changing innovation by its very nature always leads to change and conflicting results with winners and losers. With winners and losers inside the same company a neutral communication platform is very valuable.
- Scenarios can handle both the rational and the emotional part of change. Innovation creates change, and change leads to resistance – often irrational resistance. Recognizing the emotive elements in breakthrough innovation is important for managing the process successfully. Scenarios can add a rich palette of colours to a clinical analysis of the forces of change and paint a picture of the emotive elements involved.
- Scenarios are a communication tool. Scenarios can be used to communicate the strategic intent of the innovation effort between the 'top' and the 'bottom' in the company. Management and innovators can share the same language for communicating

the strategic objectives of the innovation effort and the game-changing effects that the proposed innovation projects may have. Scenarios are a strategic tool, not only for creating strategy but also for implementing it. Keeping clear communication lines between the top and bottom in the company, and between the core business and the outside-the-box innovation effort, is an important factor for success.

- Scenarios must be fit-for-purpose. This means that they must be dedicated to innovation and the strategic intent in order to provide the right background for assessing the new games. Scenarios are built around insights and in turn can create new insights; insights are the key that changes a creative idea into a value-creating, innovative concept. Scenarios must remain focused on the trends and events in the outside world and not become biased towards preferred changes or the available capabilities of the company.

Scenarios are not part of the decision-making process, neither for company strategy nor for innovation projects. Scenarios are signposts, not key factors for success or assessment criteria. Their contributions are to provide a framework for understanding change, to trigger re-perception for a new look at the business environment, and to serve as a communication platform for supporting discussion between stakeholders about the often conflicting objectives and outcomes of game-changing innovation.

SCENARIOS TO DEVELOP STRATEGIC OPTIONS: A NEW INTERACTIVE ROLE FOR SCENARIOS IN STRATEGY

Rafael Ramírez and Kees Van der Heijden

Scenarios have been used in companies for over three decades (Lesourne and Stoffaes, 2001; Grant, 2003; Van der Heijden, 2005) and even longer by military planners and policy makers. They have been used for a variety of purposes, for example to influence stakeholders, to help different parties to identify and agree upon common ground, or to research and clarify complex issues. In this chapter, we focus on using scenarios to develop new strategy and will try to show how the management of an organization can use scenario planning to develop new options for successful action. This process involves 'co-production' – engaging communities of stakeholders to create new interorganizational value. It also – for the first time

Scenarios for Success: Turning Insights into Action   Edited by Bill Sharpe and Kees Van der Heijden
© 2007 John Wiley & Sons, Ltd

in our knowledge – involves deploying scenarios proactively to shift the boundary between the transactional environment and the contextual environment. This innovative use of scenarios enables stakeholders collectively to colonize and exploit new areas of their joint environments to obtain common strategic advantage.

The authors have worked together on the relationship between scenarios and interactive strategy since 1986, first as consultants and, for the last 12 years, as academic colleagues. The ideas in this chapter draw on the extended engagements we undertook *collaboratively* with a liquor company, a petrochemicals firm and the leadership of a major UK university, and *individually* with telecommunications companies, intergovernmental agencies, an industry association and a supplier to the shipping industry. This chapter is the first time that we have brought our joint discussions formally together. The supporting case studies in this paper were originally intended for executive development and consultancy purposes, not the development of theory on an inductive basis. We see this as a strength, however. Our understanding of the relationship between scenarios and interactive strategy design is rooted in the 'grounded theory' tradition involving reflection on practice and discovery of theory. Since the beginning of our collaboration we have adopted a 'clinical' methodology, publishing analyses in what we might call 'reflective practitioner' mode for both academic and practitioner audiences.

We propose an approach based, in order, on the following five propositions:

- Successful strategy rests on the generation of new and original options. Some of these – as described in this chapter – result in the discovery of new value-creation systems (which we call 'value constellations') that at least partially span the boundary between the transactional environment and the broader contextual environment.
- The discovery of such value constellations necessitates engaging the minds of the different stakeholders involved. However, while

this requires active collaboration between the stakeholders, the designs for collaboration can initially be devised and tested unilaterally before being presented to potential partners who then decide whether to engage or not.

- Traditional uses of scenarios in strategy do not include a formal and systematic search for new options, leaving their discovery to intuition or other approaches unrelated to scenario practice. In our view, scenario activity and option generation can be closely intertwined – and this chapter explains how this might be made to happen.

- The type of change involved in the options we propose is radical and transformational. However, change is most sustainable if it is pursued on what Winnicott (1965) first called a 'transitional' basis (see Amado and Ambrose, 2001, for an updated view).

- Scenario planning can best be developed into a tool for transitional strategic change through a prototyping process we call 'staging'.

THE ROLE OF THE 'ENVIRONMENT' IN SCENARIO THINKING

Strategy is often considered 'contingent', in that it seeks to secure a better fit between an organization and the environmental constraints it faces. It is not surprising, therefore, that the concept of the 'environment' has a long history in both strategy and scenario work. We build on this tradition but argue that successful strategy requires the discovery or generation of new and more effective ways for the organization to relate to its environment. Achieving competitive success means being able to identify promising options and develop the capabilities to capitalize on them before others do. Prime-movers (Normann and Ramírez, 1993; Ramírez and Wallin, 2000) reinvent the rules of the game – rules which less inventive and agile players then find themselves having to play by.

This process, however, is not straightforward. Like all invention, creating new strategic options involves complex subjective processes in the individual and collective minds of managers. These can, for instance, result in managers rejecting possibilities that are perceived as making their jobs unmanageable. Often concealed within the strategy search techniques adopted by managers are tacit assumptions about future roles that make arbitrary demarcations between 'what is ours' and 'what is not'. These assumptions can obscure potentially valuable strategic options. However, by engaging in exploratory thinking these assumptions can be challenged, and new options for strategic action identified. This is what Vickers called the domain of instrumental judgement.

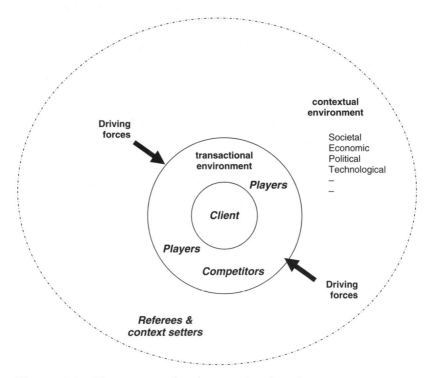

Figure 4.1   The contextual and transactional environments
Source: Van der Heijden, 1996, p. 155.

The traditional distinction between contextual and transactional environments should be seen in this light (see Figure 4.1). The remoter part of the environment that one cannot control or influence is often called the 'contextual environment'. Within it, organizations detect a range of developments which they do not believe they can control. Examples of contextual factors in business include larger developments in politics, economics, society and technology.

Although, by definition, the 'contextual environment' is that part of the environment of every organization and every individual which they see as the part they cannot influence, this does not mean that strategic planners have thought that developments within it should be ignored. On the contrary, they have fully accepted that it is helpful to have a clear appreciation of what is happening in those areas, as developments there may have significant repercussions for the organization or its partners.

The 'transactional environment', by contrast, is the more immediate part of one's environment where one can hope to exert influence. The precise limits of this influence can give rise to heated debate at the highest levels – whether, for instance, G8 leaders should address world poverty more vigorously or Shell should exercise a positive effect on governance in Nigeria.

The transactional environment is where interaction with other actors takes place. Out of the 'conversations' between these actors emerges a new, dynamic and constantly changing reality. Every player has an influence on the others, but not total control. One can compare the reciprocal situation in the transactional environment to a game in which one's actions elicit actions by others which, in turn, stimulate further rounds of action. For this reason the transactional environment is sometimes referred to as the 'playing field'.

In the context of strategy, the boundary between the two environments is to a marked degree subjective, with assumptions about roles to a surprising extent determining how far one believes one can exercise influence. 'Resistance to change', for instance, plays an important role in the distinctions that managers make between their transactional and contextual environments (see Heckscher *et al.*, 2003, for a critical overview). More adventurous management teams are generally prepared to consider a wider playing field than their more conservative colleagues.

Probing the boundary between contextual and transactional environments can not only help to flush out tacit assumptions about roles, but also challenge established beliefs about economic or technical constraints that may no longer be valid. From their rubble new strategic options can emerge. For example, the plummeting costs of memory storage now make it possible to track customer behaviour that had been economically unviable to track in the past.

As scenarios used for strategy development have tended to treat the contextual environment as a given, they are typically deployed to identify and analyse the driving forces emanating from this contextual environment. That use of scenarios has thus limited what may plausibly occur within the transactional environment. In that view the transactional environment itself has been seen as the proper domain of strategy, and it is thus only within this narrower environment that strategic options have been devised. The games played out in the transactional environment, like any other game situation, are generally thought to be less susceptible to scenario analysis, and many also tend to be considered as zero-sum. In this way scenarios and strategy development have been kept strictly separate – scenarios being used to stake out the area within which strategic options and business models can be devised. However, we have found that the use of scenarios can be more closely and effectively integrated with the creation of strategic options through a process that we call 'staging'.

FIVE PROPOSITIONS

Our approach is based on the following five propositions:

1. *A key aspect of strategy involves the invention of original options that create new value constellations along the boundary between the contextual and transactional environments*

Options represent value. We take it as axiomatic that possessing additional strategic options that others do not hold is advantageous. Even in more stable conditions, strategic success depends upon securing original strategic options, but – building on Ashby's 'requisite variety' concept where an entity has to match internally the complexity of its environment to survive – this is particularly the case in more turbulent environments (see Emery and Trist, 1965, for a full explanation).

A key part of the strategic task, therefore, is to generate more options by opening up new space in and around the transactional environment. One way to obtain this involves deploying scenarios to test in a disciplined way the accepted boundary between the two environments – pushing items that had been in the contextual environment into the transactional environment. Part of what had, until that time, been the broader contextual environment then becomes integrated into the expanded transactional environment, and thus actionable and subject to influence by joint action and co-production.

A good example is what Visa (Ramírez and Wallin, 2000, offer a full case study) or MasterCard did for the retail banks. By bringing together the banks, major retailers, telecommunications players, terminal makers and consumers, Visa and MasterCard enabled the banks to take forces converging on them from the contextual environment created by new technologies and legal payment standards, and to convert and combine them into effective processes, standards and protocols. The distinctive competency of Visa and MasterCard was essentially to transform contextual environment domains into transactional environment domains for their member banks.

Thus scenarios, with their open and inclusive vision, their ability to dramatize new possibilities quickly and vividly, and with the power to weave together previously unconsidered connections, offer an effective way to redraw the map, to reperceive the landscape, and draw together different actors in a constructive collaborative endeavour. Here we suggest they can do so to reposition the transactional–contextual environment boundary.

2. The creation of new value constellations inevitably requires rethinking the roles and relationships of the stakeholders involved

Finding new actionable space that shifts the boundaries between the transactional and contextual environments involves changing the roles of the players and their interorganizational relationships. Every assumption about roles in some way involves boundaries. Boundaries mark out and shape our relations with one another. Shifting boundaries therefore means changing one's role assumptions, engaging in new forms of interactive relationships.

This can be both liberating and disturbing. Emery and Trist (1965, 1972) showed how such changes could lead to anxiety, confusion, dissociation, disagreement and even violence. To avoid this, they suggested that such changes should be based on a search for common ground, and, further, that this ground could only be reached if common ideals for the future of the relationship were established (Trist *et al.*, 1997). We have found that scenarios not only offer a source of new strategic options, but can also be used to create a safe and neutral environment in which to explore and anticipate change and try out new roles well before strategic options are actually implemented. In this way, scenarios can be used to bring together individuals or groups drawn from a single stakeholder organization, or a group of such organizations, in a collaborative and anxiety-free quest for new actionable space.

3. *To be fully effective, the strategic use of scenarios must involve the systematic consideration of options rather than leaving them to intuition or other unrelated or unstructured approaches*

The traditional use of scenarios in strategy, known as 'S2S' (scenario to strategy), does not specifically involve discovering and developing new strategic options. S2S is generally used as a form of 'wind tunnelling' – a way to confront a set of strategic options with a range of contextual scenarios in order to test their robustness (Van der Heijden, 1996; Grant, 2003). In practice, scenario planning – and not only scenario planning of the S2S type – has all too often failed to realize the potential redesign possibilities for new forms of interaction implicit in Trist and Emery's original relational and interactive approach to the environment (Normann and Ramírez, 1993).

Over time, scenario planning has moved from Herman Kahn's famous dictum in the context of a possible nuclear war 'to think the unthinkable', to identifying the driving forces in the contextual environment that determine the transactional environment. In this way much scenario planning has ended up overemphasizing how far context limits the scope for interorganizational action. It has not been greatly concerned with how the study of interorganizational relationships in the transactional environment can push back the contextual environment and redefine the boundary between the two. This has led to a form of scenario-planning practice – particularly S2S – that is all too often reactive. Far too many strategists now base the strategic use of scenarios on a 'prepare, monitor and react' approach.

One can only speculate why scenarios have ended up lodged in this rationalist positivist corner, while its origins were of a more exploratory nature. It may be that the combination of positivist and functionalist academic writers (especially in American business school culture) and product-driven consultants selling 'market-tested' methods has proved difficult to resist.

We do not question the value, within its narrow sphere, of S2S. The technique of confronting pre-existing strategic options with a range of environmental contexts by means of a number of contextual scenarios clearly has its uses. However, we would add the proviso that, for the tests to be valid, the scenarios (the test conditions) have to be sharply differentiated from the objects to be tested (the strategic options). Scenarios based on the S2S paradigm must therefore be strictly contextual and cannot afford to stray into transactional space.

Even so, S2S makes only a limited contribution to strategy and fails to realize the full role scenarios can play. We believe that an entirely new strategic potential can be opened up if consideration is given to using scenarios to change and extend the transactional environment. We must transcend S2S and develop a new role for scenarios: searching for, identifying and even inventing new strategic options, especially options based on possible environmental boundary shifts that would otherwise escape our attention.

Our goal, therefore, is to help scenario planning to move from a predominantly reactive role to a more design-driven and interactive one (Normann and Ramírez, 1993). Developments in this direction, in our joint experience, may be effectively pursued by means of an interactive improvisation technique that we call 'staging' – a valuable but too-little considered complement to traditional S2S scenario-planning work.

4. *Change is most sustainable if pursued as a transitional activity.*

The idea of transitional change comes from Winnicott (1965), who studied how young children move from the safety of daylight and mother to the anxiety-ridden period of darkness and sleep. He noted how they invested the safety of 'mother' in a transitional object like a teddy bear which captured some of the safety even when darkness closed in and 'mother' was no longer nearby. The bear creates a sense of continuity so that the new situation has time to become part of one's context and thus of oneself. These insights have been used to generate many different types of 'transitional spaces', designed by, among others, Tavistock pioneers working with Winnicott, such as Harold Bridger who played a key role in helping POWs readjust to civilian life (Amado and Ambrose, 2001). One aspect of the transitional approach, incidentally, is that it is scaleable: it can help individuals and small groups of people as well as whole nations.

Thinking of change as 'transitional' matters in shifting the boundaries between the contextual and transactional environments, because the shift involves overcoming role assumptions. Scenario planners must take responsibility for helping stakeholders to change their role assumptions if they want to exploit the potential the scenario approach has to actually shift these boundaries. One's role assumptions tend to be 'tacit' and deeply engrained: just telling someone that from now on his role will be fundamentally different violates identity, and the client will feel as if we are inviting suicide and will resist. Discovering the potential is not enough, we also have to help people to start to see the new potential situation as 'for themselves'. Thus transitional change is highly relevant to this chapter.

In transitional change, the new does not eradicate the old: it retains and incorporates its useful aspects. While absolute change from A to B involves removing situation A and replacing it with B, transitional change creates a new B that retains key aspects of A. Transitional change acknowledges that B in part emerges from A and therefore key elements of A need to be included in B. The way Air France successfully absorbed KLM, whereby KLM continues to fly with its own colours, brand and language, is an example. Transitional change aims for change that does not violate stakeholder identity (Heckscher *et al.*, 2003) – a key precondition for sustainable change. Change agents should aim at the more achievable goal of transitional rather than at absolute change.

Another key aspect of transitional change is that it can be imagined and tried out in advance. The transitional space is staked out, as it were, within A even before B becomes a reality: imagine the mother in the safety of daylight, giving the teddy bear to the child, and explaining how he will be alone in his bed that night for the first time. The child may well use the teddy bear in a nap in the afternoon. By creating a transitional space with the help of the transitional object, one can safely experience what it will actually feel like in the new, unsafe zone; and the anxiety of entering the unsafe and unknown conditions is consequently reduced. In this way it is quite common to model what the new and unknown will feel like before it becomes real – for example, producing clay models to see the general appearance of a new BMW, and developing prototypes of dams or catalytic crackers before actually constructing them.

Transitional change pays requisite attention to the emotional dimension. A lot of inability to bring about change results from undervaluing the anxiety that change inevitably creates. Conservatism is a powerful instinct that has important survival value. But at the same time change is inevitable; we have to adapt to and exploit it, and the anxiety it may cause must therefore be constructively addressed. Damasio (2000) has argued that emotional cognition precedes other forms of cognition and shapes them. Thus, paying attention to the emotion involved in change is an important step in securing sustainable change. Because transitional objects and spaces explicitly attend to anxiety, they can help to make change more effective.

The establishment of new interorganizational relations can be achieved by 'prime movers' (Ramírez and Wallin, 2000) who have the power to impose new roles and relationships on others by mobilizing co-producing communities of interest. To be sustainable, the process requires, or benefits from, a willingness to change or accept some change on the part of the stakeholders concerned.

Such communities can best achieve progress through a process of transitional change, migrating from one 'value constellation' to another in which the new does not simply replace the old but incorporates it. Facilitating transitional change requires, therefore, a prototyping approach that is acceptable and meaningful to the full range of stakeholders.

5. *As a tool for transitional strategic change, scenario planning is best pursued using a prototyping process called 'staging'*

The new strategic capital resulting from the enlargement of the trans-actional environment is released through a process of transitional change based on interactive improvisation, especially a variant that we call 'staging' – a valuable and generally overlooked addition to scenario planning. Opening up the new action space is hard enough conceptually and emotionally for a single player, let alone a group or series of groups. One helpful way to meet this challenge is to give scenarios a transitional character by means of scenario 'staging'.

WHAT IS STAGING?

Staging builds on Moss Kanter's (2002) hint that improvisational theatre could extend the scope and value of scenarios.

Staging offers a transitional approach to change. It presents the post-change situation in the form of a plausible scenario, 'rendering' it using an approach that combines role-playing and prototyping in order to reveal how the players react. Participants learn not only how to conceptualize a post-change situation but to experience and explore it from the safety of the existing situation. Special attention is given to the feelings that the rendering provokes. In this way the players' identities are both supported and challenged during the staging.

Staging involves designing transitional spaces in which feelings can be articulated and analysed, and uses a wide range of 'transitional objects' from spreadsheets to role plays. What these objects have in common is that they give rise to an interaction that forces people to imagine and experience the future. Explicitly designing staging before scenarios are rendered is helpful in that it brings into play tacit knowledge and the emotions underpinning cognition (Damasio, 2000).

The improvisational nature of staging allows decision makers and stakeholders to see how roles and relationships play out before they are enacted in the real world. Staging presents the scenarios in ways that let the participants (decision makers, key managers, stakeholders) experience the future before it occurs. This allows organizations to check if their assumptions about their roles are viable under the scenario conditions, and to assess how it would feel to collaborate with others to redefine existing roles. It represents, therefore, a safe way to model interactive strategy and the transitions involved in reaching a desired goal. Testing also reduces risk as errors are reversible and do not incur real-life costs. It therefore encourages early acceptance.

Staging helps to redefine the boundary between the contextual and the transactional environments. The scenarios enable organizations to identify the 'prime mover' in each scenario, where they set the rules or standards by which the other actors will have to play. Examples studied by Ramírez and Wallin include Xerox with photocopying, Nokia with GSM, Visa with payment systems and Tetra-Pak with milk packaging. Other such examples are Intel with chips, Microsoft with software and the Harvard Business School with the MBA. Staging makes it possible to test how the players involved in a strategic situation might work together in reality: in other words, to assess before actually enacting how they would deal with environment factors and shift the border between the contextual and transactional environments.

After staging, groups of people are invited to write accounts of what it felt like and suggest areas that need further exploration. In some cases staging can pass through several cycles, each iteration of which makes the rendering more comfortable. By taking account of people's reactions to new opportunities, staging also allows for subsequent redesign and provides a vehicle to introduce possible new value constellation to other stakeholders who did not participate in the initial rounds.

FOUR CASE STUDIES

The following cases are intended to illustrate the preceding propositions in a grounded research manner; the engagements not only followed, but also tested, the premises on transitional change and the use of scenarios we have described above. Working in the tradition of 'reflective' and clinical forms of research-based practice, the cases we describe here were part of executive development and consultancy projects that used scenario staging as part of interactive strategy design. While it is impossible to fully capture their rich complexity with sufficient 'granularity', we have tried to indicate the major issues and developments (some of which were quite dramatic involving lay-offs and the closures of whole divisions) that characterized the situations in which these engagements took place.

Alcatel

Alcatel is a leading technology supplier, competing in a number of markets against such organizations as Siemens, Lucent, Cisco, Phillips and GE. In the mid-1990s a division of Alcatel operating in the telecommunications industry was confronting the challenge of disruptive change in its business. At the time the division consisted of two units, acquired from different firms, which had been merged to constitute the division two years before this engagement took place. Much of the division's business was becoming commoditized and was being invaded by non-traditional retail players. The rest of the business was moving 'up-scale' into knowledge-intensive niches in which this division of Alcatel could not adequately compete. Its managers needed to understand what the future held in store, what roles they would play in relation to other players, and which relationships would have to change.

We proceeded to interview 20 top executives and render the results in the form of a 'history of the organization's future' written from a point 10 years in the future, in which two happily retired senior executives recalled what had happened in their division over the past decade. They had listened to an unlikely source within the company who had advised them that 70% of their turnover would disappear within three years and they had acted in time to save the business. This draft was reluctantly received but nevertheless provided the basis for a two-day staging workshop attended by the division's 35 key managers. This was opened by the division chairman, who, with a key supplier and customer, surveyed how external forces (including globalization, EU public procurement rules, technological innovation) were changing roles and relationships among customers, producers, suppliers and competitors. The outside speakers explained how much their own businesses were challenged by change. They thus presented a scenario that fundamentally differed from the division's 'official future'. The outside speakers made a big impression on participants and convinced them that the problems they were facing were more fundamental and systemic than most of them had realized.

Participants then examined how the forces identified in the 'history of the future' would shape their transactional environment, and strengthened the draft of the history of the future to render it more plausible. When the document was distributed, initial responses to the revised draft were mixed, but eventually won warm acceptance, and participants moved on to identifying the conditions under which the division might survive and prosper. This staging process, rendering the history of the future scenario plausible and identifying how the division might survive, produced what was in effect a third scenario. The process proved to be decisive in helping the 35 managers to 're-perceive' the business of their division. Unfortunately, soon after the engagement ended, a major corporate-wide reorganization dissolved the division, and 18 months later a major crisis – the collapse of the telecommunications 'bubble' – put the very future of Alcatel in doubt. A third of the workforce of the division was laid off. The company, however, survived as an entity.

Sonera

Sonera, formerly Telecom Finland, became the main operator in one of the world's most open telecommunications markets in the 1990s, going from being part of a ministry department to a stand alone company that excelled in mobile and internet services and was for several years the leading European value-creator in its sector. One of the authors, invited by Sonera's top strategist to visit Finland, acted as a sparring partner for its corporate strategy teams between 1994 and 2000, helping them to develop thoroughly researched contextual scenarios, which the company's top management presented to the Finnish parliament in its deliberations whether to privatize the firm.

The aim of the subsequent staging was to explore the available options that Sonera professionals found most appealing, and those they wanted to avoid. The staging therefore focused on possible futures for the company itself, rather than the transactional environment. We used a five-year horizon – which in the context of their business seemed long term. A representative group of 16 Sonera professionals was asked the following questions:

- You are reading an article about Sonera in the *New York Times* four years from now: What are its three most surprising conclusions?

- You are in a restaurant five years from now having lunch with a former colleague, who has just been appointed as the new CEO. You both agree that she made her name by running a new division created only two years before: What is the division and what does it do?

- Four years from now 50% of customers no longer have any business relationship with Sonera: Who are they and how did their relationship to the company end?

- Three years from now Sonera has successfully realized a hope that you currently have for the organization: What is that hope, and how did it become a reality?

As busy executives were unwilling to fill out on-line questionnaires, face-to-face interviews were set up, the results of which were then sent to a panel of four external organization experts familiar with Sonera's industry sector. In that sense the views were 'staged' for an external audience. The interviews and the panellists' analyses and comments then formed the basis for a staging workshop. Participants were asked to develop two to six interorganizational futures centred on Sonera's organizational options and to stage the development of these, tracing the steps and events that had taken place. After identifying the current organizing principles that would lead to unsustainable outcomes and the competences that would assist survival, they produced four interorganizational futures.

The plan had been to stage the findings for the management board, and within the workshop participants staged the drafts of these options to each other in preparation. However, before this could be done, the 3G licence bubble burst and the final staging never happened. Ironically, one of the four interorganizational futures identified became a reality when Sonera was absorbed into Telia-Sonera. It is impossible to know whether, had the staging been presented to the board, action could have been taken to avoid this.

Entreprise & Personnel

Entreprise & Personnel (E&P) is a French not-for-profit professional association with 160 corporate members. Founded in 1969 by Renault and other companies who did not want to be surprised by a future 'May 1968', it studied changes in relations between employees and companies and created three 'products': research and publications; management development; and tailor-made services in support of change. However, after 30 years' successful operation, E&P's management found that its transactional environment had greatly altered. Its members – and in particular their HR functions – had changed substantially. 'Staff function' work previously done by HR had increasingly been taken over by line or top management or functional specialists. Companies had internationalized significantly and were increasingly outsourcing important areas of work. E&P faced other challenges. Business schools began moving into E&P's task environment, combining research and executive education in 'tailor-made' programmes for companies, and consulting firms were developing strengths in research and publication, invading the area of applied research that E&P had made its specialty.

Scenarios were used to investigate the broad contextual changes shaping E&P's transactional environment, but E&P felt that, in themselves, scenarios would not be enough to ensure viability, as they did not explore the roles and the relationships with others that E&P needed to develop in order to survive. E&P's managers felt they needed to find out what relations the company had to build with business schools and consulting firms as well as with its own members – opportunities that E&P was interested in exploring interactively. At the same time it was keen to find whether this 'inside-out' approach was in line with an 'outside-in' scenario analysis of driving forces in the contextual environment. So E&P needed scenarios – and also to stage roles and relationships in the context of these scenarios.

E&P adopted a staging approach similar to the one used with Sonera. Questions, similar to those used in Sonera, were sent to a range of E&P professionals who answered them on-line. Validated and made anonymous, their responses were then put on the intranet – in effect, a 'staging' for all employees of E&P. Four outsiders were then asked to comment on the staged responses, and their reports and comments were also put on E&P's intranet. In the meantime E&P strategists carried out a survey of E&P's standing among its members, a review of 10 peer organizations internationally and an analysis of the economics of their current business. Thus all three layers in the 'environmental architecture' had been investigated before the first staging workshop was held.

Participants devoted a third of the time of that workshop to the contextual environment, a third to the transactional environment and a third to E&P itself and the possible forms it might assume. They identified five interorganizational futures:

- *Continuity* – A future that assumed that no change would occur in E&P's offerings and organization, although ongoing changes would continue to take place in its environment.
- *Accelerated globalization* – A process affecting an ever greater number of companies, including E&P members, and requiring adaptation by E&P.
- *End of the community firm* – A future in which entrepreneurs and intrapreneurs bloomed within efficient markets and put an end

to hierarchy. HR would become a market, and E&P's offerings would need substantial transformation.

- *End of the HR function* – A future in which line management and outsourcing took over functions previously carried out by HR directors, necessitating radical changes in E&P's relations with its members.
- *Society in crisis* – A future in which the forces of anti-globalization and high levels of insecurity demanded a fundamental rethink of social relations and, *a fortiori*, of all relationships between employees and companies.

A summary of the five futures was presented to E&P's Management Board, and further work was undertaken to investigate their plausibility. The Board decided finally only to stage three futures to the Supervisory Board (which represents all E&P members). Taskforces of workshop participants developed fully fledged business plans for these, written up in a common format and communicated in advance of the staging for the Supervisory Board in a document similar to a theatre programme.

The whole process was designed to be as seamless as possible. The 'prototyping' inherent to staging allowed everyone to assess each option fully and test how best to stage them for a decision by the Supervisory Board. The *raison d'être* of E&P, its values and identity, to whom it wanted to relate, how it would work, what economic logic would sustain it, the career implications, even what it would feel like to work there – were all dramatized to members, allowing them, almost as theatre critics, to see the strengths and weaknesses of each staged option.

The Supervisory Board meeting was attended by a dozen people, including the Board Chairman (at the time the CEO of Pechiney), the original founding Chairman and his successors, and several HR directors and senior executives from some of France's best-known companies and the French subsidiaries of major multinationals. After a succinct staging of the three interorganizational futures, the Supervisory Board discussed each in depth, questionning and clarifying the underpinning assumptions and evaluating the consequences. As such, the meeting represented a strategic conversation of the highest order.

The Supervisory Board decided the 'Continuity' and 'Accelerating globalization' futures were plausible in the short to mid term, and the 'End of the community firm' future in the mid to long term. They asked the Management Board to prepare a three-year strategic plan costing the investments needed for each and combining them in a single coherent plan. The Supervisory Board also decided to disseminate insights to members while the Management Board communicated with them internally. One lesson from the exercise is that few individuals in this culture (whether E&P's or French culture in general) found it easy to envisage three incompatible futures simultaneously. Extra attention therefore has to be paid to the dangers of 'dissociation' (Trist *et al.*, 1997) that staging can engender.

Wärtsilä Marine

Wärtsilä Marine designs, manufactures and supplies ship propulsion systems. A staging exercise was undertaken to see how well its strategy and business model fitted the changing business strategies of its customers. The focus therefore was on the shipping industry in which its customers operated rather than on Wärtsilä Marine itself. The distinction between the transactional and contextual environments is less clear-cut when the actor under consideration is multi-organizational (Ramírez, 1996). Each organization forms part of the others' transactional environments, so no agreement is possible on the precise boundaries between contextual and transactional environments. We therefore focused the workshop on Wärtsilä Marine's ultimate contextual environment – the shipping industry.

The approach was similar to the one carried out at Sonera and E&P. The questions and the 10-year time horizon on which they were based reflected the concerns of the Management Board. However, the 28 interviews carried out were not conducted with executives within the company but with people in Wärtsilä Marine's transactional environment – customers, regulators, educators, insurers, officers of professional bodies, consultants, surveyors, naval architects, researchers, analysts, bankers and investors. Because the interviews already involved a range of organizations, and 12 transactional stakeholders (including some of the industry's most respected experts) participated in the workshop, we did not use panellists as an intermediate step. Nor did the workshop's outcomes need to be as well documented and detailed as for E&P, because a third of the key decision makers were already represented in the four Wärtsilä executives attending.

The workshop identified four plausible interorganizational futures, one of which approximated to an agreed 'official future'. This official future was based on 16 predetermined elements that people considered predictable at the beginning of the scenarios workshop. However, by the end of the workshop 5 of the 16 predetermined elements agreed in the 'official future' were judged implausible. The later staging meeting with the Wärtsilä Marine Board linked the findings of the workshop to an analysis of their strategy. Overall, the exercise identified several areas of misfit and resulted in a 're-perception' of these areas by the Board.

Unease with existing plans was palpable in the staging workshop, and the Board decided to review them more comprehensively than originally intended. It is unclear at the time of writing how much of the contextual environment has been 'colonized' as a result, partly because the shipbuilding industry has boomed since the workshop, helped by the growth of the Chinese economy and demand. The managing director says, nevertheless, that since this engagement, the company is much more concerned with its customers' customers, and takes a much longer term outlook both with regard to them and other key players, such as regulators. He reports that working interactively to reposition the transactional–contextual boundary as part of a designed strategy is much easier with those who participated in the workshop, for they all agree how powerful a factor joint 'prime-movership' can be.

ANALYSIS AND DISCUSSION OF THE CASES

The four cases are summarized in Table 4.1.

In terms of our first proposition – the importance of creating new value options along the border of the transactional and contextual environments – Alcatel failed to develop these in time and found itself overwhelmed by industry changes that overtook it faster than its managers had anticipated. Sonera did act and try to re-position this interface but failed. Its attempt involved efforts to persuade its shareholder, the Finnish State, to privatize it, but it failed to convince Parliament on the merits of doing so at the right time, and the cost of this failure to the company and to its shareholder was substantial. E&P with its partners as represented by its Supervisory Board did develop options that helped them to survive more difficult conditions. Wärtislä Marine, by engaging stakeholders in joint consideration of their collective futures, succeeded in being seen as an innovator in this regard, even though subsequent (positive) developments shifted senior management attention elsewhere shortly after the engagement was terminated.

Turning to our second proposition – the value of engaging multiple stakeholders – Alcatel was late doing this. That said, it did face a major threat: one of its suppliers, IBM, creating a JV with

Table 4.1 Summary of cases

Key issue	Alcatel	Sonera	Entreprise & Personnel	Wärtsilä Marine
Prior knowledge of the host organization by the interveners	Moderate – previous executive development engagement on the merger setting up the organization	Significant – 5 years consulting engagements with 3 successive strategy teams	Nil	Significant – previous executive development engagements for a decade
Knowledge generated on the contextual environment	Supplier and customer testimonies	Full contextual scenario analysis	Sketch scenarios, subsequently fully quantified	28 interviews; non-quantified sketch scenarios
Focus of design of interorganizational futures	History of the future, centred on the organization	On the organization	Centred on relations with members	Centred on the transactional industry domain

Table 4.1 (Continued)

Key issue	Alcatel	Sonera	Entreprise & Personnel	Närtsilä Marine
Key buyer	Division MD, sanctioned by chairman	Strategy team, sanctioned by CEO	MD sanctioned by Management Board	Division CEO & Management Board
Participants in the workshop	35 of the division's top managers; 2 external speakers	25 volunteers, all internal executive programme graduates	28; internal only	4 internal and 12 external
Audiences for the staging	CEO and Chairman of Division alone	Never delivered	Supervisory Board	Division's Management Board
Use of external expertise	Key client and supplier	4 professors	1 executive, 1 consultant, 2 professors	28 interviewed stakeholders and experts
Number of facilitators	2	1	1	2

Colonization of the contextual environment	No – the opposite happened	Explored positively and negatively: mostly the opposite happened	Explored positively and negatively	Yes – strategy focus longer, joint discussions with key counterparts to co-design viability
Strategic options created	Yes, but too late	Yes, but too late	Yes, kept steady in shrinking market	Yes, but overtaken by China trade-driven growth

one of its key competitors, Toshiba, in order to obtain scale advantages. While the relevant division in Alcatel was itself the product of a merger between two previous competitors, at the time of the engagement Alcatel did not proactively engage other stakeholders. Sonera, however, did well in this regard, and was widely regarded as a 'prime mover'. But the third-generation JV it opted for proved disastrous. By contrast, E&P's very business model was built on engaging multiple stakeholders; since the engagement it has lost far fewer members than scenarios had suggested it might, and has actually succeeded in winning some new ones. Wärtislä Marine actively used the scenarios and staging to engage other stakeholders, and became a first mover in its industry in terms of engaging others to consider viable futures over far longer terms than those that are typical in its industry.

In terms of our third proposition – the importance of the systematic search for new options – Alcatel floundered because it did not create enough options quickly enough to counter the narrowing of its transactional environment. Sonera did develop options but bet very riskily and expensively on the wrong one: 3G licences in Germany entered into with its Spanish partner, Telefonica, on the basis of a scenario – the rapid deployment of 3G – that failed to materialize. E&P, however, developed options that helped it to retain share in a shrinking market. Wärtislä Marine considered a range of possible options, and while facing unprecedented demand in its market, was and is active in preparing options for a longer term game – for example, the move from Korea to China of significant parts of the shipbuilding market, or the possibility of draconian environmental legislation.

Looking at propositions 4 and 5 – the value of scenarios as transitional spaces – the re-perceptions that took place in Alcatel, and its shift from judging the 'history of the future' implausible to seeing it as too tame, give some indication how scenarios can effectively provide transitional spaces. In Sonera, the transitional space worked for the workshop participants but not unfortunately for the Board, who did not make time for a staging. In E&P, the transitional approach adopted by its Management and Supervisory Boards was vindicated and opened up sufficient space for reflection and for the preparation of entrepreneurial initiatives that led to positive results; although even these did not materialize on the scale envisaged, due to the worsening economic climate in France. Finally, participants in Wärtislä Marine's workshop and its management board acknowledge that substantial re-perception of their customers' futures was achieved well in advance, thanks to the engagement.

Overall, how successful were these organizations generally in colonizing their contextual environments? Alcatel had lost influence over its transactional environment, as one EU directive after the other opened up previous captive markets to competitors. It could have benefited from these changes by invading other EU markets, but other players were more agile in invading its territory than it was in invading theirs. Sonera also lost control over its transactional environment because of technological convergence. E&P was facing the same fate through competition from consultants and business schools, but managed to skirt it. Wärtsilä had suffered such losses in the past, when shipbuilding moved from the EU to Asia, but had successfully repositioned itself and moved out of shipbuilding into propulsion; it now reports that it is actively engaging key partners in fields well beyond what it had considered its playing field (now including the regulators of its customer's customers) to develop new strategic relationships.

It is clear from these cases that if the reduction of the transactional environment (and the corresponding enlargement of the contextual environment) is to be countered or avoided, changes need to be anticipated and understood well in advance. Using scenarios to this end seems to have helped both E&P and Wärtsilä Marine to develop fresh options, but not Alcatel and Sonera, who acted too late.

CONCLUSIONS

The four cases we have presented offer strong, if not absolute, support for the five propositions put forward at the beginning of this chapter. They indicate that the timing of an engagement aiming to use scenarios interactively to redesign strategy is crucial, and they offer persuasive evidence to show that staging can enhance scenario planning by allowing the players to experience what the change involves, not only conceptually but also emotionally, through its combination of prototyping and role playing.

While traditional S2S scenarios explore future environmental possibilities independently of what the actors are able to do to extend their transactional environments, we maintain that proactively repositioning the boundary between the transactional and contextual environment is both practicable and advantageous, if one acts in time. As Figure 4.2 shows, a player who takes on a

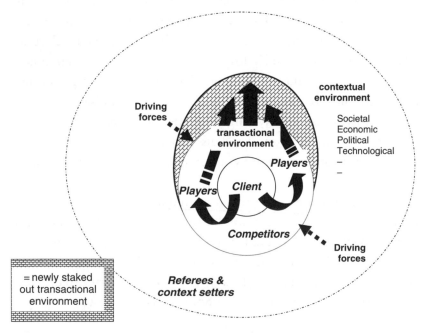

Figure 4.2   Staging interorganizational futures

'prime mover' role can beneficially encourage others to collectively redesign value constellations and shift the transactional–contextual environment boundary to their mutual advantage.

Our propositions, we believe, significantly extend the scope and value of scenario planning. The entrepreneurial use of scenarios described in this chapter to design strategy interactively has so far not received the prominence it deserves. This chapter is exploratory, but we hope that it will stimulate study that will extend its analysis and approaches. We invite new initiatives in practice and research to further the applicability and enhance the value of scenario practice and thinking.

CHAPTER 5

DEEPENING FUTURES WITH SYSTEM STRUCTURE

Tony Hodgson and Bill Sharpe

An important motive for futures work is to anticipate change and be ready for it. In strategic management the robustness of a strategy is often estimated in terms of strategic fit – that is, the degree to which the shape of the organization is congruent with and mutually supportive of its environment. If the environment changes then we lose fit and the organization starts to fail. A good analogy is the adaptation of a species to particular climatic conditions. When these change, the organisms may lose the ability to thrive. For this reason, we seek to understand predicted or possible changes in the environment so that we know how to adapt. 'The strategist, wanting to position his or her company to cope best with its industry environment or to influence that environment in the company's favour, must learn what makes the environment tick' (Porter, 1998). But the challenge in anticipatory strategy is 'What will make the future environment tick?'

Scenarios for Success: Turning Insights into Action   Edited by Bill Sharpe and Kees Van der Heijden
© 2007 John Wiley & Sons, Ltd

The problem is, then, that we cannot know in sufficient depth the nature of the future environments represented by, say, a set of scenarios. There may be four anticipated future worlds that we can imagine. We can consider the impact of each of these on our current organization, but we can then be left with the inevitable question 'So what?' One of the reasons this happens is that we cannot picture the nature and structure of these future worlds as well as we can research and picture items today. In the present and recent past we understand much through experience as well as information, but we have no experience of the future!

This chapter is about two perspectives on how we can see more deeply into the structure of alternative futures and into the nature of discontinuous change over time. Both these aspects, if aided by some additional conceptual tools, offer scope for improving our ability to anticipate what might be needed for strategic fit in the future.

How can we improve our capacity to imagine into the unknown and picture that which has not yet happened? One answer lies in recognizing that, in much of our picturing of both the present and the future, we do not understand the deeper structure that is actually causing things to be the way they are. Even our very ideas of cause and effect can obscure what may be going on because of non-linear, complex and emergent properties. Working with scenarios and other methods may trigger strategic insight in individuals, but this is inductive and tacit. This makes it difficult to share. If there are conceptual tools available that help that level of insight to be articulated, then a further layer of value can be harvested from the strategic conversation.

One of the characteristics of insight is its relationship to action. When something is seen deeply and clearly it moves us to act. This might be to switch resource application or to initiate new ideas or contingency plans. In strategy development, perhaps one of the greatest values of a well-structured scenario set is its stimulus to seek and generate a wider field of options. This way of thinking is very different from linear methods such as net present value.

In the absence of certainty people often find it hard to invest effort in generating options for scenarios that, after all, only *might* happen. However, if the kind of thinking developed in real options theory is applied more generally as a conceptual tool, then for each possible scenario in a set we need to take positions. Flexibility has strategic value. This is where deeper insight is of value. By working on the deeper structure of scenarios as described later in the chapter, stronger insight increases the motivation to generate options. In this way the quality of understanding the world of business has a direct impact on the quality of actions in the world of management. Similarly, if we can understand better the big transitions where one world replaces another, and see it coming before others do, we have energized and informed entrepreneurial action.

This chapter is about some of the ways that explicit methods can be used to help to articulate strategic insights into the future. Two approaches will be described. The first is in the field of scenario planning and introduces a way of using systems thinking to augment and capture insights provoked by a scenario narrative. This is the causal loop method. The second is a different way of relating to the future in the present, based on structural insight rather than calendar time. This is the three-horizons method.

Both methods will be illustrated by the way they were applied in a recent UK Government Foresight study of the next 50 years of intelligent infrastructure.

THE COGNITIVE TASK OF DISTINGUISHING ONE SCENARIO FROM ANOTHER

The essence of scenario thinking is the ability to entertain, mentally and emotionally, more than one 'reality'. Cognitive science refers to 'memory of the future' in which we visualize some, as yet, non–existent possible future situation. With this mental image we can see what we can learn about the likelihood of our intentions and plans working out. It is a simulation or rehearsal in the mind. So, for effective thinking with scenarios, each scenario of a set needs to be 'loaded up' into the mind and visualized clearly. Holding this visualization in mind, experiments can be made to see 'what would happen if?' Without practice, this is quite difficult. Of course, movie makers, dramatists and novelists do this but they are usually exploring only one scenario or story line at a time. In scenario thinking we must do this with at least two different but parallel stories, neither of which is our current reality.

A great strength of the scenario method is the way that multiple and interconnected uncertainties can be elegantly reduced to a small set of narratives that summarize possible future resolutions of those uncertainties. From the analytical perspective, the larger the complex of uncertainties, the more scenarios we need to encompass that complexity. However, in practice, there are cognitive limitations. This has led to different schools of thought on how many such scenarios are needed in a working set.

For many years, for example, Shell has taken the view that to have more than three scenarios is too confusing. Clearly this is the minimum set; if the scenario method is to be meaningful, there has to be an overarching uncertainty that leads to at least two distinct possible outcomes. Recently Shell (2005) has experimented with three scenarios based on a 'trilemma'. Four-scenario sets are popular because of the cognitive scaffolding provided by two orthogonal axes. Some more analytical approaches have gone as far as 8 or 16 scenarios in a set, but these really do cease to be useful in strategic conversation for executives. However, just two scenarios in a set may risk oversimplifying the real complexity, and so fail to stretch our capacity to anticipate possible futures.

Good scenario practice typically makes holding multiple scenarios in mind somewhat easier, without confusion, by means of several devices. They include:

- *Narrative* – Telling a verbal story of how we got from today to that future situation.
- *Descriptive* – Portraying the future situation by reviewing what would be seen and heard by someone residing in that future time and place.
- *Illustrative graphics* – Taking key parameters of interest and displaying them as, for example, bar charts of values consistent with that scenario.
- *Evocative images* – These may be 'pockets of the future in the present' or imaginative illustrations.
- *Causal logics* – Showing how different combinations of drivers result in the scenario's state of affairs.
- *Dilemmas* – Indicating how different scenarios tend to stabilize around a particular resolution point between polarized forces or values.

All of these are helpful but in scenario impact exercises, such as wind tunnelling, it is noticeable that mental exhaustion soon sets in and the content of different scenarios gets muddled. This loses the clarity of impact, reduces the scope for generating distinct options and loses the significance of the original uncertainties that led to the scenario set in the first place. This point will be illustrated with reference to a number of ways of framing scenario sets.

FRAMING SCENARIO SETS

In the four-box approach to creating a set of scenarios, uncertainties are grouped according to their mutual connectedness and how far their outcomes tend to get lined up with each other (like the domino effect). Two main groups then produce two contrasting outcomes, which imply a complex of the factors that have been grouped. These are then used to form orthogonal axes defining four combinations of overall outcome which represent the scenario set. An example of this way of distinguishing scenarios in a set is shown in Figure 5.1, taken from the Foresight project on Intelligent Infrastructure (2006).

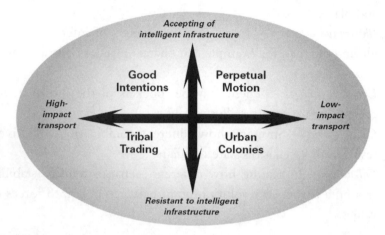

Figure 5.1 The axes of uncertainty and the four scenarios defined by combinations of those axes

The vertical axis is between acceptance and resistance and the horizontal axis between high- and low-impact transport. Taken to their extremes, the four combinations lead to very different futures represented by the four titles. However, under the pressure of thinking through multiple scenarios, people easily slip into blurring the distinctions between the scenarios. All scenarios contain similar elements derived from the fundamental driving forces and common predetermined elements. The differences often show up as different colourings of those elements. This reduces the impact of the 'wind tunnelling' and hence the value generated through the exercise. Oversimplification loses both plausibility and requisite variety.

However, when it comes to testing (wind tunnelling) a given policy initiative or strategic direction in each of the scenarios, it can be hard to make the 'what if?' question stick at the level of shaping real decisions and ideas. This is one of the reasons for the slow uptake of scenario thinking by executives; they have mental habits that cause them to

(a) want one single predictive scenario;
(b) be difficult to convince of the value of thinking in more than one reality;
(c) be disinclined to think through the impact implications of 'unbelievable' scenarios.

The cognitive challenge in a typical scenario impact workshop is to assimilate the four scenarios, single them out, and imagine the fate of a possible strategy or policy in that unique future world. That first image must then be dropped and another taken up without confusion . . . and so on. Mental overload and the tendency for memory to 'stick' from one stage to the next makes some degree of blurring inevitable. There is a strong tendency for the mind to get drawn to the centre of the four-box diagram where 'it is all the same'. Clearly, one role of a facilitator must be to remind people when they have inadvertently jumped into another scenario.

WORKING WITH DEEPER STRUCTURE

Perhaps the narrative version of a scenario that tells the story over time, and shows how each scenario unfolds differently into its distinct future, is the most powerful cognitive stabilizer, aided by suitably evocative titles. However, there need to be additional ways to bring out the distinctions. Techniques have been developed to this end to differentiate between scenarios at a deeper structural level, and even to enable the basic modelling of behaviour over time. This approach is based on a particular technique from systems thinking called *causal loops*.

A useful framework for understanding the role of systems thinking in scenarios is a triangle of deep structure (Figure 5.2). Generally we are aware of events taking place and this awareness is in the present (the first layer of events).

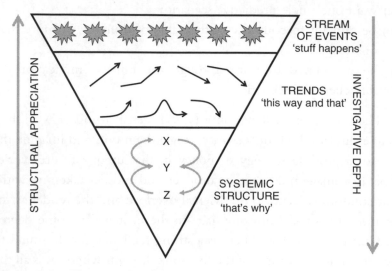

Figure 5.2   The triangle of deep structure

We may see such events coming, but we are often taken by surprise. If we delve more deeply into what is going on we identify trends (the second layer) and these give us some degree of anticipation. However, trends can be deceptive, in that there can be trend breaks and discontinuities. We are too easily trapped in assumptions of linear change and so also miss the implications of exponential change or cyclical behaviour. The third layer is structure, where we gain some understanding of non-linear causation. At this level we discover a key principle that *structure drives behaviour*. Some key aspects of that structure are that effects can be causes, and that feedback determines the behaviour of systems more strongly than linear change.

The proposition relating this framework to the scenario differentiation question is that any scenario, to be plausible, will have a basic archetypal structure that sustains its dynamic while it lasts. To keep the application of this idea at the technically simplest level we apply two types of causal loop in combination. One is called a *reinforcing loop* and the other a *balancing loop* (Figure 5.3).

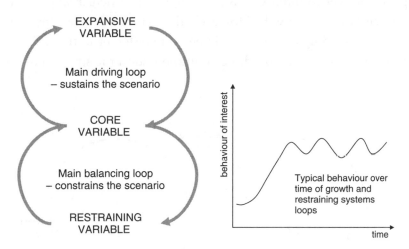

Figure 5.3   Causal loops in combination

A reinforcing loop is composed of a variable that positively drives another variable, which in turn feeds back and increases the original variable. An example is the application of interest to a principal sum of money, which in turn increases the principal, which in turn increases the accumulated interest, and so on. A balancing loop is composed of a variable that positively drives another variable but, in contrast to the previous loop, inhibits or reduces the original variable. This has a dampening effect on the reinforcing loop. An example would be: accumulating a sum of money leads to spending that then diminishes the original sum. The feedback often has a delay factor which complicates the behaviour, and leads to an oscillating behaviour called 'managing cash flow'.

The two loops combined represent a structure that is not very complex but can explain quite complex behaviour, such as the relationship between predators and prey in an ecosystem. The double loop is a structure that endures at any moment of time. However, it is also a structure that drives behaviour, as explained in Figure 5.4.

A key variable in the overall scenario arena is reinforced to grow in a particular way in a given scenario. Equally, since it will not grow for ever to infinity, it is restrained in a particular way. There will be limits to growth. However, the nature of these loops and their surrounding conditions will be quite different in the different scenarios. If they are not, this calls into question the strength of the scenarios.

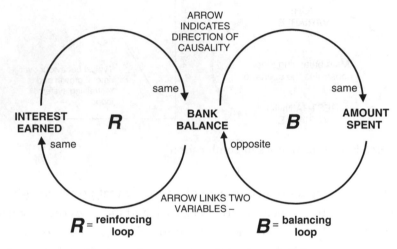

Figure 5.4   The dynamic structure of simple cash flow

Now the basic procedure for applying this technique to a deeper structure can be explained. The first assumption is that, should the conditions arise for that scenario to predominate, it will have a distinctive and enduring underlying structure. Of course, any scenario will have a life span, but for its lifetime this structure persists. Since the scenario is emerging from the present (which is not the scenario itself but must contain the potential for it) there must be growth into that state of affairs: this is the fundamental growth loop. However, this growth will not be unopposed, and will reach some sort of equilibrium position for the duration of the scenario. This may be fairly steady or it may oscillate. The greater

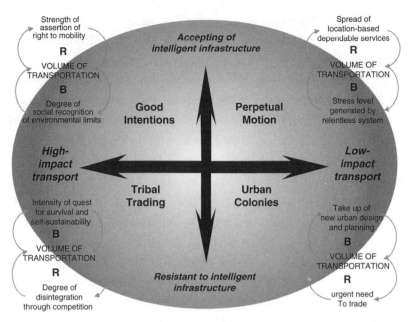

Figure 5.5   The four distinct double loops

the delay in feedback, the more likely oscillation becomes. Thus the behaviour of the double loop structure can give the intuitive insights of the scenario narrative a rational support based on basic systems theory. It creates a dynamic hypothesis for each scenario.

The four different double loops that characterize each scenario are shown in Figure 5.5. Notice that in the top two scenarios the dynamic indicates an increase in the volume of transportation, whereas in the lower two the volume is tending to reduce. This is determined by whichever loop is reinforcing. Each scenario is a dynamic battle between the two loops.

TRANSLATING SYSTEMS MODELS BACK TO NARRATIVES

These four distinct causal loop models become key anchor points to reinforce the distinction between the scenarios. However, this all takes place against a much more complex set of drivers and uncertainties. So the core model can now be elaborated with secondary loops, some of which augment the growth loop, and some the balancing loop. For example, in the scenario 'Perpetual Motion', the upper reinforcing loop ('spread of location-based dependable services') is likely to be further reinforced by a combination of increasing demand and increasing adoption of technology. However, the balancing loop of 'stress level generated by relentless system' is also strengthened by such factors as the take-up of alternatives to travel (e.g. virtual working) that reduce the travel stress. (For more complete examples of this see Curry *et al.*, 2006.)

Once we have developed a more complex elaboration of the core model, it is possible to return to the narrative form to help to visualize the implications of the deeper structure. The technique is often referred to as 'vignettes' – that is, small stories around particular aspects of the scenario that also bring to life the dynamic. These short stories fill in illustrations of the big story of the scenario. The example shown in Box 5.1 is taken from the same 'Perpetual Motion' scenario.

Box 5.1   A Family Get-together

Andrew was looking forward to the family reunion. He had spent many hours juggling with the integrated travel system to find the easiest and cheapest way to get his two sons and his five grandchildren together for 24 hours.

They were coming from Southampton and Glasgow to near Nottingham using the latest fashion, the 'family meeting caravanserai'. These were located at different hubs in the country designed on the lines of a hi-tech village with actual and virtual gathering rooms and accommodation. They were specifically designed to make use of the new intelligent modal integration which had evolved over the past 20 years to exploit the breakthrough in low-cost transport energy.

He remembered his own childhood, when it had been difficult and expensive to meet up for family events because of the high cost of fuel and the fragmentation of travel systems. His two sons, however, were plotting to persuade him that the twice-a-year get-togethers be reduced to one, and instead to install the new 'home virtual meeting' system so that they could schedule impromptu exchanges. Then they wouldn't need to be tied up helping him to play with his grandchildren. It was proving hard to persuade him that a virtual hug was as good as a real one.

His response was to try to persuade them to spend the money on one of the new hydrogen-powered cabervans that he could plug into the automated motorway network and drive safely to see them despite his age.

The negotiation is still proceeding!

The application of systems thinking to scenario insights is not a linear process. It is a reiterative interplay between the background material, the structure, such as drivers and axes, the world view perspective, the angle of interest in the scenarios and the system thinking methods themselves. When shared between scenario builders and decision makers, this search for the dominant loop in each scenario strengthens their feeling that this world is plausible: it might well happen. This, in turn, energizes the search for options that exploit entrepreneurial opportunities, in the sense that the mind becomes primed to pick up the signals that a given scenario is emerging. It also helps to increase the resilience of the strategic thinking, and awareness of the full range of underlying uncertainties and their implications.

THE DEEPER STRUCTURE OF TIME SPAN

The second main approach to deepening our understanding using system concepts begins by looking at discontinuous changes over time and how they occur. This can happen on many different scales from one civilization displacing another, to changes of political system, to one technology overtaking another. When such changes take place there are a number of features to bear in mind.

- A sudden discontinuity has usually been incubating, unnoticed by most, for some time.
- The dominant system sustains a prevailing mindset that makes it difficult to notice the emerging signs of change.
- Developments that trigger discontinuity are themselves uncertain; for example, there are many unsuccessful innovations running parallel with a successful one.
- Because of the dominant loops described in the previous section, the dynamics of change are quite messy and non-linear.
- When a change of phase is imminent, it may take only small events to precipitate the change.

We can explore this with an analogy. Imagine you have bought a house that has a large but overgrown garden. The garden was, at one time, laid out formally but has been neglected for many years and has grown wild. The trees have grown up and there is dense undergrowth. What you have acquired is a well-developed ecosystem in balance with its broader environment, but it is not the one that you want. You have in your mind's eye a vision of an area of meadow surrounded by trees, with a rich variety of wild flowers, and you set about clearing the brambles and smaller undergrowth, digging up the weeds, sowing the wild flower seeds, and creating conditions for new incoming species. This is hard work, and the weeds have been there a long time. Despite your efforts in the first year the weeds just grow back and swamp all your new seeds – in fact many of them benefit from the extra light they get as you clear the undergrowth. This little ecosystem is quite resilient, and is not going to be changed easily. You keep going, year after year clearing small patches of weeds, protecting niches for the wildflowers, and gradually shifting the balance of the whole system, until eventually you get to a point where the meadow has become the new dominant system.

In this little example we see some basic ideas about change. First, as we have discussed in the previous section, there is the idea that you can characterize a whole state of affairs with a dominant loop, and that this state emerges through some growth logic from a previous state of affairs. The garden has moved from a formal cultivated state, to a wild one, and now we are taking it to a new relationship with its environment where we are trying to align natural meadow ecology with its broader setting. In important ways this high-level description is more helpful than a discussion of individual plants – their ability to survive and thrive is a property of the overall system.

Secondly, we see very clearly the role of a human activity system in the outcome. As was discussed in the 'Overview' to this book, we can think of societal systems as stable patterns of behaviour that, in a sense, 'lock-in' – they are the ways that, as a society, we have settled on getting something done so that we can each play our individual part. By saying they are locked in, we are intending to stress how hard it is to shift them: all the species that are currently thriving have an interest in the system and will do their best to keep going; we have to change the whole system to get rid of the weeds. In the example we see that in each stage of the garden a pattern has become established and is being maintained by the natural system and its human gardeners. As in our daily lives, systems that are not sustained by activity will quickly fall into disuse and 'go wild'. The garden's three stages show a shifting balance between the activity system and its broader environment: in the first the formal garden has to be maintained with strong defences against the wild stage to which it defaults when the activity stops. In our new garden we try to align the system more with its environment, creating a wild garden with less need for maintenance. We can imagine having created the new design by using the Ramírez and Van der Heijden 'staging' approach (Chapter 4) in which we explored the boundary between the garden and its surrounding environment to find a way to appropriate its setting to create supporting dynamics, such as surrounding meadows.

As well as seeing how each state is a distinct pattern of activity, this simple example also illustrates something important about the dynamics of change from one dominant state to another. In order to achieve our new desired state we have to work very hard against the current system in order to shift the pattern of natural dynamics in favour of our new meadow and away from the dominant weeds. There is a stage when it is only the work of nurturing and protecting the new that allows it to grow and become the dominant system.

These types of system modelling of change have been widely explored by many writers, especially those interested in how new technological regimes can be realized. For example, Moore's model of technology markets draws attention to a 'chasm' that occurs between the initial efforts to introduce new technology to the market and its adoption by a market niche that enables it to start growing (Moore, 1999). This is like the step from defending a patch of the garden against the weeds to finally establishing a self-sustaining meadow.

Notice in these descriptions that there is a linear version of time and there is the qualitative shift to a new pattern of things. This distinction is made in the Greek notions of Chronos and Kairos. Chronos is the view of time as sequence, duration, the passage of time. Kairos is the view of time as the moment of opportunity, as in 'seize the day'. Kairos implies a qualitative shift or meaningful moment. The implication for scenario thinking here is that if we concentrate simply on chronology and timelines of events we may miss the important structural changes that affect strategic fit. On the other hand, if we simply concentrate on significant images of the future, we fail to see how we could possibly get there from here, so there is no basis for crafting strategy through time.

In Figure 5.6 three regions are plotted placing Chronos and Kairos as a fundamental dilemma of time. The labels H1, H2, H3 refer to three horizons of time that create a 'timescape' (Selin, 2006) which will now be described as three different orientations to the future: these relate to the kinds of actions people take and the bets they place on future outcomes.

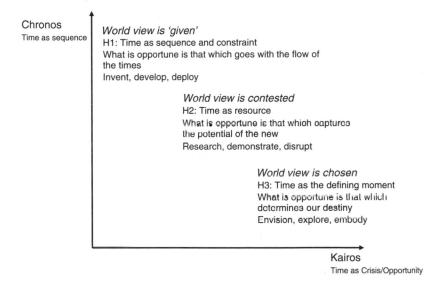

Chronos
Time as sequence

World view is 'given'
H1: Time as sequence and constraint
What is opportune is that which goes with the flow of the times
Invent, develop, deploy

World view is contested
H2: Time as resource
What is opportune is that which captures the potential of the new
Research, demonstrate, disrupt

World view is chosen
H3: Time as the defining moment
What is opportune is that which determines our destiny
Envision, explore, embody

Kairos
Time as Crisis/Opportunity

Figure 5.6   The horizons of time

Horizon 1 (H1) thinking is that which governs the continuation and extension of the current societal systems that define our culture – artefacts, behaviours, laws, institutions, and so on. Since these have certain ways of dealing with questions, issues and problems, any emerging challenge or constraint is framed according to their capabilities and possibilities. The most efficient way to handle new problems or potentialities is to extend the old – never underestimate the power of the existing system to reach further than it has before. The horizon in question is as far as we can see, and we form plans within the scope of our ability to see and plan. Time is viewed as sequence and duration, since it is the frame within which we act in understood ways to carry out plans and procedures and meet societal commitments. Much effort goes into ensuring that outcomes are as expected, that uncertainty is eliminated or managed, and that commitments are met.

An H1 mindset puts us very firmly in the present reality, extending our current system out towards the future as far as we can see, expecting, as with the real horizon, that as we move ahead our opportunity continues to expand. It is the manner of thinking that regards the current way of doing things as entirely appropriate to emerging conditions as long as we continue to extend and develop it. The dominant loop is already visible, and we anticipate the continued allocation of resources to its extension in ways that we understand. For example, in the Intelligent Infrastructure (IIS) case, a H1 model is to assume that we go on building roads and manufacturing cars for the developing world's population in the way we have for the developed world. A lot of the world's innovation happens within H1 as we build smaller, cheaper, faster, etc., products. Implicit in such systems is a broadly understood notion of what 'better' means. These are the systems that are 'locked in'.

Horizon 2 (H2) thinking looks both ways and is inherently ambiguous. The changing circumstances present us with constraints and new opportunities. Should we meet them with old systems or new? What does this choice mean? Are we on a slippery slope? Do we want to be seen as more of the old, or a break with the past and a harbinger of the new? And who gets to decide? Does our legitimacy come from the old world view or the new? We can see our path ahead, because we are using the potential of the present, though we do not know whether we will win or lose our chosen contest. Roadmaps are much desired to help us to narrow our choices and recruit others to our expedition. Evidence is available and carefully scrutinized for every clue it can give us.

The H2 mindset is an orientation to the future that is fundamentally entrepreneurial. It looks at all the potentials for change and seeks to harness them to introduce something new to the world that will grow and thrive. Such new offerings will, in some important sense, change the dominant loop by introducing new system elements that, in turn, configure other system actors to lock in a new pattern which dislocates the H1 momentum. Such change is often characterized as 'disruptive' innovation, meaning that it disrupts the pattern of value creation enjoyed by the incumbents in the current dominant system. We call it H2 to emphasize that it lies beyond H1, and so before it emerges it is only visible to those who participate in the H2 mindset.

Horizon 3 (H3) thinking views the present moment in the light of meaning and destiny. An alternative pattern or paradigm is espoused as a set of principles, a vision of a different world or an alternate reality. Time is the opportunity to take a stance and make a step, however small and insignificant, in the current world dominated by H1 and H2. Deep uncertainty is faced, and a choice is made with the resources to hand, in the knowledge that the choice is existential. We choose a way and let it define the steps. The time of fulfilment is both now and the extended future; and events are left to unfold, interpreted from the standpoint and values we have chosen. In this way H3 selects those innovations of H2 that support its principles and reject those that are seen as bolstering H1. These are considered to have been 'captured'. Great leaders are known for their kairos moments which take whole societies down paths to peace or war, prosperity or peril, and individuals face them as their lives unfold in their life-changing decisions. Equally, grass roots changes in H3 may gradually grow until they reach a tipping point and become the next ecology. Horizon 3 exists as possibilities brought forth by values and beliefs that we feel have a better fit with the future. They are a commitment to a destination over the horizon of the known, guided by a compass rather than a map: 'In order to discover new continents you must have the courage to lose sight of the land.' You can prepare for the expedition, but you cannot possibly have a roadmap.

The H3 mindset is seeing beyond our current systems, motivated by vision, values and beliefs. If an H2 entrepreneurial mindset is concerned with anticipating and capturing changing values, then H3 is concerned with driving such changes. The H3 orientation is one that looks at the values that underpin the dominant loop and takes the stance that they should be different, and that a change is the precondition for a desired new dominant loop. Thus the organic food movement promotes an outlook on how food should be grown that is fundamentally different from the dominant model of the last few decades. Another example would be the Transhumanist movement that is promoting the possibilities of human enhancement made possible by emerging technologies, and taking up the discussion of values that permit or deny this.

Horizon 3 is, in some senses, outside 'time' as understood in the first two horizons. An H2 entrepreneurial orientation is bound to the flow of events, attempting to capture momentum and appropriate resources to a new opportunity; it is possible to be too early as well as too late with such initiatives. In contrast, if you are committed to organic agriculture you will look for ways to pursue it with whatever resources can be found, challenging the current dynamics regardless of timeliness, with the intention that sooner or later the values will start to drive broader adoption. Pursuit of values or vision is a way of bringing the future into the present; it is a commitment of resources that asserts the possibility of a new system and seeks to bring together the activities that realize it. While the same can be said of any entrepreneurial activity, what we intend to show is that H3 is about the world view that prevails broadly in society and determines the sort of value systems that will survive and thrive.

This distinction between H2 and H3 orientations to change can create different types of dynamics and ambiguities in the structure of change. In particular it becomes possible to see that many H2 opportunities lie in an ambiguous state between H1 and H3. For example, returning to the IIS case, all major cities are facing increasing problems of traffic congestion and one solution is to introduce congestion charging, as has been done in London. The London authorities are dealing with the emerging limits of their H1 system with an H2 innovation. However, with an eye on the longer term issues of carbon emissions and sustainability, electric zero-emission vehicles are exempt from the charge. This may seem straightforward until you think about the surrounding value system. Suppose that I use this exemption to switch from using public transport to driving into London, or perhaps to switch cars, live further away and drive in at the same cost. Neither of these changes in behaviour is desirable from the longer term perspective of shifting to sustainable patterns of behaviour. This can be seen as a failure to think through the H3 dynamics; the new technology is being captured by the H1 value system instead of creating a shift to H3 values.

Relating this back to scenario practice as discussed in the 'Introduction' to this part of the book, we can see that H2 dynamics will tend to be dominated by 'hard' systems, that are amenable to rationalistic analysis because, in a sense, they are forces 'out there' that we are attempting to see and understand. In contrast, H3 dynamics are 'soft' and relate to the stories we tell ourselves about the journey we are undertaking, the meanings we are making, and the worlds we might want. So as scenarists we will look to intentional communities, science fiction, and fringe activities of all sorts to see the pockets of the future where new values are being put forward and experimented with. The evidence of the future in H3 is that someone sees the possibility and is promoting it.

Figure 5.7 gives a visual representation of the three-horizon framework.

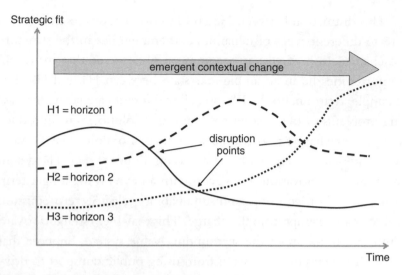

Figure 5.7 The three-horizon framework

This timescape approach was used in the very early stages of scenario building for the 50-year IIS project as a way to enable a diverse set of experts from different disciplines to share mainstream, innovative and 'off the wall' thoughts without the inhibition of having to compile it into a homogeneous category of 'the future'. It enabled different orientations of mind to be legitimized in relation to each other, and gave the scenario-building team a head start in exploring the complex set of components to take into account in the scenario building. It also served as the basis of a Technology Forward Look that could break out of the usual restrictions on technology roadmaps (Sharpe and Hodgson, 2005).

CONCLUSION

This chapter has explored the use of system concepts to help to reach deeper insights in our scenarios of the future. We have put forward two key ideas: the first is that by searching for a 'dominant loop' in an imagined future it is possible to exhibit and contrast the essential dynamics of our scenarios; the second is that, by considering the evolution of the future as three different orientations to the present, we can reach a richer understanding of the dynamics of change.

We believe that these tools can help the decision makers to see when they are at what we call an 'entrepreneurial moment' – an opportunity to act with strategic intent because they understand the flow of events, and they have reached a deep confidence in their own ability to act in a way that is in tune with the unfolding logic.

Such methods may appear at first sight to be rather technical. They are certainly founded on a great deal of research and intellectual effort by a wide variety of workers. The art or craft of application is to find the simple but profound forms that resonate rapidly with the tacit knowledge of both the scenario creators and the decision-making community who need to anticipate the changes.

CHAPTER 6

FROM SIGNALS TO DECISIONS

Alexander Fink, Philip Hadridge
and Gill Ringland

This book originates from discussions during the Oxford Futures Forum (www.oxfordfuturesforum.org). Strategy practitioners had a particularly lively discussion about how scenario planning sits within the wider field of strategy tools: from detecting and sorting signals from outside the organization, from the inside, and from the future through to the decision-making processes. The question was asked: Where precisely within all this does the scenario approach make its contribution?

This chapter focuses on this question, concentrating on the 'deciding what to do' aspect of decision making, rather than on implementation aspects, as the main territory where scenarios come into their own. But even within this we realized that many tools and approaches were used to capture and analyse information from

Scenarios for Success: Turning Insights into Action   Edited by Bill Sharpe and Kees Van der Heijden
© 2007 John Wiley & Sons, Ltd

'the world' and provide a context for decision making. We asked the question: Which approach or tool should be considered in what circumstances and where does the scenario approach fit?

SCOPING THE TASK

Before we discuss the scenario approach in the context of other strategizing tools for negotiating the 'trip' from signals to decisions, we need to set a framework in which we will consider such tools. The framework adopted is shown in Figure 6.1. Notice that

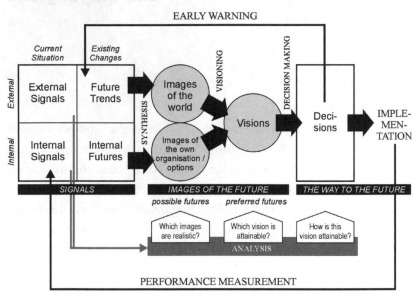

Figure 6.1 Process from signals to decisions – and back

- Four sorts of signal inform organizations: (1) from the current external world, e.g. competitors, the economy; (2) from the anticipated external future – external trends or potential new factors in the environment; (3) from inside the organization; and (4) from factors that may affect the organization internally in the future.

- The route from signals to decisions goes via possible futures and preferred futures. It includes activities such as synthesis, visioning and decision making.
- There are feedback loops from decisions and implementation back to prioritizing the important signals.
- Implementation takes place in the context of ongoing signals from the external and internal environments, which should be watched as part of the process. However we are not explicitly considering implementation in this chapter.

With this schematic of Figure 6.1 in mind, the discussion below is divided into a further six short sections, representing six idealized steps in this process:

- Capturing and categorizing signals
- Building an image of the world
- Creating images of the future (options) of the organization
- Envisioning preferred futures
- Decision making
- Early warning, loopback from decisions to signals.

In real life, steps do not necessarily follow each other in this order. For instance, a manager may be appointed because a decision is needed, and he may commission horizon scanning or business analysis work. In other organizations, an ongoing horizon scanning activity may highlight events or trends that cause management to make decisions based on these. Or – as often happens – as a preliminary to the strategic plan cycle, a CEO or CFO may commission analysis of the existing portfolio or a visioning exercise to set a context for the planning of individual units. A sequential structure is probably an exception in real life, but will be used as a framework for the discussion to follow.

In each section we describe the core task, the role that scenarios play, and list some other tools that are relevant. There are many more tools than we discuss here; our list is meant to be illustrative only.

CAPTURING AND CATEGORIZING SIGNALS

All strategic thinking starts with perception. How do we know what signals to look for? The task is to provide a set of questions that are general enough to avoid missing unexpected signals but narrow enough to avoid retrieving unfocused data and overloading the system.

We find this task at both the front end and the back end of the process. At the front end the task will be prompted by the awareness of a looming issue or opportunity that should be explored, for example 'What is this nanotechnology stuff, and do we need to do anything about it?' At this stage it is necessary to open up to all sorts of inputs to start to build up a base of information and ideas on the strategic issue that is being explored. Many of these will be thought of as 'drivers' of change – things that have a clear direction and momentum that will, over time, reshape our arena of action. For example, demographics, and the way different generational cohorts may have different values and behaviours, is one of the commonest of these drivers.

There is no shortcut to this information and it is the stuff of any good business research and planning group. Table 6.1 shows some of the tools that may be used, and each industry will have its own specialist examples. The chapter by de Ruijter (Chapter 9) discusses how in-depth trend work provided the ground work for their financial scenarios. Scenarios are not a tool in themselves for generating this information; this stage feeds into scenario building. However, it is here in particular that the linear organization of strategy steps is most misleading and we need to take a quick detour to our sixth stage – Early Warning.

At the back end of the process the value of scenarios is in the way they give us a means to discern importance and relevance in events in the world. From the position at the start of the process, where we have an unstructured and general concern about an area, we can reach some more precise set of signals such as: 'If company X starts

Table 6.1 Capturing and categorizing signals

Creating a broad base of information for scenario building		
Tool	**When to use**	**Type of organization**
Time trends	Demographics and economic variables	Public sector
Cohort analysis	Cultural factors, especially when looking for new behaviour	Public sector
Multi-variate analysis	Needed when more than one variable is involved, as in location and ethnic origin	New markets
Scanning	Covers web, journals, conferences, media – all unstructured data – use when looking for weak signals	In private sector sometimes called Business Intelligence

doing Y, then we'll need to step up our own nanotechnology efforts and get a product out.' In scenario planning particular attention is paid to identifying such signals or 'turning points' that indicate that a key threshold has been passed or uncertainty resolved. This is the way in which the whole process loops back. We move from seeing an area that needs examination for strategic impact, collecting information of relevance, all the way through to a much deeper appreciation of the exact type of information we should be looking for.

Seeing the end of the journey is essential to how we undertake the beginning. As we start to scan the environment the list of things we might consider relevant continually grows and ramifies, and if we are opening up to possibilities we will quickly create an enormous, and confusing range of material. We are then bound to start selecting and filtering using some idea of relevance. This is, however, a source of danger; until we have really understood our strategic situation we do not know what is relevant.

Richard Slaughter (1999) at the Australian Foresight Institute highlights the importance of knowing yourself and your perception filters and asks the question: 'What will you miss?' He discusses the process of building a model for making sense of signals, in that way guiding the horizon scanner towards a set of relevant potential signals. As the subsequent steps show, the role of scenarios is to create such models and link them to possible events in the environment.

Thus, the strategic process keeps cycling, while we continually extend our understanding of relevance of trends and refine our perception of significance of events.

BUILDING AN IMAGE OF THE WORLD

Perceptions need to be internalized into images and narratives. Organizations use images of the world in three ways:

- In short-term operations companies strive for a clear image of the future world, on which plans can be based.
- In tactical decision making, organizations have a medium-term perspective based on local interpretation of data.
- In setting strategy one needs to take the long-term inter-connections between factors and trends into account ('systems thinking').

As this list shows, there is a clear contrast between tactical and strategic decisions. Tactical decisions can only be made, and plans formulated, within some assumptions about how the world will be in the immediate future – we just have to make a judgement on what can be relied on to continue according to the current pattern. In contrast, as other chapters in this book make clear, scenarios come into their own when there is a high level of complexity and the issues at stake are likely to require a response that goes beyond 'business as usual'. This is the core purpose of scenario planning.

A scenario is 'an internally consistent view of what the future might turn out to be – not a forecast, but one possible future outcome' (Porter, 2004). By creating several such pictures we give ourselves a method by which to explore and test tactical decisions to find which are robust, which create options, which may have value only if executed quickly before key uncertainties resolve, and so on.

There is a whole spectrum of scenario practice that extends from those that are organized to deal rapidly with tactical issues, to those adapted to long-term assessment of major strategic questions. Scenarios are mostly built specifically for the job at hand, although exceptionally general-purpose stories are imported 'off the shelf'. The choice of approach depends on the timescale of attention of the organization: if an organization is not used to looking long term it may still be possible to work with pre-built scenarios, which extend the imagination of the range of challenges the organization may face, and improve the transparency of the decision making (see Case Study 6.1).

Case Study 6.1   India/China: Scenarios for India and China: the Implications for the City of London

The scenario project on India and China to 2015, addressing possible challenges for the City of London, is an illustration of 'synthesis', i.e. creating an image of the world that people and decision makers can relate to.

SAMI Consulting and Oxford Analytica worked together on a project for the City of London to develop alternative scenarios of the long-term development of India and China up to 2015, and their impacts, positive or negative, on the City of London

---

Case Study 6.1 (Continued)

financial services sector. The job included considering what further analysis may be necessary and what actions might be taken to maximize opportunities and minimize threats. An overall report was prepared on conclusions reached that can be used to stimulate wider debate and appropriate action among City financial institutions, government and other interested parties.

All this was based on a series of workshops and interviews. Oxford Analytica led the development of the scenarios. These were produced by separate teams, followed by a joint workshop to brainstorm the main drivers, with the consultant team writing up the scenario stories.

We then discussed the implications with key players, including the Bank of England, the Association of British Insurers, the China – Britain Business Council, Lloyds of London.

This was followed by three workshops in the City to explore the implications of the scenarios for different sectors of financial services. These implications formed the bulk of the recommendations in the report, published by the City of London in October 2006 and available from the City of London's website: www.cityoflondon.gov.uk.

The City of London is planning to host a symposium to discuss the implications, in early 2007.

Cross–impact analysis is an example of a tool specialized for the short term. This involves identifying a large number of potential events and conditions that appear to influence not only the outcome of the decision but each other as well. The events, trends and conditions typically have probabilities assigned to them, and a computer is used to sort through different combinations of probabilities and cross–impacts.

Andrew Curry (Chapter 13) discusses when to use scenarios or cross-impact analysis in his contribution to *Scenarios in Marketing* (Ringland and Young, 2006). He suggests that for short-term decisions, cross-impact analysis can provide a good support tool – though he cautions that consumer behaviour in the short term can often be better understood by considering longer term drivers using scenarios.

As Schwartz comments in Chapter 1, there is no shortcut to understanding complexity, otherwise it wouldn't be complex, and for those organizations that need to reach a deep understanding, scenarios can be deepened by exploring their underlying systems structure. This is explored in depth in Chapter 5 by Hodgson and Sharpe.

Finally we include the **Delphi** technique in this section (see Table 6.2). This technique was developed by the RAND Corporation in the 1950s as a method for gathering information about the future. In an iterative process, the goal is to get expert opinions on the future to converge by allowing comparison of your own answers with those of other experts. Delphi has proven itself useful for technology-based foresight.

Table 6.2   Building an Image of the World

Scenarios unearth shared assumptions and shape confusion into systemic uncertainty

Tool	When to use	Type of organization
Delphi	Forecasting technology	R&D organization
Systems thinking	Understanding interplay of forces	Complex environments, e.g. regulation
Cross-impact analysis	Short-term decisions	Fast-moving consumer goods

However, the classic study by the Japanese Foresight Programme (see, for instance, Ringland *et al.*, 1999) into accuracy of projections over 25 years found that projections made by experts of only the field were far less accurate than those which brought in experts in neighbouring fields. Although it can help to provide some anchors for images of the future, it is not geared up for building complete pictures in the way that the other techniques do, and may be regarded in some ways as a forecasting extension of the first step – giving a future perspective to visible trends.

CREATING IMAGES OF THE FUTURE (OPTIONS) OF THE ORGANIZATION

Decision making is essentially based on surfacing and deciding between the options that are open to you. Within organizations the task involves creating sufficient common ground among the people involved to allow them to do that (see Case Study 6.2).

Case Study 6.2   CSS Insurance: Developing strategic narratives for CSS

CSS Insurance is one of the leading health insurance companies of Switzerland, with a market share of 15 %.

In 2005 CSS decided to update its long-term corporate strategy. The first stage was to consider external questions such as the future of the insurance industry, the future of health care and the developments in the general environment, in a scenario conference, held by the Management Board and selected experts. The result of the conference was a set of six scenarios describing alternative possible futures of CSS' business environment.

However, the opportunities and threats that were derived from the scenarios did not lead immediately to a new strategy. There were too many interactions between the separate options to consider them separately. Therefore, a smaller number of higher level amalgamated optional strategies so-called strategic narratives (see Fink *et al.*, 2005), were developed during a second scenario conference. These were clustered and mapped according to their similarities in a 'map of the future'.

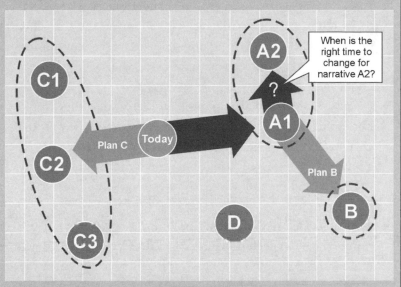

Figure 6.2   Strategy Mapping at CSS Insurance
© Scenario Management International AG, www.scmi.de
Source: Fink/Siebe: Handbuch Zukunftsmanagement, 2006.

The seven strategic alternatives shown in Figure 6.2 were then tested against the previously developed scenarios for the business environment. The outcome of this were two strategic narratives, A1 and A2, which the management could envisage as a basis for steering the company.

Following this a strategy was designed, consisting of four modules:

- *Module 1: Core strategy*. In the nearer future the central course of action of CSS points in the direction of strategic

Case Study 6.2 (Continued)

narrative A1. A further analysis showed what needed to change and what to remain 'as is' for this module to work.

- *Module 2: Long-term strategy.* The long-term goal of CSS is to switch to strategic narrative A2. However, the feasibility of this change depends fundamentally on market conditions. For this reason, a further analysis shows the specific change conditions to be met.

- *Module 3: Plan B.* Participants considered that they could not entirely reject the strategic narrative B, because of some current developments. Hence, it was necessary to work out a 'Plan B' for this case. Any long-term switch to this strategy option would be conditional on a strengthening of certain business units.

- *Module 4: Plan C.* While the previous three modules were supported by expected changes in the environment, it was considered desirable to evaluate other less likely but more extensive changes of market parameters. In this context it was assumed that a switch to the strategy narratives C1 and C2, and even C3 if necessary, could be meaningful. Therefore, an additional 'Plan C' was needed for this case.

The main advantage for CSS of this strategic options approach, compared with a more conventional approach to strategy development, was to enable them to think through alternative courses of action in a thorough and consistent way. Anticipating transitions between the various alternatives, and the conditions under which this would happen, made the outcome considerably more robust.

Table 6.3 Assessing options

Scenarios support exploration of options – is this a new game, and how could we play to win?

Tool	When to use	Type of organization
Modelling	Well-understood application, e.g. hotel utilization	Mature business
Customer segmentation	Understanding customer behaviour	Most companies
Core competencies	Understand organization capability	All organizations
Ansoff matrix	New product or market decisions	Most companies
SWOT	Strategic planning	Most companies
Porter's forces		Most companies
Market Attractiveness/ Capability (MA/C) matrix	New product or market decisions	Companies with a portfolio of businesses

Here, as Table 6.3 shows, we find a wide variety of tools tuned to specific ways of analysing decisions, and we can see the emerging pattern of how the use of scenarios relates to this range of approaches.

On the one hand, there can be no substitute for using all the specialist tools available to illuminate the particular question in front of us. If you are on the verge of introducing a new product into a category that may or may not become mainstream, then you would do well to use whatever customer segmentation and new product decision tools you can find.

On the other hand, you have to be very careful that the application of these tools does not force the new into the assessment criteria of the old. Scenarios allow us to reframe our decisions so that the same information can be seen in multiple contexts: Will this new product be seen as competing with functional extensions of an old category, or is there an underlying dynamic that is creating quite a new pattern of demand? Without understanding how we are framing the decision, we cannot undertake the detailed analysis. Some tools will themselves illuminate this question and so interact with the use of scenarios as a framing tool.

The chapters by Verloop (Chapter 3) and Ramírez and Van der Heijden (Chapter 4) develop this role of scenarios in enabling managers to envisage the new game and what their own role might be within it (see Case Study 6.3).

Case Study 6.3   Fijitsu Services: Using a MA/C matrix with scenarios

Fujitsu Services used the MA/C matrix as a way of summarizing the effect of scenarios on projects or businesses. The MA/C matrix maps business options on the basis of the attractiveness of the relevant market and the level of capability of the company to play in these markets. Attractiveness of market segments was scored using Michael Porter's list of market forces – Market growth, Barriers to entry, Market size, Cyclical trading, Competitive structure, Power of buyers and Regulatory position.

The relevant capabilities are different for each business, but the method of scoring each business is similar.

The businesses considered are then ranked and displayed on the matrix. Figure 6.3 shows how each square suggests a different management strategy.

In this case management was faced with the decision concerning which of the seven options, grouped into three potential new businesses, to invest in. They first developed two scenarios (Coral Reef and Deep Sea), addressing the question: What

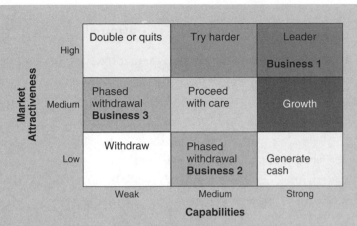

Figure 6.3   The MA/C matrix

would be the market attractiveness in 10 years' time, and how strongly would company capabilities fit with these markets. In order to score different scenarios they were decomposed into about 20 aspects. Some of these were trends common to both scenarios, while others were scenario specific.

Plotting the initial position of each business (B1 through B3) under each of the two scenarios on the MA/C chart leads to the following observations (see Figure 6.4):

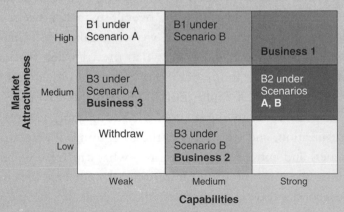

Figure 6.4   Portfolio under the scenarios

<hr>

Case Study 6.3 (Continued)

- Business 1 remains an attractive market, but under both scenarios our capabilities became less well targeted.
- Business 2 seems more attractive and oriented better to our capabilities under both scenarios.
- Business 3 is part of an unattractive market in the Deep Sea scenario, although it fits well with our capabilities. It remained a 'Phased Withdrawal' business under both scenarios – not a candidate for investment!

Surfacing the changes in markets and competencies, and the resultant changing positioning of the businesses on the matrix, allowed Fujitsu to think about the seven potential new options and make the necessary investment decisions.

<hr>

ENVISIONING PREFERRED FUTURES

In this step a scenario can again play two distinct roles: as a tool for this particular step, to be used alongside others, and as a framing for specialist tools that links into the overall strategic process. As an envisioning tool in their own right, we refer again to Chapter 4 by Ramírez and Van der Heijden in which they develop the idea of 'staging', in which the future of the organization in its environment becomes the subject of exploration. This puts the use of scenarios centre stage as a way to engage creativity in imaging new roles for the organization, and will bring to the foreground the question of uniqueness and entrepreneurial vision – what can we uniquely do to capture the momentum of future trends to our best advantage.

The second way uses scenarios to frame the challenge, but harnesses other techniques for creative exploration of the business offering. So, just as a composer might set himself the challenge of writing a piano piece only for the black keys, so a scenario can set up a challenge 'This scenario would need us to create a product that can be completely recycled and appeals to this group of customers. How could that be done?' For exercises of this sort, design scenarios known as 'vignettes' or a 'day in the life' are used, which make a future world concrete in terms of a particular user in a particular situation. There are many approaches to stimulating and harnessing creativity of this sort, and specialist design consultancies make a business out of them. By combining these two approaches it is possible to overcome the problem that can arise when creativity tools are used to stand alone: when these approaches are linked into a well-defined process for organizational change – as within a change management programme – they can be very effective; however, in stand-alone mode they create staff dissatisfaction due to their inability to influence organizational direction. By using scenarios as the bridge it is possible to create a link all the way from the specific business offering to the implications for the strategic future of the organization.

Creating strategic visions, used as a basis for strategy development, requires original invention and creativity. Many creativity methods used to imagine alternatives arise from the work of Edward De Bono on lateral thinking. (see, De Bono, 1992). Examples of visioning techniques include Future Search (Weisbord and Janoff, 2000) and Fluent Visioning (see www.infinitefutures,com). They are both methods for group use to ensure shared vision through the convergence process (see Table 6.4).

Of course the two types of envisioning we have described here feed off each other – a particular business idea is useless without the ability to create particular offerings that win in the market, and the breakthrough idea needs to be encircled by the entrepreneurial understanding of how to build a sustainable business around it. In practice, therefore, creative techniques will move back and forth between ideation and strategic shaping (see Case Study 6.4).

Organizations are often faced internally with many different perspectives on current problems, unsolved conflicts, different

Table 6.4 Envisioning preferred futures

Scenarios help the search for the prime mover opportunity – what can we uniquely do?

Tool	When to use	Type of organization
De Bono	When there is a defined implementation process	Most organizations
Future Search	Need to create a shared vision	Communities
Fluent Visioning	See De Bono	Most organizations
Strategic narratives	Aligning visions	Fragmented organizations

rating of the levers for change, inconsistent compromises, different prioritization of measures and resources, and different interests. It is helpful in negotiating through this to develop strategic options into 'strategic narratives' to explore together the internal 'window of opportunities' (Fink *et al.*, 2004, refer to 'strategy scenarios').

Case Study 6.4   Pharmaceuticals in Africa: Scenarios to develop Corporate Social Responsibility policies for a Pharmaceutical Company in Africa

A pharmaceutical company needed to rethink their Corporate Social Responsibility policies for Africa. They were investing in Africa on a large scale but were concerned that this could become unstuck in the area of Corporate Social Responsibility.

The company asked SAMI Consulting to help. We suggested that the study be based on the UNAids scenarios (http://aidsscenarios.unaids.org/scenarios) developed with the aid of Shell. These three scenarios to 2025 present three possible case studies for how the AIDS epidemic in Africa could evolve over the next 20 years, based on policy decisions taken today by African leaders and the rest of the world.

The scenarios set out to answer one of central question: 'Over the next 20 years, what factors will drive Africa's and the world's responses to the AIDS epidemic, and what kind of future will there be for the next generation?'

The scenarios allowed the Corporate Social Responsibility team of the company to discuss the situation in five representative countries in Africa and evolve strategies for each, taking into account the likely evolution of each country.

DECISION MAKING

Jim Collins, discussing decision making in organizations (Collins, 2001), defines two categories of organization – foxes and hedgehogs. Foxes pursue many ends at the same time and see the world in all its complexity. Hedgehogs simplify a complex world into a single organizing idea, and anything that does not relate to this idea is dismissed as not relevant. He argues that successful organizations are hedgehogs: that they seize upon an organizing principle and drive its implementation fanatically. However, hedgehogs cannot easily recognize when the boundaries are blurring and the organizing principle needs to change.

Decision makers need to be clear on the minimum set of decisions required to maintain the logic of the organization on the one hand, and boundary flexibility on the other. A concept helping executives to articulate this minimum package of central control is called the Business Idea (Van der Heijden, 2005). It is the subset

of an organization's business model that contains the essential success formula driving the organization's survival and development; it
helps management teams to focus their decision making (see Case
Study 6.5).

**Case Study 6.5   The Man Group: Recognizing
Change at the Man Group**

The ED&F Man Group's origins went back to the 1700s,
trading sugar from the Caribbean. The business extended over
the years into other products, from trading to refining and
sourcing, and into stockbroking, investment management and
insurance.

Gill Ringland was asked to help the Group anticipate changes in markets, for instance to reduce losses
on trading in sugar derivatives. We used a Board meeting – at which the Divisional Directors and their immediate teams were present – to run a Workshop the
next day. The scenarios chosen were 'London in 2020'
(Figure 6.5), for the future of financial services in the City
of London.

The four scenarios in Figure 6.5 look at how the City
as a leading home of Financial Services companies might
respond if:

- the world is 'global' and Information Technology (IT)
  becomes pervasive (Globetech);
- Europe, Asia and North America divide into competing
  trade blocs, all using IT successfully (Fragtech);
- a global world uses very little of IT (Slowglobe); and
- the world is broken-down, with fragmentation of trade and
  little dependence on IT (Fourth World).

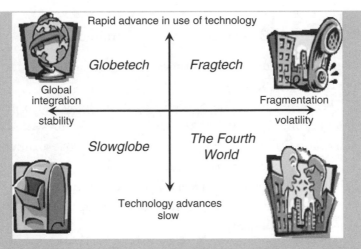

St Andrews Management Institute (SAMI)

Figure 6.5 City of London in 2020

At the Workshop Divisional Directors and their teams role-played, addressing the question 'What are our strengths in each of four scenarios?'

The answers proved very different for each business. The Division trading primary and secondary sugar products felt comfortable with Slowglobe. Other businesses discovered they had built their business plan on assumptions corresponding to Globetech, Fragtech and the Fourth World.

The discussion on the reports returned from each unit was revealing to the team. They had not realized the differences in assumptions across the Group, perhaps due to the underlying dynamics of the businesses, their history and their tacit assumptions. In particular the Division concerned with land-ownership, refineries and logistics had a very different worldview from the other businesses which relied on trading using IT.

Soon afterwards, the Group divested the sugar products Division, and later the insurance and stockbroking arms were

> ### Case Study 6.5   (Continued)
>
> aligned to the derivatives business along the lines seen during the discussion of the scenarios.
>
> This shows the value of scenarios in bringing out implicit assumptions. Although the scenarios were presented as describing 2020, the discussion brought out that a different scenario was recognized by each of the four Divisions, highlighting the source of management tensions. Surfacing this allowed a fundamental decision to be made on the future shape of the company.

Few articles on decision making refer to the use of scenarios or other futures methods as a basis for improving decision making. The focus is on the shortcomings of the human cognitive system. Why does there seem to be so little discussion of the use of tools to augment group performance in decision making?

One problem is the difficulty of obtaining benchmarks or other review data that confirm or deny a proposition that decisions made using synthesis or analysis tools are better or worse than those made by 'gut' (Buchanan, 2006). A reason for this could be that a good decision can be badly implemented, or a bad decision can be ameliorated by run–time corrections by staff on the ground.

But what is a 'good decision' anyway? It is not the same as a good outcome, as a lot can happen between the decision and the outcome. While the outcome is there to be seen and evaluated, it is mostly impossible to decide in retrospect whether a decision was good, bad or indifferent, in the absence of any knowledge 'after the fact' on the outcome of a different decision. This is why Janis (Janis and Mann, 1977) prefers to talk about **vigilant** decisions rather than **good** decisions, as something that can be tested. Janis considers contingency planning (i.e. multiple scenarios) as a key constituent part of vigilance in decision making. It seems clear to us that scenarios are becoming the key, and possibly the only, tool that managers have to communicate that the past is not necessarily the best guide to the future and that alternatives need to be considered. Table 6.5 identifies the roles of scenarios and uncertainty impact matrices in decision making.

Table 6.5 Decision Making

Scenarios bring decisions into focus and test them against uncertainty

Tool	When to use	Type of organization
Business Idea	Identifying the key decisions	Any organization
Scenarios and uncertainty impact matrix	Shared assumptions, discussion of options. Exposing default assumptions	Any organization

EARLY WARNING, LOOP BACK FROM DECISIONS TO SIGNALS

While many companies have significantly improved their process of decision making and strategy implementation over recent years, organizations continue to be repeatedly surprised by dynamic changes in the environment, realizing late – in some cases too late – that old strategies had been maintained for too long.

With hindsight, these 'sudden' events often have been preceded by so–called 'weak signals', which could have been detected in their early stages (Table 6.6). The recording and evaluation of such information is strategic early warning, which is closely interconnected with the processes of decision making and strategic planning.

Table 6.6   Early warning

Scenarios prime the individual and organization for environmental scanning

Tool	When to use	Type of organization
Scanning and Future Maps	Flagging 'unexpected' events	Any

Indicators are integrated into most strategy implementation processes – but are usually built upon the specific strategy, and conform to one dimensional external perspective. New trends are not usually obvious from these kinds of indicators. To recognize 'weak signals' in time, managers have to widen their horizon to the areas that are not part of their current strategy – and often beyond their current mental models.

Relevant future trends and events are often seen in parts of the company outside the traditional planning process, e.g. in business development, in product and innovation management or in disjoint foresight activities. As a result of these, new issues can be identified. Companies need an additional perspective of 'early warning indicated planning' or decision making.

Scenarios can play a significant and new role in combining the well-structured planning process with the often less-organized and in some planners' minds more 'chaotic' early warning processes (Fink *et al.*, 2005):

- *Scenarios define the scope of the monitoring processes.* When companies focus their strategy on selected scenarios, the scenarios that are not adopted are important sources of 'weak signals'.
- *Scenarios are needed to identify 'weak signals'.* Early warning processes focus on 'weak signals', which appear first in less plausible alternatives to the current mental models. Scenarios are an important tool for clearing the way for these new ideas into the strategic thinking.

- *Early warning processes initiate new scenario processes.* Often topics which suggest a closer examination in the form of scenarios are the result of an early warning process.
- *Scenarios and early warning systems use the same kind of information.* Well-structured knowledge about future developments can be used to reduce the time to develop new scenarios as well as to improve their quality; well-written scenarios can return into early warning systems as new information.

In traditional performance measurement approaches, companies continuously observe their performance and ask: How is the implementation of our current strategy going? Today, many companies also include external strategy premises into their performance measurement systems and ask: How are the premises of our current strategy developing? But this approach fails if the new dynamics are outside the current strategy. Here a future scorecard could help companies by encouraging the monitoring of:

- not only the premises of the current strategy but also the critical market indicators based on external scenarios that are not taken into consideration within the current strategy;
- not only the internal performance indicators but also the change indicators from alternative strategy narratives that are not part of the current strategy.

The combination of strategy premises, critical market indicators and strategy indicators leads to a Future Scorecard, which is an addition to existing performance measurement approaches. This approach is described in detail in Chapter 12 by Heathfield.

SUMMARY AND CONCLUSIONS

Scenarios are part of decision making in organizations. This chapter has focused on the use of scenarios at different stages in the process from capturing signals to decision making, comparing them with other tools in a manager's tool portfolio.

- At the scanning stage, there are a number of ready tools based on historic analysis that can be used to project forward into the future. Scanning across all available sources is much harder with overload, making it difficult to find the 'relevant' data. Scenarios have a role in prioritizing the scan, to search for early indicators of a specific scenario.

- Synthesis (creating an image of the world to which people can relate) can be achieved by forecasting tools such as Delphi, which are successful if the rules do not change; and by scenarios if the rules do change. Systems thinking is often used as a tool on the basis of which a storyline can be developed supporting a Delphi forecast or a set of scenarios.

- Assessing options is a topic with a multitude of tools to choose from. If such tools are only based on historical data, they often produce a 'garbage in, garbage out' problem. On the other hand, they are powerful when used with multiple scenarios to expand on the implications of differing futures. The main tool is the Options/Scenario matrix.

- The creation of strategic visions, and derived strategies, involves original invention and creativity.

- Decision making in the narrow sense has very few tools directly attached. The difficult question of what constitutes a 'good' decision underlies this problem. The notion of 'vigilant' decisions offers help.

- Early warning uses some of the same tools that are used for scanning, but with an emphasis on events flagged by scenarios.

In conclusion, this chapter has aimed to provide background on how to think about scenarios in the context of the overall organizational 'perception to decisions' process.

Scenarios are not good for everything; they do not substitute for special tools for particular tasks. What we have tried to do is to outline the ways in which they can be most profitably used against a bigger organizational learning and decision-making background.

Their particular contribution can be seen in the way they can hold together and work alongside the many other tools available.

The potential benefit of scenarios in decision making is too powerful to allow it to be lost in the noise of ill-informed and superficial practice.

CASE SUMMARY

6.1. *Synthesis, creating an image*
Scenarios for India and China and their use in addressing possible challenges to the City of London.

6.2. *Assessing options, scenarios vs strategic narratives (scenario/options matrix)*
Allowing CSS to think through alternative courses of action in a thorough and consistent way. Anticipating transitions between the various alternatives makes strategy considerably more robust.

6.3. *Assessing options, scenarios vs strategic narratives (tools)*
Combining scenarios with a Marketing Attractiveness/Capability matrix illustrates the way in which this type of analysis can change received wisdom. The MA/C case.

6.4. *Visioning, inventing a new strategic outlook*
The UNAids scenarios used to consider Corporate Social Responsibility priorities illustrates the use of off-the-shelf scenarios. The Africa case.

6.5. *Decision making*
The Man Group using scenarios to provoke a dialogue that had not been previously possible, and hence facilitating a decision.

CHAPTER 7

WHEN STRANGERS MEET: SCENARIOS AND THE LEGAL PROFESSION

Karim Medjad and Rafael Ramírez

Scenarios have been used in companies since at least the 1970s (Lesourne and Stoffaes, 2001), and longer by military planners and policy makers. In business, Shell's successful use of scenarios to anticipate oil crises gave them prominence in the private sector (Wack, 1984a; Schwartz, 1991; Van der Heijden, 1996). In none of these cases has it become apparent that the legal profession has been a core user of scenarios.

An exception we are aware of is a set of scenarios for the world in 2015 developed by Oxford Analytica for Clifford Chance, a leading UK-based international law firm. In this instance, the 'legal component' appears to have been marginal, however. Instead, Oxford Analytica studied the interaction of over 40 political, economic and social trends and uncertainties and their respective implications for

Scenarios for Success: Turning Insights into Action   Edited by Bill Sharpe and Kees Van der Heijden
© 2007 John Wiley & Sons, Ltd

the market for legal services, but the concerns of Clifford Chance did not differ significantly from those of any global professional services provider with a strong client base in Asia. In other words, the scenarios were not about legal thinking, but about how existing legal services might fare in the future environments in which Clifford Chance may operate. In this sense – although for a legal firm – this is a 'classical' scenario exercise, where the business idea (Van der Heijden, 2005) is not in and of itself questioned. In short, the link between scenarios and the legal profession seems to be mediated by policy makers. We consider here whether dis-intermediating this link may be of help.

Why should the legal profession (broadly construed here) pay more attention to scenarios? One could argue that scenario planning and legal reasoning belong to two different cultures, notably because the rules as such are seldom intended to anticipate future behaviours: they aim to sanction, channel, deter or prevent existing activities. Even rules that are presented as forward-looking, such as those set forth by the Treaty on Antarctica, are typically the outcome of a series of prior claims of some sort. This reactive – rather than proactive – nature of the law appears to have contributed to drive apart scenario planning and legal reasoning.

A second argument may be that the kind of uncertainty scenarios are meant to analyse is an uncertainty that laws, treaties, and contracts attempt to preclude. For example, senior managers of an intergovernmental organization with whom Rafael Ramírez has worked in recent years, suggested that since their task was to apply an intergovernmental treaty they needed no strategy.

In this chapter, we argue that there is in fact a 'considerable' market for scenario activity in the legal world, where different stakeholders (legislators, the legislated, law enforcers, interest groups, lobbies) must adopt in their own way the type of scenario thinking that large multinational companies, military planners and policy makers have so far dominated.

Up to now, as far as the legal profession is concerned, scenario thinking is very occasionally – and exclusively – used for the purposes of creating common values among stakeholders or for making sense of complex environments that have changed so much that they need to be reassessed by a central actor. An example of the first kind – futures thinking in law aimed at producing common values – is the work that Karim Medjad developed in designing legal options to lift trade barriers between the ethnic entities composing Bosnia and Herzegovina; the aim was to help their respective authorities to understand this aspect of their future relations in compatible ways. An example of the second kind of future legal thinking – where sense-making is an important consideration – was work that Ramírez carried out for the European Round Table of Industrialists some 20 years ago, to assess whether creating its own 'green' standards was worth considering. The objective was to make sense of how the environmental movement might in the future impact these large corporations and, after understanding this, to consider which options could be available to them.

In this chapter, we claim that there is room for a more strategic use of scenarios in the legal domain, not only for these two purposes but also as a means to sort out and test legal options before choosing one, and even to generate new ones.

In the first part of this chapter we explore how legal issues have been treated in scenario activities up to the present. We show that, because clients have not taken into consideration future professional aspects of the law, scenarios have confined legal considerations to mere environmental (contextual or transactional) variables.

In the second part we briefly describe the current state of the art of what 'law' and 'legal practice' are, and how legal practitioners work. Taking as an example the area of international corporate social responsibility (CSR) – from the point of view of a hypothetical NGO eager to increase the obligations of Multinational Corporations, ('MNCs') – we argue that neither 'pure' legal reasoning nor, scenario reasoning, however well documented and compelling, that pays insufficient attention to legal considerations is adequate: each will generate predictions plagued with expensive strategic blind spots.

We suggest that it is only in combining scenarios with legal thinking that truly valuable – that is, truly innovative – strategic insights are produced. To support our claim, we show that scenarios created to make sense of complexity (such as the Shell scenarios) can be most helpful when deployed instead for the strategic purposes of generating legal options and wind-tunnelling them; they can effectively improve and refine strategies stemming from legal reasoning.

In the third part, we show there is a cost for not deploying scenarios in the legal arena for the purpose of generating new options. Using the example of the ongoing battles between the tobacco industry and a number of stakeholders, we develop, from the standpoint of a hypothetical anti-tobacco NGO, a set of scenarios that highlights unexplored but pertinent legal areas that could provide more 'bang for the buck' return of invested effort for the NGO than the health-centred anti-tobacco lawsuits and legislation they have focused upon so far. Some of the blind spots created by this rather narrow focus have already been identified. In an interesting example of scenario thinking (but not of actual scenario making) in relation to legal thinking, it has even been suggested that medical legislation actually strengthened the tobacco industry's monopoly on nicotine (Bates, 2000). In pursuing our thought experiment, we further suggest that had anti-tobacco NGOs used scenario practices and thinking in conjunction with legal reasoning, anti-trust legislation would have emerged as a key strategic arena for them. To our knowledge, this critical legal avenue has been overlooked so far by the legal professionals advising anti-tobacco NGOs.

More importantly, our thought experiment shows that relating scenario thinking to legal thinking allows for the plausibility of a future legal condition which would otherwise remain an unrealistic – or even unthinkable – paradox. This specific example shows how fertile it can be to link legal and scenario thinking.

In the last part of the chapter, we conclude with practical considerations on why and how scenarios could be developed for, and by, the legal profession.

THE ROLE OF 'LAW' IN SCENARIOS UP TO NOW

We first had the ideas that we report in this chapter when Ramírez was a Visiting Professor of Scenarios and Corporate Planning in Shell International (2000–2003). Ramírez invited Medjad to a meeting in Shell which was attended by a mixed audience of scenario planners and lawyers from the corporate office. During his presentation, Medjad suggested that a particular US statute could in the future affect commercial practices in Europe as a result of the way domestic courts had begun to influence each other informally across borders.

The scenario planners in the audience quickly grasped that the mere possibility of this coming about – regardless of whether it did or not – would change behaviours. In contrast, the lawyers did not consider that the possibility needed attention as they did not foresee a legal change in Europe. We were witnessing intelligent, highly educated people within the same company reacting very differently to the same information. This sparked an ongoing conversation between us on the difference between scenario thinking and legal thinking; the co-writing of this chapter has helped to further this discussion.

If laws are reactive to events, they do not appear to react to *possible* future events well. Let us look a the UN Framework Convention on Climate Change, better known as the 'Kyoto Protocol'; it is a reaction to small amounts of global warming that have already begun to be experienced, but it is poorly equipped to address the more radical implications of how global warming could develop in the coming years.

Our hope is that if scenario thinking can 'converse' with legal thinking it will help legal thinkers to become more proactive. Grant (2003) suggested that strategic planning is no longer the primary decision-making path for strategy, but instead 'is a device that is able to enhance internal communication, integrate different capabilities, and coordinate organizational activities across different functional areas' (Hutzchenreuter and Kleindienst, 2006). If this is what strategic planning is becoming, then better 'conversation' between scenario and legal thinking will produce better strategic insights.

When scenarios examine future environments, whether of the private (corporate) or public (public policy/military) sectors, it is the decision makers in those areas who are the key actors; the legal profession and its 'products' (laws and regulations) are just part ot the context. Thus, the future of, for example, an Italian rail network would look at how municipal, regional, national, EU, and WTO rules and regulatory moves could affect this network. To our knowledge, the law itself (a rule, contract, treaty, charter or covenant) has never been considered the 'central actor' in a scenarios exercise. Instead, the law has been considered a 'driving force' extending from the outer contextual environment into the transactional environment. In the transactional environments, many counterparts to the central actors may have their core activity in the legal profession (e.g. courts, legislators), but relations with them are taken in a very broad sense and are very rarely – if at all – considered primarily in legal terms within a scenarios-based intervention.

In this chapter we present two examples where the legal actor, legal thinking, and legal practice are put in the centre for wind-tunnelling purposes. In the first example – the future of corporate social responsibility (CSR) – scenarios are used to test the legal expert's forecast as regards the evolution of the area. In the second example – the future of the legal fight against tobacco companies – scenarios are used to identify additional weaknesses in the legal armour of the tobacco companies and to reassess the allocation of an imaginary NGO's legal resources.

CHALLENGING LEGAL THINKING WITH SCENARIOS: THE EXAMPLE OF INTERNATIONAL CORPORATE SOCIAL RESPONSIBILITY

Practical approach to CSR

When legal practitioners look at legal rules from a practical standpoint, they tend to follow a binary approach. Accordingly, the law can be 'hard' or 'soft', that is, consisting either of binding or mandatory rules such as, say, criminal law; or consisting of facultative or voluntary rules (e. g. the Kyoto Protocol).

This elementary breakdown remains of limited practical interest until it is further refined with additional analytical layers: obviously, the actual 'softness' of a non-mandatory rule (e.g. 'you must attend church on Sundays') may vary considerably depending on whether one lives in, say, the gay neighbourhood of Mexico City or in a small isolated Mexican village dominated by a strong traditional priest.

In the case of 'hard' law, a rule can be more or less 'hard' depending on its social acceptance while, technically, the prohibition of murder and tobacco smoking in public places are equally mandatory, the authorities in countries such as France or Spain find it much easier to enforce the former than the latter. Likewise, the quality of the institutional context makes the same mandatory rule (e.g. the prohibition of patent infringement) an immediate and tangible threat in the USA and a vague and remote one in Russia.

From this standpoint, the nature of international corporate social responsibility (CSR) legislation seems quite composite: a handful of indirectly relevant multilateral treaties (mainly in the area of human rights), a few non-binding texts such as the Global Compact (UN, 1999), and finally, a large portion of non-mandatory, self-regulatory devices (codes of conducts, best practices, etc.). While it is fair to acknowledge that international law has accomplished substantial progress in the area of CSR, it is important to bear in mind that the bulk of such improvements has taken place within the realm of soft law.

Again, this is not the whole picture. The tremendous success of CSR over the past decade is the result of a virtuous circle that has created a 'mandatory/voluntary' paradox: the very lack of tangible sanctions when international CSR principles are breached has greatly facilitated the adhesion to such principles by Multinational Corporations (MNCs). A viral effect has followed, turning them into not-so-voluntary rules. While technically still 'soft', these rules are becoming ever 'harder' to ignore with the help of activist journalists such as Michael Moore. Whether – and to what extent – this peculiar alchemy will ultimately impose a dose of 'hard' law in the area of international CSR remains uncertain.

This is why many activist groups – including NGOs – consider that lawsuits brought against Western-based MNCs in their home country remain for now the only 'tangible' – hard – means to impose minimum corporate governance standards worldwide. The result is the series of lawsuits initiated throughout the past two decades against corporate parents for damages caused abroad by their subsidiaries, in areas as diverse as environment, personal injuries or human rights.

Bad publicity aside, this aggressive judicial strategy has produced little result to date. The so-called 'foreign direct liability suits' have remained limited in number, and have been typically confined to Anglo-Saxon countries. In the vast majority of cases, defendants have managed to raise procedural obstacles to avoid fines or prevent key executives being sanctioned (Medjad, 2006).

A theoretical legal expert's forecast (time horizon: 2025)

From the point of view of a lawyer working at the end of 2006 for an activist NGO, the question of the future of international CSR boils down to three main questions:

- What will be the future of the so-called 'Alien Tort Claim Act' in the USA?
- Can we really expect an awakening of the civil law courts to put a 'bite' into the law?
- Will CSR eventually be strengthened by real 'hard law' rules?

First question: What will be the future of the so-called 'Alien Tort Claim Act' in the USA?

As far as liability suits are concerned, Anglo-Saxon countries in general and the Unites States in particular are known to be better venues for the plaintiffs. Larger amounts can be sought, specific procedures are available (e.g. class action), and attorneys can be hired on a 'no-win no-fee' basis. These 'big' liability claims, combined with the peculiar 'results-based' fee structure of US lawyers, helps to explain why plaintiffs, NGOs and public interest lawyers avoid civil law courts whenever possible. Moreover, in the case of foreign direct liability suits, the United States is often the only country where the judicial route is available, thanks to a 1789 Statute with no foreign equivalent, generally referred to as the 'Alien Tort Claims Act' (ATCA).

The ATCA confers upon the federal district courts 'original jurisdiction of any civil action by an alien for a tort only, committed in violation of the law of nations or a treaty of the United States'. At the time in which the Act was passed, the violations in question were primarily piracy acts, and by granting non–US citizens access to US courts, the main objective of the US Congress was to let the other nations know that US territory would not become a safe harbour for pirates. For nearly two centuries the ATCA was almost dormant, until its rekindling in the 1980s in a series of lawsuits against human rights abusers. As of the early 1990s, ATCA started being used against US-based MNCs for the damages caused by their subsidiaries abroad, making the United States a major venue for testing whether certain CSR principles had acquired the status of 'Law of Nations', that is, of rules so universally applied that they have becomes mandatory rules of international law.

Since the turn of the twenty-first century, the US administration has launched an aggressive campaign to obtain nothing less than a curtailment of the ATCA to forbid its use against US-based MNCs. While anti–ATCA activists go as far as calling it a tool for international terrorism, more serious arguments insist on the economic threat posed by the ATCA. According to a well-advertised study released by the US Institute for International Economics, ATCA-based class action lawsuits could put at risk hundreds of thousands of jobs in the United States alone, and millions elsewhere. Global trade and investment might incur a drop of over $300 billion due, *inter alia*, to mega–class action suits with a financial impact comparable to that of the asbestos litigations. To illustrate this point, here is a 'nightmare scenario' as an introduction:

> [in the next decade],100,000 class action Chinese plaintiffs, organized by New York trial lawyers, could sue General Electric, Toyota, and a host of other blue-chip corporations in a US federal court for abetting China's denial of political rights, for observing China's restrictions on trade unions, and for impairing the Chinese environment. These plaintiffs might claim actual damages of $6 billion and punitive damages of $20 billion.
>
> (Hufbauer and Mitrokostas, 2003)

In 2004 the debate reached a critical turn in *Sosa v. Alvarez-Machain*, the first US Supreme Court ruling on an ATCA case. The implications of this decision are unclear: while it clearly reduces the scope of the ATCA to exclude, *inter alia*, environmental issues, it seems to endorse the ATCA as a human rights tool and does not exclude the possibility of using it to seek redress from corporations. As a result, most activist NGOs consider that the bottom line has been preserved.

This status quo is likely to evolve. Clearly, the future of the ATCA is bleak, not so much because of its content but because of the lack of an equivalent text elsewhere. As it is perceived as setting US corporations at a disadvantage – an intolerable taint – the ATCA will at best be maintained with a reduced scope.

Second question: Can we really expect an awakening of the civil law courts to put a bite into the law?

An important consequence of the growing 'criminalization' of corporate misconduct worldwide is that continental European courts are asserting a much broader territorial competence in this area than in civil or commercial matters. Accordingly, the judicial exposure of the parent companies located in continental Europe has increased: Anglo-Saxon countries are no longer the exclusive judicial destination to seek redress for damages caused in a developing country.

This 'opening' of the civil law systems to foreign direct liability suits should contribute significantly to enforcing a minimum of CSR norms worldwide for four reasons:

1. It should provide human rights and environmental activists and their NGOs with a significantly larger legal menu with which they can threaten MNCs. For the same act, multiple 'judicial bids' may be placed in different countries, under different labels, thus improving the odds of a judicial sanction.

2. The area of criminal law allows more international interaction among jurisdictions. Domestic courts of various countries, by exchanging information about each other's case law, inevitably tend to harmonize their responses, thereby allowing the emergence of additional transnational customary law.

3. The threat of relocating headquarters, often made by MNCs facing common law courts, has lost its credibility now that civil law countries are equally open to foreign direct liability suits; and so has the threat of a 'race to the bottom' between common law and civil law courts to protect their domestic firms.

4. The important development of apparently unrelated legal fields, such as consumer law or competition law, should generate new grounds in the western world for imposing sanctions on MNCs that breach their CSR commitments. For example, the charges of false advertising or of unfair competition could become instrumental in forcing MNCs to comply fully with their own codes of conduct.

In short, the expected reduction of transnational liability suits in the USA should be more than compensated for by the foreseeable increase, in Europe at least, of CSR-related law suits in the areas of criminal law or consumer law.

Third question: Will international CSR eventually be strengthened by real 'hard' law rules?

A 'soft' law is seldom an interim rule put in place until a hard law can be devised and implemented. Quite often, a 'soft' law is intended to be exactly the opposite of a step towards anything more 'hard' or mandatory. Thus, by adopting voluntarily rules, MNCs expect to defuse the need for a mandatory rule: they want to decide the nature and extent of the restrictions they impose on themselves.

CSR is no exception to this classic strategy on the part of MNCs; it, too, can operate as a smoke-screen or a decoy to avoid hard and enforceable law from being enacted. Accordingly, more and more 'soft' law is anticipated in the area of CSR, whether it is proposed by public national or international bodies (e.g. OECD, UN) or by private firms (in-house charters, codes of conduct, etc.). And this should logically mean that little 'hard law' will be enacted in the foreseeable future.

How will the resulting 'mandatory/voluntary' paradox mentioned above unfold? It is not clear, notably because we do not know how the 'southern' MNCs (from China, India, Brazil, Mexico) will respond. The relative weight of these MNCs is now far from negligible; so if they do not follow the western-based MNCs by adhering in large numbers to basic CSR principles, these soft rules will not be strengthened by unanimous endorsement.

Wind-tunnelling legal forecasts

It is quite easy to show the limitations of the 'pure' legal reasoning developed above by confronting it with the 'generalist' sense-making scenarios that are regularly released by agencies (e.g. UN, CIA, IEA), think tanks (e.g. Rand Corporation) and corporate players (e.g. British Telecom, Shell).

Take, for example, the Shell 'Global Scenarios to 2025' (Shell, 2005); it is convenient that a version of these is publicly available, and that they retain the same time horizon as the above legal forecast. Using what it calls a 'Trilemma Triangle', Shell proposes three scenarios: 'low trust globalization', 'open doors' and 'flags'. These scenarios – whatever their original purpose – can be used immediately and without any adaptation for legal wind-tunnelling purposes, as follows:

Scenario 1: Low Trust Globalization

This scenario describes a more globalized world with more market liberalization than at present, but a world where the trust problem posed by mega corporate scandals (such as Enron, Parmalat) has not been resolved, and has caused states and regulators to be more coercive.

The scenario reveals a blind spot of most legal predictions: it shows that the dose of 'hard' law in the future global corporate governance may be quite important, after all. The reason why a legal future with a larger chunk of hard law has become plausible is simple: more coercion in a globalized world requires a better coordination of domestic authorities across borders. And this kind of international coordination is typically formalized in a treaty 'with teeth that bite', as in the case of the Interpol treaty.

Scenario 2: Open Doors

In this scenario, the world is also more globalized, but this time the trust and security crisis has been resolved, allowing more cohesive and powerful civil societies to emerge. Key consequences of this power shift include the development of more soft power and an extensive use of the precautionary principle.

The main interest of this scenario is that it challenges the traditional distinction between soft law and hard law: in this future, soft law stemming from soft power may no longer be so 'weak' and so voluntary. A critical question that the scenario does not address follows: If a 'mutant' norm does emerge, will its effects be more or less predictable than those of its 'hard' and 'soft' predecessors?

Scenario 3: Flags

This scenario envisages a less-globalized world, where states have become more protectionist and rally around the flag at the expense of economic efficiency and market-oriented values.

As foreseen by our hypothetical legal forecaster above, it is far from certain that global CSR principles will become universal enough to achieve the status of 'hard' customary principles in international law within the time frame of the scenario. But where legal analyses focus on the obstacles to a general acceptance of CSR principles, notably due to the resistance of the southern players (MNCs, governments), this scenario highlights a more temporal obstacle: under certain political conditions CSR principles may simply not last long enough in western countries. Indeed, with less open and transparent domestic borders, western-based MNCs might simply return to their old habit of applying different governance standards in different countries; and as long as the profit stream remains uninterrupted, regulators and shareholders might prefer to turn a blind eye to such practices, as they did in the past.

USING SCENARIOS TO GENERATE LEGAL OPTIONS: AN IMAGINARY ACTIVIST NGO FIGHTING TOBACCO COMPANIES

NGOs' legal resources are not commensurate with those of tobacco companies. This imbalance begs for an assessment of how anti-tobacco activists allocate their legal resources. This case study illustrates how scenarios can be used for that purpose and for identifying additional legal targets.

The tobacco industry: facts and figures

Tobacco figures (WHO, 2002) are literally breath-taking: over 15 billion cigarettes are smoked daily in the world. China is the main player: it is the main producing country (followed by the USA) and it has the single largest domestic market (over 300 million male smokers). The demand in industrialized countries is decreasing, but it is more than made up for by an increasing demand in developing countries, and by the overall increase in the world population.

On the supply side, state monopolies continue to account for 40% of total supply, but this percentage is declining. The single main producer is a private player (Altria Group, formerly Philip Morris) and so is the main distributor (BAT). Demand and supply are linked by official trade (the largest exporter of cigarettes is the USA with 20%), as well as by a considerable amount of illegal trade – smuggling accounts for one in three cigarettes.

For the largest tobacco MNCs such as Altria Group or BAT, these simple data raise a number of complex legal uncertainties. For example:

- As business moves south, will legal issues be temporarily less critical on average?
- Could joint-ventures with state-owned cigarette manufacturers contribute locally to secure smoker-friendly regulations?
- Are smugglers friends or foes? Is the answer the same everywhere?

The tobacco industry and scenarios

For the tobacco industry, part of the official future is already known: one day, there will be tobacco-unfriendly health rules everywhere. What is uncertain is the path leading to this future: will it be smooth or chaotic? Will the flow of hostile stakeholders (NGOs, public health authorities, international organizations, e.g. WHO, UNICEF, etc.) stop growing?

Every option for this official future has already been considered by tobacco MNCs, including the most radical ones: Philip Morris has even studied the possibility of quitting the tobacco business (Smith and Malone, 2003). But it won't quit the business, and why should it? The tobacco industry is virtually unsinkable. Even a giant zillion-dollar class action suit won in court could not put this industry out of business: in the USA, the famous $206 billion multi-state settlement could be brushed off with a modest 40 cents price rise per pack (Bates, 2000).

With virtually unlimited financial resources, tobacco MNCs have become more sophisticated scenario professionals in areas such as the future of tobacco regulation than any other stakeholder, whether they be legislators, enforcers, public health authorities, NGOs, or even smart and well-funded smugglers. For tobacco MNCs the game is straightforward: develop scenarios and play the options in each of them all at the same time, because in a world made of 200 different legal systems, all imaginable legal futures may plausibly coexist.

Unlike the tobacco industry, anti-tobacco activist NGOs cannot afford to put the options of all plausible scenarios into play simultaneously. Most of them are also more geographically restricted in their breadth of activities than tobacco MNCs, so the uncertainty of how a given legal regime will play out on their own turf is relatively higher. For these activists, scenarios would be primarily a means to set priorities in order to allocate limited resources. In this turbulent setting (Emery and Trist, 1965), multiple scenarios would help such an activist group even more than they would help a large tobacco MNC.

Activist anti-tobacco NGOs appear to devote a significant part of their resources to legal matters (litigations, lobbying with local legislators . . .) but as far as we know they do not use scenarios to identify how best to deploy their limited legal resources.

Thought experiment – deploying scenarios to help an NGO fight tobacco MNCs

In this section, we present a summary of a set of hypothetical legal scenarios. Neither of us has ever worked for – or against – a tobacco company. This is a logical reconstruction from available data – not grounded in any actual case. Our purpose is to show how the scenarios can identify legal options that, to our knowledge, NGOs have not pursued.

As pointed out above, scenarios would not be, for a large tobacco MNC, the way to prepare for alternative legal futures, because very different (even all plausible) legal futures may coexist. Any given legal future in any given time horizon will plausibly become accurate somewhere: more judiciary 'hardness', more 'softness', more regulation, more deregulation, more rule of law, more arbitrary action. In this context, the main purpose of scenarios for an MNC would be to distinguish these different futures from each other, to make sense of how to 'arbitrage' among them, and to rank possible actions based on their ability to play out in more than one scenario. Assuming, for example, that the prime objective of the tobacco industry was to preserve the status quo in its global market, an ideal response would be one that could contain the pressure from the judiciary in industrialized countries while slowing the dissemination of tobacco-unfriendly rules in the developing countries.

Our thought experiment led us to develop three legal scenarios for the horizon 2025 along today's legal and geographical divides: 'North Wind', 'Chinese Wall' and 'Free for All'. They are briefly described below.

Scenario 1: North Wind

This scenario describes the dissemination of a western-like logic, characterized by a high enforcement of anti-smoking rules and the development of mega-lawsuits against tobacco MNCs.

To cope with this setting, tobacco MNCs would develop alliances among themselves, notably:

- to capture the best legal and scientific expertise (both for lobbying and in defence against lawsuits),
- to ensure that their respective arguments are consistent (or better, identical), and

- to fight smugglers (to diminish smuggling-related liability, e.g. tax-avoidance, absence of proper health warning, etc.).

Scenario 2: Chinese Wall

In this scenario, the enforcement of anti-smoking rules and/or standards remains low in key domestic markets (e.g. China, India), notably because the State itself is a tobacco manufacturer and/or distributor with a vested interest in tobacco consumption. However, this scenario is not good news for tobacco MNCs because here, protectionism has replaced anti-tobacco regulation as the main barrier to entering these markets or expanding within them.

To force these countries to open their market, western-based tobacco MNCs have no choice but to form a coalition to induce their respective governments to initiate a WTO-type action. Other actions include encouraging smuggling in the region and setting complex standards in the tobacco industry to exclude small or new players. Again, the existing incumbent private companies have an interest to come together to succeed in this situation.

Scenario 3: Free for All

This scenario describes a future characterized by a low enforcement of anti-smoking rules, with accessible but competitive and fragmented domestic markets where smuggling accounts for an even larger percentage of tobacco trade than it did in 2006.

To address this situation and eliminate smugglers and smaller players altogether, western-based tobacco MNCs are forced *inter alia* to enter into alliances with their southern competitors to secure distribution networks; and to set up among themselves, even with the support of consumer associations, complex industry and quality standards.

The blind spots

Early versions of each of these scenarios already exist somewhere and will continue to do so in 2025. Whether one of them will prevail and how fast each will unfold are important strategic questions. In any case, in any of the above-surveyed scenarios tobacco MNCs will seek to grow ever bigger. For this reason, what tobacco MNCs already do to fight activist NGOs is what they are likely to continue to do in the future if any combination of the scenarios we produced continues to unfold. In this strategic mode: they will outspend NGOs in advertising (e.g. sponsoring F1 teams, which is one of the most watched sports by TV audiences worldwide); they will outspend them in lobbying legislators; they will outspend them in hiring the best lawyers; and they will outspend them in applying the lessons learned from one legal battle to cases in other settings.

Clearly, the bigger the tobacco MNC, or the more alliances it can arrange with other tobacco companies, the more it can interconnect multiple legal battles across the globe and fend off future opposition anywhere. Also, the bigger it is, or the better its connections – i.e. the more alliances it can build – the more it can improve its position *vis-à-vis* governments, particularly in small countries. So from a purely legal perspective (let alone the economies of scale in branding, marketing, production, and so on) the bigger the tobacco MNC, the more effectively it can implement these strategies.

All this is known to anti-tobacco NGOs. Their blind spot resides in the fact that in every confrontation with tobacco MNCs they are already facing giants, and they fail to see that such giants need to become bigger. If, however, as we have done in our thought experiment, such an NGO were to look at the situation using scenarios, it would discover that for reasons specific to each scenario, an important level of coordination among competing western tobacco MNCs is crucial for any one tobacco MNC in all scenarios. In effect, alliances and/or concentration emerge as the strategic preference for tobacco MNCs, 'paying off' in all scenarios.

A logical conclusion follows: anti-trust measures (broadly construed here, i.e. the prohibition of anti-competitive undertakings in the EU and in the United States, notably the restrictions imposed on concentration and on alliances) are a threat to the future prosperity of the tobacco MNCs. Accordingly, this field deserves significantly more of the attention and resources that anti-tobacco NGOs dedicate to legal efforts, especially as they will need to prepare for the counter-attack. MNCs may respond by, for example, lobbying to relax the regulations concerned, or by redefining the current relevant market (i.e. moving from cigarettes to a broader market, e.g. tobacco, or better, nicotine), thereby reducing their relative market share.

CONCLUSION

We have here suggested that, to our knowledge, scenario thinking and legal thinking have not had the conversation they might have had to strengthen each other. We have outlined a few reasons as to why this state of affairs has come to pass. However, we believe that applying scenario practices and thinking in the legal domain would be fruitful, and we have tried to show how this would be so. We have used two examples to illustrate this claim.

The first one involved considering possible futures of international CSR from a legal perspective. In applying scenario thinking to this domain, we found that apparently paradoxical situations may in effect be more plausible and/or viable in the long term. We have suggested that this finding is counter-intuitive for legal thinkers.

The second example was a thought experiment about how anti-tobacco activist NGOs might best deploy scarce legal efforts to counter the strategies of large tobacco MNCs. Here we suggested that securing anti-trust blockages to control size and alliances would be as important as pursuing health legislation or increasing the taxes on tobacco sales as a way of curtailing tobacco consumption. We have suggested that this finding would not be self-evident to an activist NGO, and could become evident if they were to use scenario thinking in determining their legal battle priorities.

We believe that if the legal profession were to use scenarios, it might be able to legislate in more proactive or interactive modes and be less reactive. The Financial Services Authority of the City of London has begun exploring this possibility, producing draft scenarios on how the future of City legislation may affect the international competitiveness of London's financial services industry. In the same way, the search-conference – like consultative processes involved in Swedish environmental legislation with key stakeholders and their future interests – was shown by David Hawk to be more effective than top-down standard setting enforced by legally trained inspectors.

An interesting research question is whether a full-blown appropriation of scenario thinking by legal professionals would change the nature of the legislative process. Arguably, it might convert legislative drafts from single to multiple texts, allowing a more conversational generation of social norms. One can imagine competitive prototype laws being sent around for consultation: imagine what might have happened to the EU constitution had its drafters embarked upon this venture with a scenario-intensive mode to generate a Plan B for the case where their proposal was rejected. Wind-tunnelling potential legislation in different scenarios has not to our knowledge been done – and doing it now, we think, would be worth attempting.

To summarize, we believe that the legal world could benefit from interacting more routinely with scenario thinking. Scenario thinking might itself be rendered more robust, and certainly more relevant to an influential population of decision makers, if it were to lend itself to this profession. We think of this chapter as an exploratory stab at this relationship, and we hope it will spawn a set of initiatives to make these two conceptual worlds meet and help each other.

CHAPTER 8

THE POWER OF NARRATIVE

Lennart Nordfors

Simplification is the mother of deep understanding – Richard Normann

Can scenarios, or any other form of future studies, capture the complexity of the modern world? In this chapter it is argued that scenario analysis has an important role to play. It still has the power to enlighten thought and guide action. Increased complexity can be handled through a better use of narrative techniques and by taking care to anchor the 'stories of the future' in observable facts of today.

When Margaret Thatcher, Helmut Kohl and others met in Berlin in 1999 to commemorate the fall of the Wall they agreed on how they had failed to foresee the full force of events 10 years earlier. The event of 9/11 took the world by surprise. Global affairs have never been simple to analyse, and developments have not made it easier. Scenario analysis was developed in a time of relative geopolitical stability: the world was essentially bipolar, and strategies could be developed on this basis. Since the fall of the Wall, and with the

Scenarios for Success: Turning Insights into Action   Edited by Bill Sharpe and Kees Van der Heijden
© 2007 John Wiley & Sons, Ltd

growing impact of globalization, the issue of the global system *as such* is up for discussion.

When explaining his concept of 'Soft Power', Joseph S. Nye (2004) offers an elegant description of modern power relations, developed since 1989. The world can be described as a game of three-dimensional chess. On the top board, we find traditional military interstate issues. This world is unipolar; the USA is the only superpower. The middle board is about interstate economic issues. In this game, multipolarity holds – it is about interplay between the USA, Europe, China, Russia and others. On the bottom board, we have transnational issues such as terrorism, international crime, climate change, and the spread of infectious diseases. Here, 'power is widely distributed and chaotically organized among state and non-state actors'. The case of Iraq is illustrative: the Bush administration thought it was only playing on the top board, and did not take forces on the bottom board into account.

It is not just about geopolitics. The business landscape is also more complex or chaotic than before. Thomas Friedman (1999) has written about a 'flat world' of digital networking, where every-one – potentially – has access and makes decisions. It is a world of instability: of an 'electronic herd' of capital that, at the tip of a hat, can move in and out of local markets. What activates this herd? Geopolitics is one of many factors. We thus have geopolitical complexity feeding into market complexity, and vice versa.

To understand this world of nested games, where outcomes on one level determine input for the next, we must create thinking tools that make it possible for us to move from geopolitics to the local market while identifying connections, risks and opportuni-ties. Furthermore, the system is unstable. The more complex the system, and the more decision points it contains, the greater the susceptibility to 'exogenous shocks' and surprises. How can we rule out less relevant factors and concentrate on 'fundamentals' in such a situation, in order to prepare an organization for change?

Scenario analysis – like all forms of analysis – is a method of simplification. The presumption is that one can cover most relevant issues by creating up to four scenarios. Experience tells us that the utility of scenario analysis quickly diminishes when one moves above this number of 'images of the future'. If there are too many, the analysis tends to reflect existing complexity rather than cutting through seemingly chaotic circumstances and delivering insight into core conditions and problems. Furthermore, scenarios are built around an interplay between conditions that are taken for granted ('givens') and open-ended questions ('uncertainties'). Another way of describing the current situation is that with complexity the proportion of uncertainties has increased. Is it still meaningful to try to say anything reasonably precise about the future using a small number of scenarios?

Of course, four images of the future are better than one, especially under conditions of uncertainty. Scenarios can accommodate more information than traditional forecasting. But this does not meet the challenge that more is demanded of *all* forms of future-oriented analysis when complexity increases. In which directions should scenario practice develop to meet this challenge?

The answer is twofold. On the one hand, scenarios will have to move closer to econometric modelling. Quantitative and computer-based modes of analysis can harbour greater complexity in the form of causal models. And the science of 'alternative predictions' is developing quickly   witness the scenarios for climate change and their development since the Intergovernmental Panel of Climate Change first met in 1988. For instance, when scenarios are used as a tool of decision support, for calculating and assessing possible effects of a given decision, such models help us to assess possible returns on investments.

On the other hand, narrative, aesthetic methods, used within the humanities, have to be further developed in the context of scenario building. They must be used when developing content for formal models and when illustrating what they actually say about the future. Furthermore, when scenarios are used for transforming an organization by innovation, or for identifying broad strategic 'thrusts' for the future, narrative is necessary. Such processes involve stimulating people to work from new points of departure – to 'see themselves from the outside'. In order to understand a possible future fully, you have to 'see' it. Witness Al Gore's film *An Inconvenient Truth*. In this film, Gore didn't just tell us about global warming – he *showed* it to the audience. As a means to help people to 'break out of the box' it was far more powerful than any model from the IPCC.

THE EFFICIENCY OF THE NARRATIVE

Scenarios resemble any other future-oriented scientific endeavour. Working with givens and uncertainties is not peculiar to qualitative scenario practice. Rather, it is the standard way of operating when constructing, say, econometric models. In modelling, the 'givens' could be said to be the properties ascribed to endogenous factors in the model: that is, which factors they are, the equations that bind them together, etc. 'Uncertainties', on the other hand, can be interpreted as similar to the exogenous variables. These are the variables that the econometrician allows to vary, identifying different outcomes when different values are allowed for in the model. This results in answers to a number of 'what if' questions. For instance, what happens, under given assumptions: If the oil price increases? If China revalues its currency? If the currency is revalued while oil prices move upwards simultaneously?

What is offered is a form of scenario analysis; econometricians present their results as scenarios. It is standard practice in long-term economic forecasting to present a 'normal' development, an 'optimistic' development and a more 'pessimistic' one. The same applies to, for instance, urban planning and its population assumptions. In this area, one is often met by 'maximum', 'minimum' and 'middle of the way' forecasts. It is a moot point whether they should be called 'scenarios' or 'alternative forecasts'; I would call them 'alternative forecasts'.

It is standard procedure when constructing and presenting scenarios to take inspiration from modelling: the process is a kind of 'intuitive modelling'. Among other things, we identify driving forces (variables), construct matrices specifying the interaction between them, and identify general outcomes based on this interaction. When presenting scenarios, we often use causal chains, showing the variables as boxes, with causal relationships depicted as arrows between them. Using the language of economics and natural sciences gives the audience a sense of scientific thought, with its rigour and logical build-up.

However, there are problems with this ideal when complexity increases. For econometricians, with their computer-based models, there is a problem of transparency. The audience (decision makers, the public at large, etc.) cannot see, let alone understand, the properties of the model. It tends to be a 'black box', assessed by its predictive performance in the past. With growing complexity and incremental tinkering, the model also tends to become a black box for the analysts themselves. This is generally not a problem, as long as the model continues to perform well in its predictions.

But in a process where intuitions play an important role – when research is brought to a facilitated seminar where the participants proceed by identifying critical turning points, formulating outcomes and giving them names, etc. – there is a very real problem with increasing complexity.

Scenarios deliver value in more ways than econometric models. Value is not just attached to the contents of the scenarios, to being able to say that we 'got it right' sometime in the future. Analyses of the effects of scenario exercises show that the process *as such* delivers a lot of value. Letting people reflect together on the future in a fact-based and structured setting opens new perspectives, creates contacts, offers a common language and makes participants sensitive to the relevance of contextual circumstances. A good workshop cannot be replaced by a computer program without loss of value. But the number of variables or driving forces that can be handled intuitively is limited: there is an indeterminate point at which things get so complex that discussion loses focus – although this probably varies from audience to audience.

It's a fair guess that the academic discipline that has to work with the most complex social phenomena is history. Understanding geopolitics is at the core of world history studies and it probably always has been. History enlightens us about historical eras, revolutions, world wars, and the rise and fall of dominant powers. But while scientific ideals and quantitative methods form a part of the discipline, many of the subjects studied are just too complex to be analysed in this way. Another method is needed: the best way to learn about the French Revolution is not by describing it with econometric techniques or by creating a model, but by telling the story; and there are good reasons why historical narrative still holds its ground.

Depicting complex situations and developments by means of narrative is a common way of making sense of historical data. The ability to tell a good story is thus more than a way of illustrating your findings – it is the core competence of the good historian and a research method in its own right.

Why is this so? The narrative is an extremely efficient way of creating insight into complex matters and processes. You seldom have to tell the whole story in order to win understanding: a good narrative is open-ended and new 'snippets' of information can easily be inserted into the plot. The trick is creating a narrative that stimulates further reflection and development, and doing this is not just a question of substance but also of form. Thus, understanding aesthetics – understanding form – is a prerequisite for good research.

One school of historians employs the method of 'colligation' (literally, 'to bind together') when creating narratives. The basic question is not 'what causes what?' but *what fits in?*. 'Colligation' is, in fact, sometimes presented in direct contrast to causal analysis. It is related to methods based on interpretation and understanding (such as hermeneutics) that were introduced into disciplines such as social science as an alternative to scientifically-based models of thought.

History, it is claimed, cannot be captured in full by using scientific 'covering-law' models ('if X, then Y'). History evolves as a continuous process where events fit into each other and form a whole. Proponents of the narrative method talk about 'process tracing', where the arrows of causality in econometric models are replaced by a story, allowing the reader to follow the process as it evolves. The concept of cause and effect is notoriously problematic within the philosophy of science. How do we know that what we see is true causality and not just simple covariance (i.e. that things just tend to happen at the same time with no necessary connection between them)? One way, maybe the only way, is to see if we can construct a story that informs us exactly how one thing led to another over time. The narrative does not just offer insight, depicting a typical series of events using the language of cause and effect; what makes us convinced that we are witnessing a true dynamic relationship between different events is that the story is understood as plausible or *meaningful*.

The important point is not only that the narrative is a more accessible and efficient way of arranging otherwise complex sets of data, but that it adds dimensions that other ways of describing reality cannot capture in full. The narrative adds depth that cannot be found in formal modelling. It solves the problem of explaining connections between events by using hard-to-interpret arrows of causality. A well-told story has the same flow as reality itself, and we can (intuitively) see how its different parts hang together and form the whole. Furthermore, the narrative can capture how reality develops in one, unique, case. By contrast, statistical modelling works with many cases, since the basis for its conclusions is systematic variations over many examples or over time.

The way historians work with narrative is not exactly the same as the way scenario practitioners work out scenarios (using concepts such as drivers, givens, uncertainties, etc.), but there are similarities. Just as scenario practitioners start by defining the 'focal issue' with which they should deal, scholars working with colligation start by defining what they call the 'colligatory term'. This term refers to the subject of the narrative and forms the framework for selecting events that can fit into the overarching story. The 'colligatory term' might be a 'revolution', or a historical era ('Renaissance'), system ('feudalism') or process ('evolution'). Scenarios are formed in much the same way. Scenario plots might depict 'the rise of the e-society', 'the breakdown of globalization' or 'the development of services within the pharmaceutical industry', to name three examples.

Ogilvy and Schwartz (2004) describe some typical plots for constructing scenarios. They are well known (and thus, according to the authors, archetypical). Stories can be told about winners and losers (e.g. 'an ascendant Asia Pacific bloc vs Europe in decline'), about crisis and response (e.g. 'the greening of Russia'), about 'the lone ranger' (e.g. 'Apple Computer vs IBM'), etc. This might also work when constructing stories about the future. Given that we are speculating, we have the freedom to choose from a number of well-tested ways to spin a good yarn.

Historians, on the other hand, are faced with a mass of data about historical events. The method has to identify events and show how they interact. Ideas concerning how this is best done vary. The scholar should define the dimensions of the narrative (e.g. social, temporal and geographical settings). He should take as a further point of departure theories about which 'motors' (Hmimda and Hultén, 2005) drive history. Events might interact in an evolutionary way, following a life-cycle pattern; develop 'teleologically' (driven by, for instance, purposeful enactment); or proceed 'dialectally' (where conflict is the driving motor behind change).

Constructing the historical narrative is an art. History lacks a strong, generally accepted, theory that tells us which kinds of events and connections are the most important. The object is creating the narrative that best fits the facts. A parallel can be drawn to the way lawyers work when arguing a complex case: 'As litigators of complex cases have increasingly realized, the more complex the facts, the greater the need to forge a simple, elegant, and compelling narrative for the fact finder' (Gavil, 1999, quoted in Dumez and Jeunmaitre, 2006). Research progresses when existing narratives are challenged by new ones that are based on hitherto unknown facts, or that offer more compelling or elegant interpretations of well-known events.

Conveying meaning is a core task. Describing phenomena in a way that gives them meaning supports understanding. This is where aesthetic ideals and techniques enter the game. Another way of describing the importance of aesthetically well-scripted stories is that these make it easier to understand intuitively 'what fits in', and add meaning to complex sets of data. Seen in this way, scenario analysis is not just intuitively – performed econometrics, but rather employing the method of the historical narrative to issues of the future. Historians sometimes do it for amusement – witness the public success they have had with hypothetical history such as the 'What If' books recently published. This brings us to a few conclusions:

- The first is that aesthetic and artistic skills will grow even more important when creating scenarios (not just when communicating the final results).
- A second conclusion is that what Van der Heijden (1996) calls 'deductive scenario structuring' is probably more appropriate when handling complex issues. This way of working entails first establishing key events or trends; then describing a future state;

and proceeds by creating the best possible story that leads up to this end-state. Here the question can be asked 'which factors or events fit best in such a story?' and new facts – maybe not uncovered by previous research – can be inserted.

- A third is that the 'core narratives' of scenarios must be presented much earlier than is often done in the process, aiding the participants in an 'association game' in which they can identify 'what fits in and how' in the story they are writing together during the exercises. Causal links might enter the discussion – but as part of the story, offering deeper understanding of the plot.

Scenario practitioners thus have a lot to learn from history and the humanities in general when constructing stories of the future. But, it may be asked: How should we create scenarios that go beyond capturing the imagination? How can we create stories that are plausible? Historians do not face this problem. Their narratives are about well-proven, identifiable facts of the past. Telling 'stories of the future', however, is about speculation. Depicting them in the language of scientific, econometric modelling would, it can be argued, give the stories the feel of 'hard' science and help audiences used to this kind of language to accept them. But is it possible to convince an audience that a scenario is plausible, and motivate people to take action 'just' by telling a story?

THE POWER OF THE NARRATIVE

The use of 'storytelling' has during the past few years surfaced as a tool for corporate leadership. The narrative as a way to coordinate and guide collective action is, of course, nothing new; it has probably been around as long as mankind. So what can explain its growing popularity today? One of the pioneers in developing storytelling as a vehicle for corporate change, Steve Denning, claims that the answer lies in increasing complexity: 'Stories are the only way to make sense of a rapidly morphing global economy with multiple wrenching transitions under way simultaneously' (Denning, 2005). But succeeding in storytelling means meeting the challenge noted above: how to reconcile the world of 'left-brained managers' – used to reasoning in rational/cognitive categories – with the 'right-brained world' of storytellers?

Denning's answer is a story in itself. As a programme director at the World Bank in the mid-1990s, he set about introducing knowledge management in the organization – 'a strange notion...at the time'. Traditional rational/cognitive techniques didn't work, no matter how compelling the PowerPoint presentation. Somehow, he got around to telling a very simple story, which catalysed necessary change within the organization:

In June of last year, a health worker in a tiny town in Zambia went to the Web site of Centres for Disease Control and got the answer to a question about the treatment of Malaria. Remember that this was in Zambia, one of the poorest countries in the world, and it was a tiny place six hundred kilometres from the capital city. But the most striking thing about this picture, at least for us, is that the World Bank isn't in it. Despite our know-how on all kinds of poverty-related issues, that knowledge isn't available to the millions of people who could use it. Imagine if it were. Think of what an organization we would become.

Later, this kind of story was labelled a 'springboard story': one that shows how successful change was implemented in the past, and allows listeners to imagine how it might work in their situation. It is a simple story, and Denning claims that such stories are best kept simple. It does not use archetypical plots. Simplicity (one place, one protagonist), and the fact that the story is true (dates are given, facts can be checked), explains its power to move an organization, together with the fact that it illustrates the need for specific change and what might happen without it.

A powerful 'springboard story' should thus not be too elaborate. The important thing is that it is to the point. Furthermore, a simple story invites listeners to do the elaboration for themselves, to internalize its message: 'A springboard story told in a minimalist fashion . . . (creates) a vehicle that encourages all listeners to craft similar stories, each of which is still the listener's own story. The result is personalized coherence across large numbers of people.' A good image says more than a thousand words; so let people fit in the words for themselves.

The experience of Steve Denning tells us that narrative can motivate change when figures and graphs fail to do so. Stories can do a lot of other things too, according to him (like strengthen brands, transmit values, foster collaboration, stimulate knowledge sharing) provided they are true and touch a nerve within the organization. But what about stories about the future – like scenarios? Here we run against the problem presented above: stories about the future cannot be tested against existing reality. Furthermore, they tend to run into more opposition than other uses of storytelling. Accepting stories of the future is an act of will, and 'the truth is that people don't want to believe a future story that involves significant disruption'. This experience is probably shared by many scenario practitioners. Organizations that have experienced some kind of a jolt or external shock are more susceptible to scenario planning than complacent ones (even if the latter often need them just as much).

In this situation it is tempting to fall back on the language of econometrics – in other words, to supplement the narrative with the formal language of forecasters and planners. However, this is a short-term fix. With increasing complexity, causal chains tend to be long and complicated. To quote Denning once again: 'The longer the chain of causation, the greater the chance that one or more links will break, as some unexpected development throws all predictions into chaos.' This does not necessarily mean that the scenario is less relevant or less plausible. As a rule, there are many ways in which a given future might come about. What it does mean is that it is unwise to invite belief in a scenario by insisting that it will evolve in any particular way.

So how do professionals of 'storytelling' go about supporting change or innovation through stories of the future – stories they agree are crucial for these ends? Denning's solution, to shorten the time span of the narrative ('reduce the length of the causal chain'), is not helpful. Scenarios are about looking round the corner, in other words about taking the long view. Another suggestion is to increase the aesthetic qualities of the story ('using consummate artistry'). This might take us some way, but it is not enough. As pointed out, aesthetics help the audience to 'live' the scenario and aid them in adding new elements to it, but a well-told story does not, in itself, make the narrative plausible. It does not necessarily make the depicted future convincing as a *realistic* version of the future.

However, a third option is possible: connect the narrative of the future to a springboard story. This story is about the past; its facts can be checked. If it could be shown that the springboard story is the first step towards a given future, it would add plausibility to the scenario. Indeed, what makes a springboard story interesting is its implications about the future. The above story about Zambia is not just about some African who happened to use the internet. It is a story about an emerging *global internet society*, where it would be disastrous for the World Bank to be left behind. Denning does not make a point of it, but the power of the springboard story depends on the strength of the scenario it implies. Thus, the scenario practitioners' 'narratives of the future' and the storytellers' 'springboard story' depend on each other for effect.

Nothing of this is especially new for the scenario practitioner. For what Denning calls a 'springboard story' is nothing other than the 'pocket of the future in the present' discussed in the introduction to this part of the book. Identification of such pockets is often a result of participating in a scenario exercise. Participants tend to see news items in a new way during such a process; they use the scenarios as categories to understand developments in the present.

The techniques of storytelling tell us how crucial this effect is. It is when the audience can connect scenarios to the present – experience the feeling 'My God, it is already happening!' – that scenarios become fully plausible. When presenting a set of three or four scenarios, one should also present a set of 'pockets of the future' to correspond to each of them, showing a reality where the scenarios play out against each other. The scenarios are then grounded in narratives of the present, and show the interplay and conflicts between different driving forces. In this way, using scenarios does not only mean showing alternative futures. They also depict an ongoing 'struggle for the future', which can be followed up by posing questions such as: Which 'pockets of the future' are developing? How are they developing – what is the causal logic? Can the observed developments be fed into the scenarios, creating richer narratives of the future?

Our previous conclusions were about how scenarios can be developed. The findings from storytelling tell us how they can be used:

- The users of the scenarios should be helped to find the 'pockets of the future in the present' that correspond to each scenario. This can be done through the method of colligation, where the scenario is the 'colligatory term' guiding us to identify exactly which events should be included when describing the present, and how it has come about.

- The scenarios should of course come into play when discussing strategies and innovations; but they should also be used as a means of tracking current developments. Through systematically studying the development of identified 'pockets of the future', information about relevant market and geopolitical developments is gathered. An important part of the follow-up of scenario projects should be setting such a knowledge-gathering process in place. This means actively supporting the use of scenarios as a vehicle for conversation within the organization; fostering 'adaptive learning', as it is called in the introduction to Part II.

CASE STUDY: FUTURE OF SWEDISH FARMERS

At the end of the 1990s, there was a strong need for Swedish farmers to reinvent their business. They had just been through a turbulent period, and expectations were that more was to come. Farming had been deregulated only to be re-regulated when Sweden joined the European Union in 1995. The leadership within the Federation of Swedish Farmers was not certain of the result of all these changes, but they were convinced that it would necessitate a change of attitude among the members. They had to stop seeing themselves as recipients of public support, and continue a transformation to a more business-minded attitude. In order to succeed, members had to understand the necessity of change and begin identifying possible business opportunities that they would lose if they clung to a more political outlook.

A point of departure was a set of scenarios authored by Bert Levin and Lennart Nordfors (1999). These were purely geopolitical scenarios, telling stories about the distribution of power in the future. Four worlds were described, using the narrative form of a PhD thesis in 2007 (in other words, 10 years later). Special care was taken to 'colligate' a narrative of the present (i.e. 1997) as an introduction to each of the scenarios, leading on to the scenario and lending it credibility. The four scenarios were, briefly:

- A future of free trade, rapid globalization, burgeoning entrepreneurship and innovation, weak politics, decentralized network economy and strong competition.

- Strong, large-scale global businesses, concentration of capital through mergers and acquisitions, centralized decision making. The global economy (and global politics) dominated by Fortune 100 companies.
- Trade wars and blocs of trade, a strong and increasingly federalistic European Union, inward-looking values, strong politics.
- Weakened European Union, strong nation states, rapid globalization but less migration of experts between countries, adaptive national policies, competition between different models of national development on a global market.

These scenarios said very little, if anything, about the future for farmers. So we performed a series of seminars with the leadership of the Farmers' Federation where they were invited to write a continuation of the stories. This was done in a traditional manner: participants wrote 'newsclippings of the future', describing the development of relevant business environments. By analysing the proposed clippings, we were able to construct consistent business narratives corresponding to the geopolitical master-scenarios and use these to identify 'pockets of the future in the present', supporting them as plausible stories of the future.

Finally, we gave participants a description of the typical (or the least untypical) farmer as the beginning of a story. Participants were then asked to describe what happened to this farm when the farmer had seized the business opportunities identified in the four scenarios. This produced a new narrative: of a typical individual and his or her business in each of the futures. Using geopolitical scenarios as a point of departure, we had already produced narratives on a business or federation level. But this was not enough; to enable members to see possible futures, the narratives had to be brought down to an individual level where each member could envisage his or her possible futures.

This was done through further use of the narrative. A journalist was assigned to create four versions of a newspaper – *Tomorrow's News*. Using pictures and text, we filled the pages with a large number of articles. Not all of them had obvious relevance to business; some were just used to create atmosphere. These were stories about what people eat ('recipe of the month'), how they travel, what happens to well-known politicians and why, developments in the labour market, developments within the arts, etc. In each of the futures we presented a named farmer, with a photograph, who told us about her business. For example:

- In the first scenario, she had teamed up with other farmers selling food on the internet, circumventing the large food-chains.
- In the second scenario, her farm had been acquired by Unilever and she held a middle-management position within this corporation.
- Scenario number three told a story of increased competition on the European market and how our farmer had developed products and found distribution channels to this market.
- Finally, our farmer had adapted to a re-nationalization of agricultural policy. But this policy was more about helping farmers to find competitive niches on an international market than about traditional subsidies. For instance, it indicated an emphasis on quality and organic food.

The narratives formed a tabloid brochure which also included endorsements from known personalities within Swedish farming and a 'how to work with scenarios guide' for the reader. Readers were told to think through the narratives, to take them further by adding possible developments relevant to their business, and also to identify 'pockets of the future'. They were told how to fit their own business into each scenario ('wind-tunnelling' the business) and substitute themselves for the farmer portrayed in the brochure to create their own narrative. Finally, we asked them to draw a few strategic conclusions, and answer the question: Where would your business be if you *didn't* change? This material was widely distributed to members (30,000 copies were sent out), and local seminars were offered on demand. Not surprisingly, a certain concentration of interest was found among members of the youth section, Young Swedish Farmers.

It is important to see that the object of the exercise was not to define one new strategy. The Farmers' Federation has 163,000 individual members, encompassing a wide range of different kinds of businesses. The object was to change attitudes within the organization, helping members to 'break out of the box', to begin to envisage alternative futures, and to reach a common understanding about the necessity of a more business-oriented attitude.

It was about setting the stage for change on the federation level, stimulating a new kind of conversation within the organization and urging individual members to think through their business ideas. Today, a few years later, there is evidence that the scenario exercise made important contributions to this end. The Farmers' Federation now presents itself as an organization for 'Green Business', with a stronger interest in new offerings within areas such as energy and tourism. A more international outlook is also present. According to the current leadership of the Federation, the scenarios played an important role in the early stages of this development.

CONCLUSION

When working with scenarios, dual modes of presentation are often used. On the one hand, they can be presented as econometric models, specifying variables and causal relations between them. On the other hand, there is a narrative, storytelling, component; scenarios are 'stories of the future'. Increased complexity means that more attention has to be given to the power of storytelling. As methods employed by historians have shown, the narrative has a great capacity to capture complex phenomena, adding both depth and scope where formal models fail.

That the narrative has power to enlighten and move organizations is shown by recent interest in 'storytelling' as a tool for innovation and change. Furthermore, it is important that scenarios are seen not just as stories of the future: they make visible 'pockets of the future in the present'. This adds credibility and focuses attention when studying ongoing processes. They do not just tell us about possible futures; more importantly, they help us to identify the significant issues in the world of today.

SCENARIOS IN THE WORLD OF MANAGEMENT

INTRODUCTION

So far we have discussed strategy making, and the part that scenario thinking plays in it as a mental activity that is carried out on behalf of the organization as one unitary actor, in interaction with other actors in the world, in an attempt to decide on the best way forward. We also saw (page 67) that strategists are called upon to make three judgements, on the basis of their personal understanding of the situation: (1) about the reality in which the organization will be operating in the future; (2) on whether the organizational value system suggests that something should be done about it; and (3) on the organizational potential for action and available action levers in the anticipated future world. In Part II we discussed strategy making as a rational thinking activity on behalf of the unitary organization, based on these three logical key judgemental steps (see Introduction to Part II).

However, strategists can think on behalf of the organization as a whole, but actions are taken by individuals. If no individuals take up the resulting challenge, the strategy exercise has been a waste of time. Strategists must pay attention to activities undertaken by

Scenarios for Success: Turning Insights into Action Edited by Bill Sharpe and Kees Van der Heijden
© 2007 John Wiley & Sons, Ltd

individuals; this is what Curry (Chapter 13) calls the 'transition from the appreciative to the instrumental'.

In addition, we need to consider the question: Is it a reasonable assumption that an individual can think objectively on behalf of the organization? Thinking is done on the basis of mental models that have been built in people's minds through years of personal experience. Everyone has different experiences, therefore everyone has different mental models determining what they see and understand. Thinking strategically is a deeply personal activity and everyone will do it differently. Furthermore, people in organizations interact and influence each other's mental models. This interaction between acting individuals is what Hodgson (Chapter 11) calls the 'real strategy work'. Organizations consist of large numbers of people, each with their own interests and views, understandings and levers for action. A particular individual will have a particular view – one of the many existing in the organization. The task is how to combine such diversity of appreciation and initiative into the three unitary judgements needed as the basis of strategy of the organization as a whole.

One way forward is to interpret strategy making as the privileged thinking activity of a CEO or another influential agent with sufficient power to move others along. However, this does not seem to be a realistic representation of the strategy-making situation in most organizations. While the all-powerful CEO is a popular figure of myth, the reality is that most CEOs are strongly aware of the limits of their power in their organizations, which normally does not include dictatorial powers on strategy. While thinking in the world of business (WOB) is crucially important to make a strong reality judgement on where the organization is heading in its business environment, it needs to be supplemented by thinking in the world of management (WOM) where we recognize the range of thinking and acting contributions of individuals to value and instrumental judgements, and the consequent emerging behaviour of the organization.

THE DOMINANT VIEW

A way to resolve the paradox is to define something that could be called the 'dominant view in the organization'. The underlying assumption here is that through internal communication processes people will gradually align their views on important decisions facing the organization. In Part III of this book we will take this view. The idea of the dominant view allows us to realize that action does not necessarily require full consensus. The degree of alignment is a variable, stretching from total consensus on everything on one extreme, to everyone insisting on their own view, and lack of interest in anyone else's, on the other. Both extreme situations can be described as organizational pathologies that can be observed frequently in the real world. The fragmented organization has in fact given up the intrinsic advantages of doing things collectively, while the consensus organization suffers from an impaired ability to observe and read the business environment, as people have given up the richness of their own individual perspective in exchange for 'groupthink' (see Janis and Mann, 1977). Organizations try to position themselves somewhere between these extremes, where there is not only space for maverick views to be considered, but where people also accept that members of the organization occasionally have to accommodate each other's views if they want to move forward.

In such a strategizing organization there must be a lot of attention to processes that help or hinder the attainment of strategic closure on the three judgements that have to be made. Most of these processes escape the control of top management; however, management has a number of levers they can use to promote an open perspective on non-traditional views, and combine this with the ability to build an emergent dominant view on strategic direction. This is a key responsibility of management, and without it the best thought-out strategies are likely to fail. Active attention for such processes is an example of 'thinking in WOM'. This is distinct from thinking towards developing optimal strategy, as discussed in Part II, which is what we call 'thinking in WOB'. While in the world of business we construe the organization as one unitary actor on the playing field, interacting with competitors, customers, stakeholders, etc., in the world of management the organization is considered as a collective of many individuals, each with his or her own agenda, trying to bring together many individual actions that hopefully cohere as a way to ensure survival and success. As we suggested in the Introduction to Part II, good strategy requires superior skills in both thinking domains.

This is not a trivial task, and people will make very different judgements based on their different situations. For example:

- People are different in nature; some feel most comfortable in a well-controlled stable environment while others prefer the adventures of exploration of the unknown.
- People have different interests; for example, some may be up for promotion while others don't see themselves moving very far from where they are now.
- People have very different perspectives, depending on what they do in their daily jobs. Organizations are based on the principle of the division of labour, which provides very different inputs to different people and creates very different perspectives on the strategy question.
- People may operate from different belief systems, based on their different origins. Curry (Chapter 13) refers to conflicting beliefs about values that stand in the way of the development of a shared view of the context. This is often particularly pernicious in systems that are vulnerable to disruptive change or disruptive innovation.

One can see the task of dealing with this diversity as a complication that top management has to deal with to bring the organization to a level of mutual accommodation without which action is impossible. One can also see all this variety in the organization more positively as a source of richness that can be mobilized in the search for strategy to come to a superior result. As we saw in Part II, there is no one right answer to the question of the 'best' strategy. The process of strategy making is fundamentally judgemental. The complexity of the strategic question is only one reason for this. More fundamental is the insight we gained in Part II that a strong strategy is always based on an original invention. Making an original invention – something that has never been considered before – cannot be only a rational thinking process, but is based on the inspiration and intuition of an individual.

Fortunately strategists live in a relative world where one does not have to produce the 'perfect' answer; the art of successful strategy making is based on being one up on one's competitors.

THE STRATEGIC CONVERSATION

In Part III we are concerned with the WOM aspects of strategy. The focus is on process and the strategy practice as it lives among the individuals involved. This raises some fundamental questions. How can the rational thinking process underlying strategy encompass all diversity in perspectives available in the organization (or imported from the outside world) to maximize richness of insight? How can we involve all thinking and thinkers, including those with a 'doing' perspective? Even more fundamental: How can we take account of the fact that no one in the organization is a solitary thinker as they are all influenced by the thinking network of which they are a part?

All this is the subject matter of Part III. We will find that the answer must be in the networking that goes on in every organization, both horizontally and vertically in the hierarchy. We are not only concerned with the top-down process of involving everyone down the line in 'strategy implementation', but also the recognition of the bottom-up communication that fundamentally affects the thinking at the top. The rationale of everyone, including the authoritarian CEO, is fundamentally determined by the networked thinking down the line and the mental model filters applied to this thinking by individuals while listening to each other. Bradfield (Chapter 10) goes into some detail on the thinking traps that are faced by individuals in this process. Recognition that no one in the organization has the monopoly of knowledge is a good starting point for these internal processes.

We will be looking at the two-way communication processes between strategists and the organization, in which the organization injects their views into the strategy, and in which the strategists gradually bring the organizational agents to the insight that strategic action is required. This conclusion can be reached only if people are prepared to accommodate thinking that is different from their own, giving priority to the strategic needs of the organization as a whole. We call this two-way communication process the 'strategic conversation', without which the organization will prove to be unable to develop coherent action and will become paralysed. Heathfield (Chapter 12) refers to the frequent complaints about strategic planners not being heard. Such complaints are always a manifestation of a weak two-way strategic conversation. Very often people will refuse to listen until they are aware that they are also being heard, and this applies both to the strategists as well as to the operators in the organization. And listening is the key to a successful strategic conversation; people will not act until they understand why this action makes sense.

SHARING OF VIEWS

The first requirement of building an effective strategic conversation, therefore, is to provide space in the strategy process where participants can contribute their own divergent views of what needs to be considered in strategizing. Chapter 9 by De Ruijter, the first chapter in Part III, deals with a case study describing the creation of such a WOM network and process in a retail banking system, creating a dimension to the strategy process that cannot be expected from a formal 'strategy department'.

Emergent contributions from anywhere in the organization can be in any of the three judgement areas. Some people in the organization need to be able to post their views on the reality of the organization in its business environment. Others need to be able to post what they consider should be the values steering whatever the organization does in the world. And some people need to be able to post their views on how the organization could propel/steer itself towards a desirable future by positioning itself in a new way in its playing field.

Introducing all these views in the strategic conversation, and taking them all seriously, feels like a huge complication in the strategy development process. However, help is at hand. Part III contains a number of contributions on how this task can be cognitively simplified. Hodgson (Chapter 11) shows how diverse strategic thinking can be facilitated, and Heathfield (Chapter 12) refers to the knowledge infrastructure that can be used in the strategic conversation through, for example, the group creation of a joint strategy map.

Once ideas are made visible they can be grouped (intuitive coupling), duplication can be removed, and higher level ideas can be built together towards reaching a logical outcome. Heathfield's suggestion is to express all ideas in terms of their effect on past, present and/or anticipated events, creating a so-called event field that can be organized into strategic futures. Bradfield (Chapter 10) points out how scenarios as such are a powerful tool that can be used to provide templates for diverse and disparate ideas, building them into logically ordered stories about the strategic future.

What is common to all these approaches is that space is provided in the strategy process for posting one's ideas in the strategic 'workspace' next to those of others, assuring contributors that they have been heard and allowing them to consider contrasting ideas contributed by others. As in other brainstorming approaches, the underlying principle is 'the suspension of disbelief'. All contributions are considered to be equally valuable. The same space should then be used to show how the relation between individual ideas and the developing strategy is maintained during the strategy development process. Bradfield suggests that good process involves more than just making contributions visible; they must also be introduced into the overall strategic conversation, requiring good process and facilitation. He suggests that this issue gets a lot less attention from strategists than it deserves, leading to his observation of 'methodological chaos' in many strategy efforts. Hodgson provides a systematic and rich overview of what can be done in this area.

It is fundamental to good strategy design that contributing ideas should come from all the different units that make up the organization. Organizations exist to exploit the advantages of specialization and, as a result, are organized by discipline. Knowledge is subdivided and stored on a departmental and disciplinary basis. Individuals bring with them their disciplinary orientation, and finance people will emphasize very different things from marketers. Hodgson refers to this as 'thinking within functional islands', which fundamentally interferes with 'strategy work' that needs potentially to incorporate everything. And the strategic listening and display space where views surface, and are combined, needs to accommodate all these disparate ideas. The approaches included here are all based on expressions in colloquial spoken language, used to express constructs, events or stories. A more formal quantified modelling language would quickly reduce the ability of participants to express what they mean to their own satisfaction. This is why scenarios are such a key tool in the strategic conversation.

Heathfield (Chapter 12) highlights a formidable competitor for attention that the strategic conversation faces, namely the needs of running the business day-to-day. He suggests that unless the process makes it clear how the long-term strategy has repercussions on the short-term operational decision making, it will be moved aside. The problem here is that often 'short term' is associated with what we called in Part II 'business as usual', while 'strategic' implies a change of direction.

ROLE ASSUMPTIONS

The difficulty of a change in direction relates to new role assumption emerging in the organization as part of the instrumental judgement underlying the strategy. As we saw in Part II, 'business as usual' is essentially based on a traditional set of role assumptions for the organization that have served it well in the past, while future strategy is based on the invention of another new and more effective role the organization can adopt in the future. Role assumptions are deeply entrenched in our minds, are often held tacitly, and powerfully determine our actions. They tend to be at the core of how we define ourselves. For example, if we see ourselves in the 'energy business' we can be quickly convinced that our strategy should include the photovoltaic solar panel business, even if we have no experience or particular skills in this area.

Role assumptions limit strategic thinking and a good strategy process should therefore challenge them. This is the contribution of instrumental judgement as part of the strategy process. The strategic conversation will have been successful if it produces the shared insight of a new role the organization can play in society, in a process that Ramírez (Chapter 4) has called 'colonizing their contextual environments'. There is a fundamental conflict here with the short term, where the business-as-usual view does not as yet recognize this new role, and the strategic conversation should address it squarely. Hodgson and Sharpe (Chapter 5) suggest the use of a 'Three-horizons framework' to do this.

THE ONGOING STRATEGIC CONVERSATION

Finally, the strategic conversation should be seen as much more than a periodic exercise to revisit and redesign the organizational strategy in, for example, an annual planning cycle. We have looked at the strategy-making activity as an exercise in which everyone has an input and/or can be called upon to take the initiative to act. People don't stop thinking strategically or talking about it once the annual exercise has been completed. We have discussed how important it is that the conversation has a structure that ensures that everyone can contribute their views as a precondition to having a productive conversation resulting in strategic action on the ground. We saw how important it is that everyone has the ability to communicate with everyone else, to ensure that one's contribution is heard.

But in many organizations such a conversation seems difficult to mobilize for the common good. Often areas of interests are diverse and unrelated, and the common ground is lacking where the gap with the views of different disciplines can be bridged. Hodgson suggests that how we interpret information is through pattern recognition of meaning. What is already in our heads determines the meaning of what we see, and therefore what we can observe consciously. If we don't share in the organization a critical mass of understanding of what is going on in the world, we can't share meaning and the conversation stops.

In order to have a meaningful conversation we do not have to share each other's entire operative knowledge. Vygotsky (1986) suggests that we will have a meaningful conversation if we share part of what he calls our 'zones of proximal development'. This zone includes all exploratory ideas that stick in our minds, not because they are well-integrated with our operative knowledge, but because we intuitively feel that they may relate to it somehow without as yet having worked out where and how. People who meet each other regularly start to share some of these ideas, and the conversation may help in 'scaffolding' them into our operative knowledge, making it operationally accessible. In an environment where people are accustomed to conducting a strategic conversation there will be overlap, and therefore development of the zone of proximal development. Where such a conversation is only incidental there may not be enough overlap to compare and contrast what things mean to us. Management cannot expect that the 'range of meanings in the room' (Heathfield) can be bridged if the conversation is episodic and not part of the day-to-day culture in the organization. The strategic conversation cannot be limited to an episodic strategy exercise, for example, as part of the annual planning cycle. Heathfield has stated that the strategic conversation is ongoing, or it does not really exist.

CHAPTER OVERVIEW

The WOM perspective of strategic thinking is illuminated in six chapters, as follows:

Chapter 9 – Viewing Futures Network: Collaborative Learning and Innovation at Rabobank, by Paul de Ruijter

We begin Part III with a case study illustrating the contrast between WOB and WOM, and why it is important to put both on the agenda. Sole attention on the WOM without any clear WOB logic leads to a yes/no debate and fragmentation in the organization. The WOB perspective is fundamental in providing the logic for the WOM processes. As De Ruijter says: content comes first.

But WOB logic needs to be realized in the real world and, as the case illustrates, requires new and innovative initiatives at the level of individuals in the organization. This is not only about implementing a WOB logic once it has been developed, but also about mobilizing all thinking resources the organization has available to develop the best possible business logic in the first place. This is the content of Part III: how to facilitate the internal strategic conversation that creates a business logic, as well as translate it into a successful strategy and business.

Chapter 10 – Cognitive Issues in the Scenario Development Process: Some Lessons for Facilitators, by Ronald Bradfield

Preparing the ground for our discussion of how to make the strategic conversation work for us, Bradfield gives us an overview of the many dangers that threaten effective thinking by individuals and groups involved in scenario methods. He considers the flaws in thinking that stand in the way of good strategy but can be overcome with scenario work. The key is involvement and interaction of multiple perspectives in the group. However, from his research he concludes that there are too many loosely defined procedures with little theoretical justification or empirical validation, none of which is immutable. Paying attention to this field will lead to a more effective practice.

Mental traps is a subject that has been heavily researched in cognitive psychology over the last 50 years, but the scenario community lacks awareness of its results. Bradfield suggests that the human thinking apparatus evolved when there was a premium on quick and decisive thinking 'in the moment'. But the subject of this book is strategy, i.e. projecting our thinking over a wider territory and a longer time scale. Some of our built-in thinking routines become counter-productive in this context. Scenario planners need to master this field.

Chapter 11 – Appreciating the Future, by Tony Hodgson

Having discussed with Bradfield the many possible thinking flaws that lurk in the background of strategic decision making, Hodgson considers what can be done about it. And we find that a lot can be done. He goes back to the five fundamental dilemmas of scenario planning developed in the introduction of Part II, and provides us with tools to negotiate each of these. The discussion deals with coping with flaws in individual thinking, as well as group thinking. The latter brings in the area of people communicating with each other, and, in the context of this book, engaging in a strategic conversation. Most scenario work takes place in groups within organizations, and Hodgson makes clear the importance of good process. The people in charge of the scenario process, normally referred to as facilitators, need to internalize this material. Hodgson illustrates all this by means of a comprehensive case study.

Chapter 12 – Building a Comprehensive Strategic Future Management System: A Future Map Approach, by Don Heathfield

While Hodgson emphasizes facilitation, Heathfield draws our attention to the importance of good knowledge infrastructure for the strategic conversation to take off. The strategic conversation process is made possible by management providing a 'common space' where people feel free to learn about the strategic views of others, get an overview of the total picture and where they are motivated to contribute their own insights as part of the process. A key element of this is that individual contributors have the confidence that their voice will be heard. Today such a future-based 'space' is likely to be virtual, and Heathfield gives examples in some case studies of how this can be implemented.

Chapter 13 – Acting on the Future, by Andrew Curry

With the field having been prepared in this way, Curry takes us into the real world of scenario processes driving the strategic conversation. He emphasizes the social scenario process, and the degree to which understanding and appreciation of the strategic situation is a social conversational process. In such a process individuals can reach a point where they reframe their understanding as a result of conversation and negotiation. A successful strategic conversation is based on relationships and trust. The strategist's first responsibility is to create or foster this, based on equality and absence of coercion. For this reason an effective strategist must be a skilful facilitator. He or she needs to bring the relevant people together and ensure that the full range of meanings in the room can be expressed and heard. The role of the scenarios in such a process is multifaceted. One interesting perspective considers that scenarios are 'systems in disguise'. Their narrative structure, and the requirement that they are plausible and coherent, enable people from multiple disciplines who are typically untrained in systems thinking to have useful conversations about causality. He calls this systems thinking without systems specialists.

Curry raises an interesting issue that is part of all scenario work, and most often overlooked, known as the granularity problem. It relates to the level (macro, meso, micro) at which the scenario framework dimensions should be conceptualized to create the 'superior story'. As Curry points out, as soon as you discover that all scenarios developed could be happening simultaneously ('parallel futures'), you may want to go back and reconsider the granularity question.

Chapter 14 – Backwards to the Future: Scenarios as Routines for Organizational Health, by James Tansey

Tansey takes the strategic conversation into a policy debate involving a multi-organizational consultation. He describes how such a large-scale intervention helps a wide range of people to learn, improve and enhance their understanding. The challenge is to connect scattered and unconnected knowledge with a growing pool of shared understanding that is continually questioned and upgraded, with the ultimate aim of discovering a new and unique perspective that can be the raw material of a new successful policy.

In this connection Tansey introduces the idea of a normative scenario discussion. If the need for change is understood, the question is change into what, and the perspective becomes normative. In Vickers's terms, a value judgement has to be made, and the scenario work and strategic conversation widens out from developing understanding into articulating and sharing value systems. The case concerns a question of government policy that involves large groups of people who need to take position in the long-term future, where possibilities can be considered that are unconnected with the present (the third horizon, see Hodgson and Sharpe, Chapter 5). Having decided a normative future in the third horizon, the next step is to consider what needs to be done now to get there. In an iterative process that confronts people with the consequences of their expressions of desirability, the process converges on a result where a compromise is achieved between long-term desirability and costs to get there.

The case shows how difficult it is to make people take such a proactive stance. Adopting the role of a passive observer seems so much easier. It is not always productive to ask people what they want. Tansey observes that people often cannot articulate what they want. Either participants project the political struggles of the present in their expressions of desirability, or the consultation processes are treated as fleeting encounters. The best to hope for is to find out what they don't want.

IN SUMMARY

De Ruijter shows how successful strategizing is not only a rational thinking process but also requires intelligent activities in the WOM, which is the focus of Part III. Bradfield considers the flaws in thinking standing in the way that can be overcome with scenario work. Hodgson shows how good facilitation makes this possible and considers the tools available to the facilitator, enhancing the quality of the strategic conversation. Heathfield emphasizes the importance of building the communicative infrastructure in order to mobilize all resources available in the organization. With all this in place we turn our attention towards the actual scenario-based process of learning as it takes place in the group. Curry gives examples of effective processes within organizations, and Tansey takes it wider into the multi-organizational situation such as encountered in government policy development.

CHAPTER 9

VIEWING FUTURES NETWORK: COLLABORATIVE LEARNING AND INNOVATION AT RABOBANK

Paul de Ruijter

When the number of customer visits to your bank drops from 200 million to 2 million, what do you do with your network of local banks and branches? And with share prices and the number of IPOs at an all time high, should you take your 'old fashioned' cooperative bank to the market? These are just two of the strategic questions the Rabobank faced in the year 2000. Answering these questions needed a clear view on the future of banking. However, banks have plenty of data about the past, but not a single fact about the future. At 'Rabobank' a network was set up to deal with the problem of exploring the future beyond the limit of the historical data set. This network, called the 'Oog voor de Toekomst network' or, in English, 'Viewing Futures Network', is still active today as

---

a collaborative learning and innovation network to deal with these and the many other strategic questions that followed.

START OF THE VIEWING FUTURES NETWORK

The beginnings of the Viewing Futures Network can be found in the year 2000. My client Philip J. Idenburg then started his job as corporate strategist for the Board of the Rabobank Group. What struck him in the first period working there was that all the questions he was asked by the Board or its individual members came from what, in this book, we call the 'world of management' (see Introduction, to Part III). Discussion revolved around questions about internal issues, like top-structures, processes, governance; or about the interdependence and mutual relations of the different local banks and companies within the Group.

The highest management levels within the bank were predominantly inward-looking and operated from old perspectives. But maybe this was not so strange. After all, until almost the end of the twentieth century the Dutch financial world was very stable and predictable, with only a few major retail banks, very little competition, no major foreign parties and all the elements of a traditional oligopoly. Dealing with uncertainty was therefore not really 'in the genes' of the organization.

However, in 2000 major changes were happening in the financial world, both internationally and also within the Dutch market. When analysing the competition, Rabobank only looked at other major Dutch retail banks, but in 2000 other channels of distribution for mortgages were springing up, and quite successfully. More than 15% of all mortgages were sold through specialized so-called 'mortgage shops'. The same was true for stocks. Specialized internet brokers were making a successful entrance in the market. At that time, 20% of outstanding debt on credit cards in the USA had shifted from the traditional banks to retailers, car manufacturers and airlines. Within Rabobank, Philip noticed that very little attention was given to market developments like these.

Two strategic questions

At the top of Rabobank the 'world of management' seemed to dominate the focus. The orientation was mostly inside out, seldom outside in. When historical data showed that in the last 15 years the number of visits by clients to the 1400 or so branches of the 218 independent local banks had dropped from over 200 million to less than 2 million, the Board wanted a discussion on how many local banks should be closed in reaction to this. But to Philip, another perspective on the same issues was more pressing. He first wanted to know how the needs of the costumers would develop in the future, concerning the proximity of bank offices, and only then look at the role of the local banks. He wanted to shift the focus from today's world of management to the future world of the banking business.

Next to the urgent question of the number of bank branches, in 2000 there was also a major discussion about the future of Rabobank as a cooperative bank. Rabobank is a cooperative owned by 218 local banks, which are in turn owned by their 2 million members. Many former mutual or cooperative organizations have demutualized and become companies with shares listed on the stock exchange. What about Rabobank? In this discussion there were two dominant 'camps' within the organization: 'orange' and 'blue' (which are the two colours of the Rabobank logo).

Blue stood for rationalizing operations and services, with consumers becoming more and more individualistic, focused on their own interests, without much taste for solidarity. This development would undermine the basis for the cooperative structure and in time the value of such a philosophy would disappear.

The orange camp, on the other hand, claimed that individual consumers – now having to carry more responsibility and more freedom in an increasingly complex financial world – needed more than ever the security of a cooperative structure not focused on shareholders.

These arguments all have their merits, but the identification of the two sides (clearly identifiable by name) resulted in a game of 'yes' and 'no' where each side tried to convince the opposite party by presenting supporting data. This ended in an inconclusive debate, instead of a constructive dialogue.

These were just two strategic questions that convinced Philip Idenburg that a new way of looking at the outside world and the changes within the financial service market was long overdue and therefore necessary.

External uncertainties

Developments in the outside world only enforced his arguments. In 2000 and 2001 the internet bubble on the stock exchange imploded and then there was 9/11. The year 2001 saw the beginning of a political crisis in the Netherlands, symbolized by the rise of a new populist political party run by Pim Fortuyn, who was later murdered. All these developments contributed to a growing sense of insecurity and discomfort. Society was suddenly confronted with complex and drastic changes, and the end did not seem to be in sight. Turning to their strategist, the Board would ask: 'What will happen in this or that field in the future?' He could only answer that he did not have the answer. Long-term predictions were expected but could not be given. In the relative stability of the sector, people often preferred seeming certainties, to an uncertain reality.

In a presentation for the Board, Philip Idenburg stated that, in his opinion, a different way of looking at the future was necessary: that scenarios were the way to learn to cope with uncertainties and create more sensitivity to the above-mentioned issues. The Board thought this a 'very interesting' and important idea, but 'not right now'. There were always more urgent and pressing internal issues that occupied their agenda.

The managers in the next to top level, however, were more enthusiastic, and eventually a small number of them became advocates of the idea. They recognized that a scenario project could be a way to give room to new ideas. Here the cooperative structure of Rababank worked to Philip's advantage. In such an organization there is room to start an initiative without the explicit permission of the Board. With the back-up of a group of sponsors or advocates from within the organization and a cooperative environment one can go a long way. In such an environment there is tolerance for, as Arie de Geus calls it, 'activities in the margin' (de Geus, 1997). According to Philip: 'Any other bank would probably have fired me before I could have even started.'

So, in order to anticipate and be prepared for possible changes in society in general, and in the financial world in particular, Rabobank's Strategy Group initiated a scenario project called 'Viewing Futures'. Based on positive experiences with earlier scenario projects in the organization, Philip began by building a network of supporters and participants. The vehicle was a scenario project.

DEVELOPING A SCENARIO PROJECT

The goal of the scenario project was twofold. Firstly, the scenario process would provide a set of alternative images of the future, which would serve as a basis for answering strategic questions. Secondly, participating in this process would sensitize bank employees towards recognizing change as a first step towards building a lasting competitive advantage. In Philip's own words:

Scenarios make you more sensitive to changes in the environment and changing customer needs, and therefore more manoeuvrable. They are not predictions but sensitivity-analyses. They give you a sense where new opportunities might emerge or where your business model is vulnerable. As a result it strengthens your ability to signal market changes before your competitors do.

Mobilizing intellect

When Philip Idenburg had the green light to continue (or at least he did not get a red light to stop him), he went to his sponsors to make their support more substantial. The different departments helped him to select people throughout the organization who might be interested in participating. Philip realized that, especially during the early stages of the project, the budget was not the most important thing. To create support for an increase in market sensitivity throughout the organization, and to start a serious dialogue to this end, it is critically important to involve many smart people from many different departments. A network is stronger than just one individual or one department. And with the right process, a crowd can be smarter than one expert. Eventually the network, facilitated by his Group Strategy department, included almost 1600 people from many different departments and organizations throughout the Rabobank Group. Not only (top) management and strategists, but people from marketing, communications, HR, functional departments, from the local banks and other companies within the Group were asked to participate. The commitment of the people in the network is illustrated by the fact that almost everyone involved participated in the project in addition to his or her regular work. As a result, the trends, scenarios and strategic implications were felt to be owned by everybody in the network, and not seen as just another report written by a department.

Although the beginnings of the process were humble, with no allocated budget and without strong commitment from the Board, the project did have potential. The sponsors and the people who were asked to be part of the network confirmed this impression. But further steps had to be taken to lift the whole process to a higher level.

The scenario process

The scenario-planning process was performed in four phases: trend analysis, modelling, scenario building and strategic conversation. The first phase was the trend analysis. It was decided to make this a fully-fledged analysis, as an intrinsic part of the whole process. Two years before the start of Viewing Futures, Rabobank had spent a significant sum of money on a 100-page trend analysis by an external consultancy firm. The impact of that research was almost zero for Rabobank (even if it did provide very good learning for junior consultants working for the consultancy firm).

Philip decided to learn from this mistake, because he assumed that a thorough trend analysis, in addition to being a solid basis for a scenario project, is also a necessary ingredient in all strategy and innovation processes. An in-depth trend analysis unavoidably raises the question: 'If these are the historic trends, then what are the uncertainties for the future?' Furthermore, by having 100 employees of the Rabobank Group participating in the research, he basically trained his own internal network and its advocates.

Exploring trends

In the first workshop, early in 2002, in which approximately 20 people participated, one of the participants asked Philip: 'What's your mandate?' Looking back Philip realizes that the whole process could have crashed right then and there.

Luckily I was very resourceful at that moment, so I answered: 'We are all here, therefore the 20 of us think it's important'. That seemed to resonate with a new kind of awareness in the organization. It helped to articulate the view that the question is not whether their bosses wanted them to do this, but whether they themselves thought it was important.

In the six months that followed, around 20 workshops were held on five themes: economy, technology, social society, politics, and ecology. In this part of the process more than 200 people from different parts and departments of the bank participated. Most of them became advocates of the scenario process. They talked about it with others, showed their enthusiasm and so broadened its support. During these six months they not only participated in workshops, but also did desk research and, importantly, talked to people from the outside world. Some went to Brussels to talk about European legislation, some spoke with politicians and policy makers in The Hague, others went to universities, to financial experts, or to interest groups.

In retrospect one observes how most of the information developed could have been gathered from the internet or from other easily accessible sources. Looking at the process, however, this stage is of invaluable importance:

- It created a sensitivity towards the outside world – one of the major goals of the process.
- It also introduced the message of uncertainty – confronting people with so many different points of view, so many different data, so many different 'truths', makes them susceptible to the idea of thinking in multiple futures.

Philip remembers to have witnessed this change in some of the participants:

One of the participants in the process told me that since we started the trend analysis, he read the papers differently, no longer as a result of the past, but as a signal for a possible future. Another participant, somebody from the economic research department, told me he could not yet deliver his material, because he didn't know precisely how the trend was developing. He mentioned that he was confused; he had data to show both the trends of globalization and anti-globalization at the same time. So he wanted more time to figure out which trend was true. When I told him we would be interested in both trends, then he suddenly realized what the whole process was about.

In September 2002 the trend analysis resulted in 500 pages describing 42 trends and 'counter trends', published in five internal publications (Rabobank, 2002) on the five pre-set themes. A lot of time and effort was put in to these five booklets. Philip wanted the bank's senior management and the members of the Board to have them on their desks, in the hope of turning them into advocates. The booklets were a serious report of the analysis, but also served as a marketing tool to raise more support for the process. Therefore the trend analysis was also put on CD-ROM and distributed to the local banks and departments within the bank. Some of these used the analysis in their business planning; this provided a strong justification for all the efforts of Philip and his team: they had made a thorough analysis that was actually being used within different departments of the bank.

In October 2002 a two-day workshop was held with the Board about the trend analysis. Arie de Geus also attended the workshop and presented the concept of scenario planning and his experiences within Royal Dutch Shell. The reaction of the Board was more or less the same as before: they thought the whole process an important initiative, but still did not really embrace the concept of scenario planning. Again, there were more urgent internal issues to discuss. For Philip there was a consolation, however. The Chairman of the Board, when asked by Philip what he should do now, said: 'Continue.' This, of course, was not a formal commitment by the Board, only an informal one by the Chairman, but it resulted in some latitude for the network and support to advance to the project's next phase: the actual development of scenarios.

Content first

The network was now firmly established within the Rabobank organization. Interestingly, Philip always spoke about the content of the project, never about the process of collaborative learning and innovation, either with the participants or with the senior management or the Board. As Philip puts it:

> In order to be a legitimate conversation partner you should keep the eye on, and talk about, the real strategic issues that are at hand. People want to talk about content and the hard stuff, and many find talking about all this change-process and learning organization stuff fluffy and immaterial. The project and network had to be seen as generating serious content and expertise for the business to be taken seriously. I only discussed the 'soft side' with a limited group of external scenario planning and change management experts.

So, although the Viewing Futures Network was not formally named as such, it was from the start conceptualized as what is now known as a Collaborative Learning and Innovation Network or COIN. A COIN can be defined as 'a team of self-motivated people with a collective vision, enabled by the web to collaborate in achieving a common goal by sharing ideas, information, and work' (Gloor, 2006). Working with a COIN was beneficial, because it released synergy, reduced costs and cut time to market. There are many smart people in a large organization such as Rabobank, and this network helped the talent in the organization to become visible and feel rewarded for their expertise. Recall how, during the first workshop, Philip had addressed the question of mandate by suggesting that the shared feeling of importance was the best possible mandate. This is why working in a COIN can be so rewarding. There is a feeling of peer recognition: a willingness to work together with friends and colleagues and thereby win their respect. Other motivators for working in a COIN include fun, and financial rewards of knowledge. For the participants, it makes visible the value of being part of a cooperative organization, in the literal sense of the word.

From trends to scenarios

After the completion of the trend analysis two courses were followed almost simultaneously, starting in December 2002. One was the development of scenarios on the future of the 'price of money'. Key variables for the Rabobank are long- and short- term interest rates: 80 % of the turnover of the bank is interest payments, and 60 % of costs are interest costs, so scenarios about interest rates address the core of the banking business. The modelling and writing of these scenarios were done in a small group of financial specialists, with a very specific goal, to support Group Treasury and the Balance and Risk Management Committee in their decision making. These scenarios were published early in 2003 (Rabobank, 2003).

The other course of action was the creation of four scenarios (Survival, Support, Growth, Meaning) on the future of society in general and consumer needs specifically: a much broader subject with a much broader scope. The key question in this scenario project was: What will Dutch society at large look like in 2015 and what does that mean for consumer behaviour? These scenarios were to be used as a basis for answering general strategic questions, and signal and identify threats and opportunities.

Both scenario projects could build on the trends and counter-trends from the trend analysis (illustrating that a trend analysis should not be limited in scope too much). Philip had strategic reasons to start these two different courses; they would help to legitimize the whole process by showing these different possibilities.

Interest rate scenarios: the price of money until 2010

Using the same set of trends, a small group of financial market specialists worked together on the most important question for any financial institution: How will the long-term (10-year bond) and short-term (Euribor) interest rates develop in the period up to 2010? What are the consequences for the financial results of the Rabobank Group and its strategy? Experts from the Strategy Department, the Economics Research Group, Financial Markets Research Group, Rabobank Japan, Group Treasury and Finance & Control were involved.

They were asked to do something they initially found counter-intuitive. Traditionally the question is what the future will bring. It is their official job to have an opinion about where the markets will go; such that the bank should take a position. But this time, the experts were asked to develop divergent scenarios to sketch what might happen. They were asked to focus on the uncertainties rather than the certainties. And for those who were convinced that the interest rate would go up, it was quite upsetting to conclude that they could almost as easily argue for the opposite with the same data.

Through interviews and workshops the following driving forces and uncertainties were selected. These were assumed to be the most significant in their effect on the future interest rate:

- Monetary policies
- Inflation
- Government policies
- Economic growth
- Trust (consumer, market)
- Capital flows
- Macro-economic savings.

Three scenarios were developed in a workshop (Figure 9.1). Use was made of a number of studies using international, historical

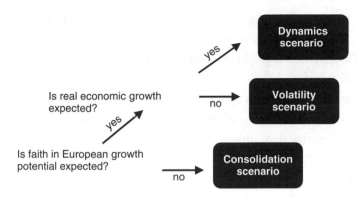

Figure 9.1 Interest rate scenarios

analogies. The scenarios were called Consolidation, Volatility and Dynamics.

In the **Consolidation** scenario Europe remains stuck in a long-lasting period of recession. A weak climate of trust, uncertainty about future pension provisions, restructuring of debt positions of companies, families and government combined with deflation form an important breeding ground for higher savings and low spending and investment growth. Both short- and long-term interest rates decline further in this scenario.

In the scenario called **Volatility** both financial and energy markets, as well as world trade and politics, are highly volatile. This leads to violent swings in the economic cycle and extreme levels of inflation. Central banks are therefore forced to adjust interest rates more often and more vigorously. In addition the European potential for growth is still hampered by a lack of structural reforms. Both short- and long-term interest rates follow a highly volatile pattern. Furthermore, the interest structure is temporarily inversed in the period up to 2010.

In the third scenario, called **Dynamics**, the first few years are marked by the restructuring of balances by companies, families and the government. Willingness to implement economic reforms is high. Furthermore, the Euro area profits from investment opportunities, accompanied by extensions of the European Union to Middle and Eastern Europe. Short- and long-term interest rates show an upward trend.

Following their conceptualization the scenarios were quantified and both calculations and narrative scenarios were used by the Group Treasury department and the Balance and Risk Management Committee for financial policy purposes. It became apparent that Rabobank faced three real strategic risks. The first was the danger of a flattening of the yield curve, with both long- and short-term interest rates declining. With a flat yield curve it is difficult to make money as a bank, since there is only a small difference between the short-term interest rate at which the bank borrows and the long-term rate at which it lends. The bank's margin would be almost zero in this scenario. At first most experts thought such a Japan-like scenario was impossible in Europe, but they changed their mind following the scenario analysis. This risk was real and should be taken seriously. The second risk was that of an inverse yield curve, which means that the short-term interest rate increases and is higher than the long-term interest rate. This hasn't happened often in history as it would normally indicate a recession, and can have drastic consequences for a financial institution. If unhedged it means that the bank will lose money on every euro it lends. And thirdly, the most positive scenario saw interest rates going up. But this is also a risk. The bank has given out billions of loans at a fixed rate. If the short-term interest rate at which the bank borrows rises above the rates it has guaranteed to its customers, it will potentially lose money. Not only that, rising long-term interest rates could put downward pressure on the housing market, and this would reduce the value of the underlying assets against which the bank had financed the mortgages.

The two strategic questions with which the exercise began no longer seemed so essential; there were more important questions to solve. How could Rabobank survive and protect its customers in all three scenarios? The three interest-rate scenarios indicate how the bank should monitor these risks and make sure it is properly hedged against all of them, all the time. Early indicators have been identified, which are constantly monitored. Traditionally Rabobank, like every other bank, calculated many thousands of scenarios in their asset and liability management studies, but with these three narrative scenarios, the organization now has a language and a mental picture of what might happen and how it can respond.

After the interest-rate scenarios had been used internally to review the financial strategy of the bank, they were published for the use of the top 2000 clients of Rabobank. This allowed the clients to more easily manage their own risks. And if the bank's clients manage their risks better, this in turn reduces the bank's risks as well. A true win–win that fits with the bank's cooperative spirit.

Consumer scenarios

Parallel to the interest-rate scenarios project, the consumer scenario project was launched. This made use of the same trend database as a basis. But while only a limited group within the bank is specialized in, or responsible for, decisions regarding the financial strategy, almost everyone else is involved with the customer service strategy. Hence, many more people were part of this process. Several workshops were organized in which the trends were translated into key uncertainties, which were then used as the basis for the consumer scenarios. The actual writing of the stories was done by a small group of five, during the Christmas holidays of 2002. Even though so many people had been involved in the process, the decision was made to use only a small group of people to draw up the scenarios. In the writing of scenarios a consistency in style is required, based on a feeling for nuance, for what can be written down and what can not. The scenarios must meet the threefold requirement of plausibility, relevance and surprise – a minimum requirement for all scenarios. How this is filled in is of course highly dependent on the organization for which the scenarios are written. What is relevant in one organization is not necessarily so in the next. However, a watered-down compromise is unlikely to produce a result that meets the threefold criteria satisfactorily. A final consideration for Philip, when deciding on a small writing team, was that he didn't want to go too far 'out of the box', since Rabobank was rather new at the process, and dealing with uncertainty and creativity (out-of-the-box thinking) was not the strongest quality of the organization at the time.

In January 2003, after the modelling phase had been carried out in workshops, supported by research and quantification, the first drafts of the four scenarios were ready to be presented to a group of proofreaders in a 'test run'. They concluded that the language used was too abstract and too theoretical. People from the local banks emphasized that a mortgage means a serious, long-lasting obligation for customers who are worried whether they will be able to repay the mortgage when the economy slows down (recall that these were scenarios on the future of consumer needs). It was decided that the writing had to be refocused more on a micro level. Also the language used had to be made concrete for the audience – for example, words like 'individualism versus collectivism' were changed to 'alone versus together'.

The scenarios could have easily focused on important macro factors like new financial regulation, consolidation in the industry, the impact of mobile communication technology, and so on. However, after several interviews, workshops and long discussions, the insight emerged that what was required was a strengthening of the customer focus. Internally 'strategic' questions were somewhat different, focusing on: what do our customers need and want from us (bearing in mind that customers are also the owners of Rabobank, because of its cooperative structure). Not only today's customers but also those in the future, when the results of strategic actions play out.

In addition to the core question concerning consumer needs change over the next ten years, four sub-questions were formalized to further focus the scope of the scenarios:

- Who are our consumers of the future?
- What will society look like in 2015? What will be the main themes that concern people, the economic situation, social and political relations and so on?
- What ambitions, wishes and needs will consumers have in 2015?
- What wishes and needs do consumers have in regards to financial services? And what do they expect from their bank?

As a result of the analysis of trends and uncertainties, two specific, critical uncertainties were defined which were believed to dominate future consumer needs. The first involves consumer ambitions, which will either continue to be aimed at individual welfare, or change towards collective welfare, based on groups and social

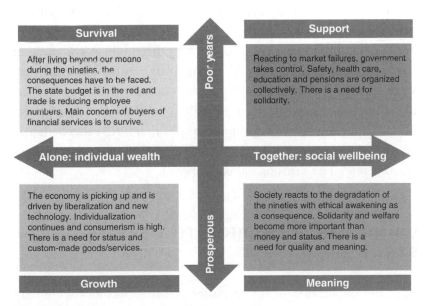

Figure 9.2 Consumer scenario framework

arrangements. The second key uncertainty underlying future customer needs relates to the economic position of clients of financial services, which might deteriorate, or eventually strengthen again. Based on these key uncertainties a framework of four scenarios were shaped, as shown in Figure 9.2.

SURVIVAL OF THE NETWORK

In May 2003 the consumer scenarios were published (Rabobank, 2003). Once again the network proved its value when the new Chairman of the Board at that time decided to abolish the Group Strategy department. Had the whole project been firmly established within that department this would have been the end of scenario planning within the Rabobank Group, as has happened in many other companies. However, the network proved to be able to function without the existence of a formal strategy or scenario department. The members just continued to meet and discuss the future. Philip, who became head of the product management, marketing and sales support of the local banks' asset management portfolio, ran the network alongside his official job. A colleague in the network, Sanny Zuiderveld, was granted permission by the network members in the Economic Research department to continue to facilitate the network from there. The internal intranet-site was hosted by Group ICT, so nothing changed there. All other activities of the Group Strategy department ended when it was dissolved, but not this one. The virus had already spread.

USING THE SCENARIOS TO DEVELOP STRATEGIES

After the publication of the scenarios, many workshops were held with over 1600 participants within the Rabobank Group from local banks, daughter companies, the internal project organization, Communications department, Human Resources department, Market management, Group Treasury and others. With the disappearance of the Strategy Group Philip was more than ever dependent on his sponsors and advocates. This can be seen from a positive perspective, because the budget for all workshops had to come from the departments and the local banks that participated. Philip managed to get additional funding every time a department or local bank wanted to join in, and this commitment indicated that they considered the scenarios interesting and important enough to put time and effort into organizing workshops to create focused strategies.

Scenario films

The workshops were facilitated by Philip's virtual team which limited the scope considerably. Therefore it was decided to narrate the scenarios on film. These were simple, 10 minutes each, but proved very effective: one narrative per scenario, a voice-over and pictures, and specific music supporting the story. Using new technology the cost of the four films was below 8000 euros.

Philip recalls making these films: 'It was a bit weird. Here I was, working for this major Dutch bank and we had practically no budget to make these films. I remember that during one weekend I was searching for music and photos, that needed to be free of copyright.' With the films a broader audience opened up. Departments or local banks could order the films and start working with the scenarios without being completely dependent on one of the internal facilitators.

The films made it possible to start discussing future customer needs with big groups of employees from diverse training backgrounds. This would have been more difficult with the well-researched and data-rich original scenarios. Instead of complicated trends and theories, the films provided four rich images of the future that provided a common playing field for everybody, from bank clerks who often 'recognized' the customers depicted in the films, to highly trained senior executives, thus providing a starting point for discussions on a wide range of issues.

The future of the cooperation

As well as all the strategy workshops, three major meetings were held in August 2003 in which over 600 people, representing about 100 of the 218 local banks, participated. In these meetings the participants were taken through the four scenarios. In four different rooms symbols of the four different worlds were provided. In the room representing the 'Meaning scenario' (see Figure 9.2) participants found only organic food. In the 'Growth scenario' room, however, the scenario was celebrated with champagne and caviar. Actors were invited to play out the relations between bank and clients in 2015. In the Meaning scenario a client comes to the bank to talk about sustainable investing. The reception is polite and the client is offered a cup of coffee and a chocolate and then the client refuses to continue the conversation about his investments. What has happened? It transpires that the coffee and chocolate have not been produced sustainably and organically, a small and negligible detail for 95% of clients, but a proof of integrity for the other 5%. After the workshop Rabobank decided from then on only to serve 'ethical' coffee, and to switch gradually to using only 'green energy' – an example of one of many small changes that resulted from the strategy workshops.

The official aim of the three meetings was to discuss the future of the cooperative structure of Rabobank, one of the original strategic questions. The outcome was used to reposition Rabobank, and for the first time in years Rabobank seems proud again of its cooperative identity, now reaffirmed with new meaning. In the workshops the question had gradually changed from: 'Should we be cooperative, yes or no?' to 'How can we give valuable meaning to our cooperative nature?'

Product innovation

The scenarios were also used to think about new products that would correspond with the future needs of consumers. For example, in the discussions on the identity of Rabobank the question was asked: Do we just sell mortgages, or do we want to play a more substantial role *vis-à-vis* customers? Three of the scenarios – Survival, Growth and Meaning – showed a need for home owners in difficult times to be able to free up and use the wealth accumulated in their houses. The product developed is a variation on 'sale and lease-back', which allows people to use the assets they have built up without having to leave the house and move. A key consideration was that Rabobank will also be a major real estate player in times of serious economic crisis. When people can no longer afford their mortgages, Rabobank will not profit, because most houses will be sold with considerable losses. So developing a product that helps clients to get through the worst benefits both parties.

In addition, 'sale and lease-back' can also prove its worth in a booming economy. Rabobank has recognized a change in consumption behaviour among baby boomers. More healthy and active than their parents, their spending is often higher than their pension plans were designed for. The generations before them would probably have saved for their children, but the baby boomers feel more at ease with spending their resources. Freeing the capital tied up in their homes will help to fund their preferred living pattern and may help them to finance other projects, such as a second house in sunny Spain or France.

Externalization

After many internal workshops and three larger meetings the process was extended beyond the scope of the bank itself. Local banks started to invite their business relations and partners to discuss the consumer scenarios. Meetings were organized with independent mortgage intermediaries, and also with construction companies and healthcare institutions. Collaborative learning and innovation were, with the formal approval of the new Chairman of the Board, taken beyond Rabobank. Some of the parties who were introduced to scenarios through their contacts with Rabobank have now started their own scenario projects.

RESULTS

The Viewing Futures Network still exists today and is active in strategic conversations about the future of Rabobank and society at large. Many parts of the organization use the scenarios as input for their business planning and new product development, and markets and services are being developed as a result of this. The scenario method also continues to be used for marketing and financial management purposes. Scenarios have, within the Rabobank organization, become a lasting approach to thinking about strategic questions, the future and uncertainties. The original strategic questions with which the process started have changed; but the overarching question continues to be: How can we add value to society as a cooperative organization, and how can Rabobank best serve its customers? If that means that fewer local banks are needed, so be it. Many local banks have decided to merge with each other, not because they were told to, but because they came to the strategic conclusion that this is best for their customers and members.

The Viewing Futures Network has recently updated the trend analysis and upgraded its presentation, from booklets and

CD-ROMs to a self-maintaining wiki. From now on all 65,000 Rabobank Group employees can access, and contribute to, the further expansion and updating of the megatrends database that forms the basis for all strategy development, scenario planning and innovation within the organization. A similar approach for a wiki-database of the accompanying options for innovation is being considered.

Rabobank has not only embraced scenarios as an important instrument, but has also embedded these in a wider strategic conversation in COINs. The learning process during the scenario project has validated new lines of innovation with new approaches. Hierarchical considerations have become less important than the quality of the input by participants.

An interesting dilemma has emerged. On the one hand, the success of the process was dependent on the initiatives taken by the participants themselves and therefore on their 'self-organization'. On the other hand, some direction was needed. Aspects of the process had to be initiated by Philip (or later by Sanny) who, for example, took responsibility for the communication between participants and the remainder of the organization. As Philip puts it:

> Especially at the start I found it interesting to manoeuvre in this way, because I had to use the energy and the enthusiasm of those involved. After all, as a strategist, I had practically no budget and no hierarchical line position. At the same time I had to steer a clear course and define the conditions.

In 2005 Philip Idenburg published, with the explicit consent of the Board, the book *Viewing Futures: About Marketing and Consumers in a Changing Society* (Idenburg, 2005) which was subsequently nominated for the prize for the best and most innovative marketing book in 2005. Currently, the bank is engaging with other organizations in the joint development of scenarios about topics like insurance, shipbuilding, water, home care and the Dutch manufacturing industry. Not only can the outside world now profit from the experiences of the project, but also the enormous amount of work done by the network has received recognition.

At present, Philip Idenburg is no longer officially with Rabobank, but with their support he continues to help other organizations to develop their scenarios and strategies.

CHAPTER 10

FACILITATING SCENARIO DEVELOPMENT PROCESS: SOME LESSONS FOR FACILITATORS

Ronald Bradfield

Scenario techniques have a long history, a multiplicity of applications, and are widely used in both the public and private sectors, as is demonstrated by the examples in this book and the wider literature on scenarios. Despite this there are few areas in scenarios on which there is widespread consensus; the literature reveals a large number of different and at times conflicting definitions, characteristics, fundamentals and methodological ideas. Even the term 'scenario' itself is not a precisely defined concept; it means different things to different people and accordingly is defined and applied in widely divergent ways. The consequence according to Khakee (1991) is that 'few techniques in futures studies have given rise to so much confusion as scenarios'. This confusion results from the

Scenarios for Success: Turning Insights into Action   Edited by Bill Sharpe and Kees Van der Heijden
© 2007 John Wiley & Sons, Ltd

fact that there is a paucity of systematic research in the scenario domain, hence, unlike other long-range forecasting methods, there is as yet no solid theoretical-based foundation underpinning scenario techniques. This can be attributed to the fact that the growth in popularity of scenarios since their modern day emergence in the late 1960s has happened for practical reasons rather than theoretical ones; and this does not trouble practitioners, who defend this state on the basis that scenarios are more art and craft than science.

Within the 'intuitive-logics' scenario methodology, the most widely discussed of the scenario techniques in the literature, the assorted tasks comprising the scenario development process are generally undertaken in facilitated groups, are primarily creative, and rely heavily on the subjective judgements or 'disciplined intuition' of the group members. However, there is a notable absence of discussion in the literature on the individual cognitive and group behavioural factors that have been shown to affect group process in other domains, and can therefore reasonably be assumed to influence the scenario construction process.

This book makes a start at addressing this omission in Chapter 11 by Anthony Hodgson, who discusses a range of 'mental traps'; these lead to false dichotomies, and scenario facilitators must be on the watch for them lest decision makers fall in. The objective of this chapter is to expand on these mental traps by reviewing the body of empirical evidence from cognitive psychology concerning intuitive human judgements, and to identify the cognitive phenomena most likely to be prevalent when there is a multitude of inherently uncertain and complex situations to consider (as is generally the case in scenario work). Inevitably these cognitive phenomena influence the scenario development processes in terms of how and what information is searched for, what data is accepted or rejected and so on; as such, facilitators need to be aware of them if the process is to achieve the transformational strategic thinking attributed to scenario-planning techniques.

THE SCENARIO DEVELOPMENT PROCESS

The first comprehensive model for the development of scenarios to be published in a journal was that provided by Zentner in 1975. Since then numerous models have been published, and the literature is replete with descriptions of prototypical patterns or models for generating scenarios ranging from the simple to the elaborate, highly structured, recipe-type techniques. Most of the models and techniques discussed are highly prescriptive in nature, each identifying a number of discrete steps, varying from 5 to 12 or more, depending on the scenario approach used and the features of scenarios that are highlighted or ignored. Although there are notable differences between the models, in broad terms they appear to adhere to a similar structure consisting of a series of distinct phases completed sequentially. In most cases, however, specifics of the construction process are generally vague, and some 20 years ago Jungermann (1985a) reported that 'most techniques discussed in the literature are only loosely defined procedures with little theoretical justification or empirical validation and none are immutable'. Eight years on, Bunn and Salo (1993) maintained that notwithstanding the considerable changes that the scenario approach had undergone since its rise, protocols for scenario development were still 'ad hoc and not very defensible'. Despite the outpouring of books and journal publications on the subject of scenarios over the past several years, the situation remains essentially unchanged.

Earlier in this book (Chapter 1), Peter Schwartz suggests that scenario practice has endured so well because it is really operationally easy relative to other techniques; conceptually it is not a hard idea to grasp and it 'is an easy fit to the human brain – storytelling is what people do, it is how their brain works'. It would appear, therefore, that the scenario development process is relatively straightforward; constructing scenarios is simply a matter of progressing through a series of well-defined, sequential steps.

While this may be true for experienced practitioners, anyone who has carefully observed the development process in detail will quickly realize that it is not that simple, there is obviously substantially more going on in the process than is generally ascribed to in the literature. In fact as Napier Collyns suggests in Chapter 1, 'it's really closer to magic than technique'. However, if scenario techniques do have the ability to stretch managers' mental models and engage them in strategic conversation, to which chapters in this book will attest, then an understanding of how people 'think' is an essential qualification for anyone designing and facilitating a scenario process.

By taking a hypothetical example of an individual constructing a scenario and then tracing the cognitive activity required, Jungermann (1985a) describes what constitutes a generic, four-stage scenario generation process model, namely:

- activation of problem knowledge within the world knowledge of the individual;
- constitution of the mental model in terms of the activated problem knowledge;
- stimulation of the mental model in order to draw inferences;
- selection of the inferences which appear appropriate for scenario construction.

According to what we know from the cognitive sciences, three areas encompassing the above are likely to impact this generic development process in terms of how people think. The first of these are cognitive processes related to how knowledge is organized and activated in the human mind; the second is the area of heuristics or cognitive simplification processes, and biases individuals naturally use to deal with uncertainty and complexity as they cope with the daily flood of data; and the third area concerns inductive versus deductive thinking.

ORGANIZATION AND ACTIVATION OF KNOWLEDGE

Although it is yet to be established with certainty how knowledge is stored in memory, one widely accepted theory is that knowledge is stored and organized in the brain in the form of a 'cognitive schema' which comprises the total of our past experiences. When faced with disparate streams of complex facts and events, individuals attempt to understand the situation by automatically applying the schema according to the similarity between it and the situation facing them, relying in the process on cognitive simplification processes discussed in the next section of this chapter.

When it is used to understand a situation, this schema also includes expectations of what should happen, in what order, the alternatives that exist and the information that is required. The consequences are threefold. Firstly, the schema limits the solution space available to individuals as they comprise deep-rooted, unquestioned assumptions of the nature of a problem and a preconceived conceptualization of the available range of feasible options and solutions. Secondly, following from the above, once the problem set is established by the schema, the information search set is also then established; and, as has been demonstrated in laboratory experiments, individuals are insensitive to the completeness of information in the search set, even when data are missing – data that are crucial to the type of decision being taken. The third consequence is that where the existing schema cannot be readily applied because the individual is attempting to construct previously unexperienced patterns of events, the individual will generally force the situation to suit the existing schema, using causal inferences from his or her schema to compensate for any gaps.

Closely allied to the above is the theory espoused by a number of researchers in cognitive psychology that information is stored in human memory in the form of an 'associative network', in which various nodes representing concepts are connected by links representing relationships between the concepts. Activation of one node in the network automatically activates other nodes in a search set according to the associative or causal links between nodes. It follows, therefore, that the instances or events that are searched for and retrieved from memory, are largely dependent upon which search set within the individual's knowledge base is elicited; and the set that is elicited depends on the starting point, as it is the starting point (itself influenced by factors such as saliency) that will, by activating nodes in an associative pathway, determine the information that is subsequently generated. Consequently, activation of different search sets will generally result in different frequency and probability judgements being assigned to the same problem, because different search sets are unlikely to contain the identical availability of instances or events.

HEURISTICS AND BIASES

In the early 1970s a major line of research by cognitive scientists such as Kahneman, Tversky, Slovic and their colleagues resulted in a set of findings which demonstrated that, as a consequence of cognitive limitations, individuals tend to rely intuitively on a limited number of inferential judgemental rules, known as 'heuristics', in order to reduce the complex task of determining the likelihood of uncertain events. Although these cognitive simplification or heuristic principles are perfectly valid in some situations and can result in reasonable judgements, they can lead to biases which result in 'severe and systematic errors' in the intuitive judgement of probability (Tversky and Kahneman, 1982). The three most widely discussed heuristics are 'representativeness', 'availability' and 'anchoring and adjustment'.

The representativeness heuristic

In a series of studies, Kahneman and Tversky established that individuals intuitively evaluate the probability of an event or a sample by the degree to which it is similar in critical properties to its parent population, and equally, the degree to which it reflects the relevant features of the process by which it is generated. Thus, by extension, individuals assign probabilities to uncertain events according to how closely the events represent each individual's model of the world and an understanding of the processes that result in various outcomes; the greater the degree of representativeness, the higher the probability of occurrence assigned to the events, and the higher the confidence associated with the resultant prediction.

Reliance on the representativeness heuristic leads to predictable and systematic errors of judgement because 'representativeness has a logic of its own which differs from the logic of probability'. Tversky and Kahneman support this contention by identifying a list of biases which impact probability judgements and therefore should, but do not appear to affect representativeness, such as the base rate fallacy, insensitivity to sample size, misconceptions of random events and regression, and the conjunction fallacy. This suggests that, as in schema search sets, the expected accuracy of judgements of individuals based on representativeness appear to be unaffected by the quality and reliability of the information that forms the basis of their predictions.

The availability heuristic

Tversky and Kahneman have also demonstrated that individuals intuitively judge the probability of an event by the ease with which they can remember or imagine instances of a similar nature. In general terms this availability heuristic suggests that instances or events that occur more frequently are more readily recalled from memory than those that occur less often; thus instances or events that are more likely to occur are more easily imagined than those that are less likely to occur, and instances of larger classes are more easily constructed in the mind than instances of smaller classes. A cornerstone of availability is that the only two mental operations by which things can be brought to mind are 'recall' (retrieval from memory) and 'construction' (the process of imagining).

Both recall and construction are affected by a number of factors. In the case of recall, factors affecting retrieval from memory include:

- *Recency* – Incidents that have occurred recently are likely to occupy a more prominent position in the memory and therefore will be more readily retrieved; because they are more readily retrieved they are given greater weight than is warranted.
- *Salience* – Vivid and concrete information is likely to be more memorable, and has a greater impact on individuals and their theory development, even if it is contradictory and inferior to more abstract, pallid information.
- *Familiarity* – Events or incidents with which an individual is familiar, and can readily recall past incidents of a similar nature, will be judged, albeit erroneously, as occurring more frequently than incidents or events that occur with the same frequency, but with which the individual is not as familiar.

In the case of the process of imagining, instances or events that are not stored in the memory need to be constructed or imagined according to established rules. In these situations individuals tend to evaluate the frequency or probability of the instances or events according to how easy it was to imagine them. This leads to bias in that the most easily imagined instances are not necessarily the most frequent or most probable events.

Anchoring and adjustment

The third heuristic widely discussed in the research literature is 'anchoring and adjustment'. When required to make an estimate, individuals generally begin with some initial value (the anchor) and then adjust the value up or down to reflect subsequent information to arrive at a final answer. The initial value is either explicit in that it is given, or it is implicitly derived from the way in which the problem is framed. Regardless of what the initial anchor value is or how it is obtained, the findings of numerous researchers indicate that having established it, people tend to make insufficient adjustments up or down in arriving at a final answer because they are usually biased towards the initial value.

In addition to the three factors discussed above, several well-documented biases which are relevant to scenarios processes are mentioned below.

Belief perseverance

As far back as the 1950s, researchers such as Hovland, Janis, Kelly and Luchins had already established that individuals have a propensity to adhere to their initial opinions, attitudes and theories about themselves, others and relationships between variables, even when it is made clear that the initial data on which the beliefs are founded is fictitious. This belief perseverance or 'cognitive inertia' is inherent in all individuals to a greater or lesser degree, and it appears that once created, beliefs tend to become independent of the data on which they are founded. Subsequently demonstrating that the data are not true appears to have little effect on the beliefs, as people are selective in terms of which parts of their mental models they hold onto, and which parts they eventually change. Additionally, the findings of researchers indicate that while vivid and concrete, albeit dubious, data have the greatest impact on memory, they also have a similar effect on belief perseverance.

Confirmation bias

The confirmation bias, well-documented by researchers, indicates that, once formed, initial beliefs are not only difficult to dislodge because of belief perseverance, but they tend to structure the way in which subsequent evidence is interpreted; new evidence supporting initial beliefs is judged to be reliable, whereas evidence that contradicts the beliefs is dismissed as unreliable or erroneous. Consequently, individuals routinely overestimate evidence that confirms their theories, expectations and beliefs, and disregard or devalue evidence that falsifies them; or they engage in developing elaborate rationalizations to defend their theories. Paradoxically, in searching for and being receptive only to supportive evidence, individuals unwittingly receive repeated reinforcement as to the correctness of their theories and become convinced that these theories are correct, even when presented with contradictory evidence.

Experience bias

This bias, also called 'selective perception', postulates that the training and experience of individuals – their knowledge base – will bias how they interpret and act on information, because people have a propensity to focus on those things that they already understand. This experience bias gives rise to three interrelated problems. Firstly, the knowledge base, goals and values of individuals will naturally determine how they conceptualize the problem – a process termed 'framing' by Tversky and Kahneman. Secondly, the framing of a problem in a certain way determines which elements of the decision-maker's knowledge base are activated, effectively limiting the solution space available. Thirdly, in viewing problems from their experience vantage points, individuals tend to ignore or dismiss other aspects of information, even though they may be more relevant.

Overconfidence

This phenomenon describes the fact that people appear to be systematically overconfident of their ability to predict because they fail to recognize the tenuousness of the assumptions on which their judgements are often based. Empirical evidence in this area comes from laboratory studies associated with calibration in which it has been repeatedly observed that there is an incongruity between the confidence individuals have in their judgements and the number of correct answers they subsequently achieve in simple meta-knowledge tests. The implication of this overconfidence is that people are not generally aware of how little they know and how much more they need to know in order to make appropriate judgements.

Single outcome bias

Normative decision theory supposes that in searching for solutions to problems, individuals will specify all relevant values and outcomes, and generate and evaluate alternative courses of action. Empirical evidence, however, suggests that individuals tend to be satisfied with a single interpretation of a situation and are predisposed, at the outset of a decision process, to focus on one outcome and one alternative for achieving that outcome partly because this reduces uncertainty. This predisposition towards a single outcome is evidenced by experiments demonstrating 'bolstering', a process in which individuals magnify the perceived attractiveness of desired alternatives in order to widen the spread of desirability between their preferred and non-preferred alternatives.

INDUCTIVE VERSUS DEDUCTIVE DEVELOPMENTAL PROCESSES

Jungermann (1985a,b) has demonstrated that exploratory or deductive scenario developmental models that rely on forward inferences and causality, result in very different scenarios than would be generated by anticipatory or inductive developmental models that rely on backward inferences and diagnostic effectuality. At the same time there is empirical evidence that, firstly, people make causal inferences with a greater degree of confidence than they do making diagnostic inferences, even when they are aware that the relationship between variables in the data is accidental rather than causal. Secondly, when presented with data that have both causal and diagnostic elements, they generally accord more weight to causal data in probability judgements than to diagnostic data, even where the cause and effect provide the same information about each other (Figure 10.1).

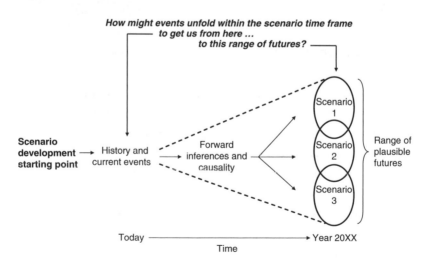

Figure 10.1 Exploratory (Deductive) Scenario Development

Backward inferences or diagnostic reasoning require 'uphill thinking' as they are at odds with the temporal order of things, and causal knowledge cannot be easily transferred in backwards reasoning; therefore, constructing scenarios by the use of this approach is more difficult. However, causal thinking is problematic given that there are no universally accepted rules for distinguishing between cause and effect; thus individuals distinguish causes from effect by relying on probability-based 'cues to causality', which include the temporal order of events, the degree to which two events occur simultaneously, the number of competing variables or explanations, the degree to which one variable can predict another, and the similarity between events and prior knowledge (Figure 10.2). These cues are related to numerous heuristics and biases, and as Einhorn and Hogarth (1981) observe, 'one must guard against the way cues to causality quickly restrict our interpretation of the past by structuring and stabilizing our perceptions of reality'. In essence, the cues are apt to focus attention on the obvious and known at the expense of creative thinking.

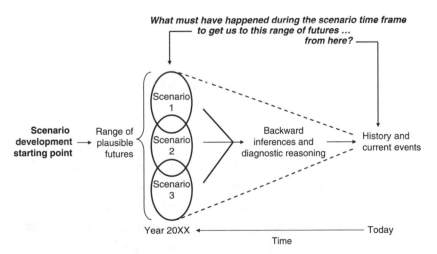

Figure 10.2 Anticipatory (Inductive) Scenario Development

PUNCTUATED EQUILIBRIUM

All the discussion in this chapter thus far has revolved around particular sets of cognitive phenomena operating primarily at the individual level. There are also, of course, equally important group dynamics and behaviourial factors of which designers and facilitators of scenario processes need to be aware. While the most obvious of these are 'Groupthink' and its opposite 'Fragmentation', there is another group phenomenon that has not been accorded any attention in the literature on scenarios, and this is a pattern of behaviour in groups characterized by periods of 'inertia punctuated by concentrated, revolutionary periods of quantum changes' (Gersick, 1988), with time being the stimulus for the transition in group behaviour. This 'punctuated equilibrium' means that instead of developing gradually through a logical sequence of stages over time and becoming more effective, as traditional linear models of group development suggest, project teams progress through an alternation of stasis and sudden change. Moreover, the group's progress is triggered more by members' awareness of time and deadlines than by completion of an absolute amount of work in a specific developmental stage.

IMPLICATIONS FOR SCENARIO FACILITATORS

Most of the research discussed above is rooted in the discipline of cognitive psychology, and relates primarily to examining the quality of intuitive human judgement of uncertain events. It was conducted more than 20 years ago, and explanations for its findings are not unanimous in the literature. At the same time, much of the research, particularly in the area of heuristics, is based on probability forecasts; and, as scenario practitioners from the intuitive logics school will be quick to point out, scenarios have nothing at all to do with either probabilities or forecasts. What then is the relevance of the preceding discussion, and how does it relate to scenario facilitators?

The cognitive sciences tell us that humans are bounded in their rationality; they interpret and make sense of what they see going on around them through unique and interacting ontological and epistemological lenses that comprise their mental models. And, as Pierre Wack has noted, 'in times of rapid change and increased complexity, the mental model becomes a dangerously mixed bag; enormously rich detail and deep understanding can coexist with dubious assumptions, selective inattention to alternative ways of interpreting evidence and projections that are a mere pretense. It is here that the scenario approach can make the difference' (Wack, 1985a,b). The contention then is that in order to exercise this leverage by exposing the flaws in the mental models of individuals and engage them in new ways of thinking, it is essential to have an understanding of how they think, the way in which knowledge is stored and organized in their brains, how they subsequently search for and then interpret information, and so on. The above can be illustrated by some examples from a research project at the Centre for Scenario Planning and Future Studies, within the University of Strathclyde Business School. The behaviour of groups undertaking a scenario process designed and facilitated by Kees Van der Heijden was covertly recorded and then analysed. In terms of exploring the potential drivers of change in the contextual environment and then developing scenarios, observations included the following facts:

- The initial search set triggered in the groups determined which variables the group subsequently explored in depth, and the trigger basically related to topical happenings highly publicized in the media. Thus, events such as AIDS and 'bird flu', the war in Afghanistan and the Middle East tensions, the situation in North Korea, the question of the sustainability of the US economy, and stem cell research were the initial issues raised in all groups as the likely dominant drivers of change. Numerous other issues were raised, but accorded relatively minor attention. Even when provided with evidence that, for example, pneumonia, diarrhoeal diseases and malaria were responsible for more childhood deaths in developing countries than AIDS/HIV, the groups dismissed this and continued to focus their discussions on AIDS/HIV.

- In exploring these recent events, each of the groups tended to have a clear view of how they would unfold within the scenario time span. Although the groups engaged in 'freewheel' thinking in terms of possible combinations and alternative future developments, they invariably returned to contemplate combinations and alternatives that were either already well known, or easily imagined. In reviewing these it was apparent that developments envisaged by all groups largely represented variations around a common, already articulated midpoint. Extreme developments were raised but lay dormant and were eventually discarded as being unrealistic and implausible. For example, in discussing global economics, the headline news at the time was that the US economy showed signs of slowing while the Chinese economy was overheating. In contemplating this, the combinations and outcomes discussed in the syndicates ranged from 'the US and Chinese economies would continue to grow' to 'the US economy would slow while the Chinese economy would manage a soft landing.' A collapse of the economies precipitating a global depression was raised, but summarily rejected by all syndicates as an implausible development.

- Once the groups had determined what constituted the most plausible future developments, they were generally insensitive to missing information, sample size and the concept of regression and correlation, among other things. Activities at this point centred largely on identifying supporting events and data that could be causally linked in a plausible manner in order to explain why a particular event would or would not occur.

- Having established the critical uncertainties and an initial scenario matrix, several of the groups were tasked with using a deductive approach to develop the scenarios defined by the matrix; as discussed earlier in this chapter, a deductive approach is likely to result in more revolutionary scenarios, potentially leading to the discovery of new options that would not ordinarily surface under a causal process. As a starting point in the deductive process, groups were told to imagine themselves sitting at a Starbucks coffee shop in a particular location in the scenario horizon year within each of the scenario end-states defined in the matrix, and asked to look around them and visualize what the world looked like – what people were doing, reading, talking about, and so on. Having imagined the state of the world in the horizon year, the next step was to work backwards to determine what must have happened in the intervening years for the end-state situation to have arisen. In observing the groups throughout this stage, it was apparent that none found this an easy process, problems in developing diagnostic reasoning were encountered, and the groups invariably abandoned the task and resorted to an inductive approach.

Again, in the same research project discussed above, the punctuated equilibrium phenomenon was clearly evident in all groups as they progressed through the stages of scenario development. However, unlike the model described by Gersick, the transition point was not in all cases the midpoint in the time allotted for the various exercises; it varied within each group. More significant, however, was the observation that once the punctuated equilibrium transition point was launched, the groups abandoned any further exploratory discussions, self-sealing on ideas already discussed. At this point, interventions by the facilitator proved ineffective; even when it was demonstrated that the ideas and supporting data being used may have been outdated and incomplete, or that the relationship between variables was more likely to be accidental than causal.

While group members appeared to pay attention to the facilitator, on his departure from the room they dismissed his comments and continued to develop their existing ideas with an escalating commitment, invoking elaborate causal reasoning to justify the ideas, and massaging data to fit the existing schema and dispel any doubts raised within the group, or by the facilitator. Some revisions were made on the basis of the facilitator's comments, but these tended to be minimal in scope.

CONCLUSIONS

The empirical evidence from the cognitive sciences clearly suggests that scenario developmental processes will be affected by a range of cognitive processes. How events are interpreted and then unfolded into the future in a scenario will, for instance, be largely determined by the existing schematic conception of the individuals developing the scenarios. The schema contains deeply embedded assumptions about what is feasible and what is not in terms of future developments. Where individuals cannot readily apply the schema because they are attempting to construct previously unexperienced patterns of events, they will invariably force the situation into their existing schema using causal inferences to compensate for gaps. Finally, once they have imagined how events might unfold in the future, it will be difficult for them to view these events from different perspectives.

In addition to the impact of cognitive processes, a range of heuristics and biases will impact scenario developmental processes in varying degrees, in terms of what information is searched for and analysed and what data are accepted or rejected. For example, factors such as experience bias, framing, saliency and primacy will largely determine the starting point of the information search in the scenario development process, which in turn will determine what information is searched for, as pathways of linked nodes in the neural network of the brain are activated. Once the search set is activated, individuals will probably be insensitive to missing information, and events that are representative, well publicized, easily imagined and generally lead to a single outcome, will dominate the thinking. Interpretation of information will be largely guided by issues that individuals already understand, and will be constrained by belief systems and cognitive anchors. Information which accords with experiences and belief systems will be readily assimilated; that which does not will be discarded. Finally, once the individuals have developed a scenario, they will be quite confident of the inherent predictions underlying the scenario.

Seasoned scenario practitioners may, as a consequence of their experience, be intuitively aware of much of the above. Practitioners at large however, appear generally unaware of, or at best only vaguely aware of, these phenomena and the effect of their ramifications on the scenario developmental process. This is evidenced by the fact that few of the articles on scenarios in the anecdotal, experienced-based literature make references to these phenomena; and in advocating particular methodologies only a small number cite supporting empirical evidence. A significant omission in the literature on scenario planning is the fact that there is an absence of discussion on 'failed' scenario interventions. However, as both a researcher in scenarios and a practitioner who served an apprenticeship under Kees Van der Heijden – one of the foremost authorities on the subject – I have observed and been a part of several scenario projects that were not successful in terms of changing mental maps, initiating a strategic conversation, generating options not previously considered, or indeed any of the other success criteria ascribed to scenario planning. In analysing these failures, I have come to recognize and understand the effects on process of individual cognitive issues, group dynamics and behavioral patterns, and to see that they have all played a significant role one way or another. Scenario planning may not be 'rocket science', but neither is it quite as straightforward and effortless as it is often made out to be in the literature.

CHAPTER 11

APPRECIATING THE FUTURE

Tony Hodgson

There are two aspects to the world of management, as described in the Introduction to Part III: the operational and the strategic. The argument of this chapter is that shifting from the operational to the strategic is difficult and requires appreciation of the future. The *operational mindset* is essentially narrow in focus and short term in its decision and action cycle; the *strategic mindset* is broad and long term. This common way of distinguishing between the two is a half-truth. Effective strategy is also grounded in the present and has depth as well as breadth. The challenge to practitioners is how to engage a decision constituency in a process that shifts them into a strategic mindset which is both focused and broad, and both short and long term.

Whereas operations are more about picking fruit, strategy is more about growing orchards. Thus the split between short- and long-term orientation often occurring in organizational management is somewhat like, on the one hand, picking fruit without retaining any seeds for future trees and, on the other, postponing the sowing of seed until a new orchard is needed. It is a false dichotomy.

Scenarios for Success: Turning Insights into Action   Edited by Bill Sharpe and Kees Van der Heijden
© 2007 John Wiley & Sons, Ltd

So a crucial and often overlooked aspect of scenario thinking is that to be effective it depends first of all on the presence of strategic thinking. To run day-to-day operations we develop an operational mindset that also acts as a cognitive filter on those issues we pay attention to. It becomes adept at picking up signals of the immediate. If we approach the understanding of longer range scenarios in this mental frame it will be ineffective. Similarly, if we try to develop scenarios while dominated by the operational mindset, they will have limited value because the 'bandwidth' of the scenarios will be too narrow. (This latter approach is referred to elsewhere (Selin, Chapter 2) as an 'atomistic' approach.) As Schwarz points out, 'scenarios really function when there is something game-changing to explore' (page 15). So the challenge is to cultivate a strategic mindset that has the bandwidth to pay attention to wider trends and possibilities that correlate with a game-changing stance.

It is difficult to recognize when the operational mindset is constraining the work, both when creating scenarios and when applying them in strategic conversation. This chapter describes some enabling conditions for strategic thinking, firstly by characterizing a number of mental traps that decision makers and their support staff frequently fall into; secondly, by pointing out the importance of certain types of cognitive skill necessary for avoiding these traps; and thirdly by describing a case example of how a strategic conversation was facilitated in a way that moved a poorly integrated set of multi-product operational businesses forward to become a coherent strategic business. As such, it is an example of a way to incorporate the world of business into the world of management at the strategic level.

THE CHALLENGE OF ENGAGING DECISION MAKERS

There are three ways of appreciating the future. The first is where we create images of the future based on our best understanding of the factors that we believe will determine the future state of affairs. This is a judgement about the reality of the future. The second is where we make connections with our current interests and intentions and what we might be able to do about them. This is an instrumental judgement about how our images of the future inform our judgement on what we can do, the instruments or levers we have, and the role we might play. The third is where we place a value on a future state of affairs and either try to make it happen or establish a value position for ourselves. These three phases, based on the concept of 'appreciative system' (Vickers, 1965) are discussed in the Introduction to Part II, page 67 and, provide a framework in which we can critique current use and misuse of scenarios in decision making.

Scenario planning practitioners have developed a rich set of tools and processes for carrying out stage one, images of the future. These can range from sketches of future possibilities using simple quick-cut methods, like four-box frameworks, to extensively researched narratives annotated with copious research and statistical background. However, these do not necessarily engage the appreciative system of the decision maker if they are simply the product of the scenario-planning support group. If the first stage does not properly engage the decision-maker's mind, then the second and third stages, which lead to decisive action, are impossible. Of course, the decision maker who is disconnected from scenarios will still make decisions, but not ones informed by that level. To get a better sense of what we are missing in efforts to engage decision makers in scenario thinking, consider the typical, but usually unquestioned, assumptions that scenario planners often make with regard to what they are expecting decision makers to do.

For example, in being presented with a set of scenarios, what is the information structure that tends to be presented? There will be more than one version of the future – often three or four – and these will be framed in various ways, such as dilemmas, trilemmas, event trees, orthogonal axes and so on. There will be a set of drivers and uncertainties that the scenario set addresses. If well researched, they may be quite unfamiliar, surprising or even shocking to the decision maker. There will be some time span of interest, with scenarios depicting a state of affairs in 10, 20, or 30 years' time. There may well be a time line for each scenario indicating how it might evolve, starting from where we are today. All this will be backed up with data, graphs, bar charts and diagrams. There may also be illustrative examples from current affairs indicating pockets of the future in the present.

The decision makers are then expected, without any preparation, to:

- assimilate the multiple images and stories
- understand how the driving forces and uncertainties ended up there
- envision scenarios that do not correspond to their current beliefs
- place their strategic intent or strategy in that context
- infer a transaction zone in terms of shifting from the 'might be' context to the 'make happen' capability of their organization
- envision options and decisions that have implications for the present.

But these conditions are complex, and their success in influencing decisions is often dependent on the decision maker's participation in generating the scenarios in the first place. It is also dependent on having a clear notion of strategic direction formulated in terms that will relate to the context and language of the scenario set. The decision makers also need the mental agility and stamina to assimilate complexity rapidly, and visualize strategic consequences and their timings. Needless to say, this is usually asking too much of time-constrained executives; and so the gap persists.

Another reason that scenario planning has not been applied as well as it might is that the thinking part of it has been treated as a given. 'Give me the tool and I will use it' tends to be the position taken by consultants and executives. If the field of interest were carpentry, the skill development component would never be separated from the tools themselves. There is the chisel, but there is also the skill and safety in using it well. A proper application of the tools must include mastery, apprenticeship and coaching. However, in the field of thinking we all too easily assume that we are born experts! In practice there are cognitive skills that both scenario planners and decision makers need to learn to get good results.

Once learned, the effectiveness of these cognitive skills can help to cut through the time limitation constraints. They function differently from academic or professional skills which seek right answers. In futures work, faced with complexity and uncertainty, there are no right answers. Any appreciation of the future is a temporary place-holder to enable action to be taken. These skills then have a feeling and a cultural component which is often experienced as uncomfortable, unproductive and unreliable by minds schooled only in the combining of evidence-based analysis and strong opinion that imbues many boardrooms and policy committees. Paying more attention to, and researching the cognitive skills of, strategic and scenario thinking may well provide a way out of the dichotomy between 'heavy' and 'light' processes (see page 16), since the overarching criterion is effective insight for decision making.

It is difficult for decision-making teams to make time to learn together at the strategic level. However, a skilled facilitator is able to take people through a strategy process that they have not previously practised and also, in the midst of doing that, inculcate many of the skills that are needed. This is because the best way of learning these cognitive skills is through active engagement. The skilled facilitator will not only run a scenario-to-strategy process but do it in a way that makes the methodology transparent and, as far as possible, devolved to the participants. We shall define this as *strategy work*.

This is distinguished from strategic planning and analysis in that it refers to the non-delegatable work that executive decision makers need to do if they are to be the active progenitors of strategy rather than the passive receivers of proposals from strategy experts. Strategy work is characterized by a combination of factors:

- It is carried out by the responsible executive team, with wider involvement from the organization.
- It is a design process not to be confused with operational management.
- It functions at the level of developing uniquely new perceptions and mental models in contrast to 'business-as-usual thinking'.
- It is facilitated by the timely introduction of strategy frameworks based on good research but depicted in a form such that everyone's experience can be mapped onto it and new insights gained.
- It requires a progressive build up of new thinking over a time period of weeks rather than days, giving time for absorption and reflection (see Schwartz interview in Chapter 1).

Given the expectations listed on page 282 and the demands of strategy work, it is not surprising that simply leaving people to talk over a strategic decision rarely leads to effective strategic conversation. The deeper causes of this relate to certain mental traps that people easily fall into because they have not developed the cognitive skills to avoid them. The role of an experienced facilitator is crucial here. The facilitator can help the team by functioning as a coach and catalyst. The role of a catalyst is to increase the productive yield and achieve it with less wasted energy. Unlike a content consultant, the facilitator does not prescribe the strategy through a process of analysis, but lets the strategy emerge through a designed process of strategic conversation. Yet this is not a detached role like a behavioural process consultation. It is a cognitively demanding task of thinking through with the client team the hard stuff of the strategy work, as indicated in Figure 11.1.

The remainder of this chapter will first develop some of these mental traps as set out by Bradfield (Chapter 10); second, it will describe some of the key cognitive behavioural skills in which the

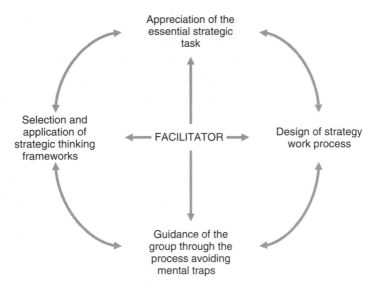

Figure 11.1   The role of the facilitator in strategy work

facilitator needs to be competent to coach the team through; and third, it will provide a case example that shows how these were orchestrated on a strategy work project.

HOW THE FACILITATOR HELPS DECISION MAKERS TO AVOID MENTAL TRAPS

In designing and facilitating a process of strategy work taking into account the cognitive skills shown a Figure 11.1, the facilitator has a number of challenges to his or her own skill. Whereas the facilitator can use codified tools and techniques designed to be fairly easy to see, there are two additional major demands. The first is the intellectual challenge of using a wide repertoire of synthesis tools and techniques as a flexible resource to draw on as the process unfolds − a kind of strategic-thinking pharmacy. The role of the facilitator here is essentially a designer of 'thinking through'. This process design must be customized: an approach very different from the formulaic technique procedures of many consultancies. The second is the cultivation of emotional intelligence in the group to withstand a creative process which may unravel the vested interests of the decision-making constituency. Absence of this emotional intelligence is demonstrated by the tendency for those engaged in strategy work to fall into a number of mental traps which can be related to the findings in cognitive research summarized by Ron Bradfield (Chapter 10). From the standpoint of a facilitator practitioner whose experience is based on working with management and policy teams, the mental conditioning referred to in that chapter as 'belief perseverance', 'confirmation bias', 'experience bias', 'overconfidence' and 'single outcome bias' all reinforce the tendency to fall into these traps.

These traps are like attractors that subconsciously pull people back into their usual thought patterns and judgement frameworks. They are symptoms of a stuck appreciative system. A key role of the trusted facilitator is to challenge the strategy work team whenever he or she notices a tendency to fall into one of these traps, for a fall virtually guarantees that critical information or perspective will be overlooked, or even suppressed. Of course, the strategy facilitator is also prone to falling in, but part of his or her education is to have explored these consciously and personally in order to have a clearer recognition of them. The network of 'remarkable' people is important here: a facilitator of strategy work who is not fairly frequently being shocked by interacting with interesting people is not likely to be on his or her toes!

The five aspects the facilitator needs to consider specifically are:

- Strategic belief
- Sequence of information
- Single-loop learning
- Time horizon extrapolation
- Intolerance of ambiguity.

Strategic belief

Belief must be distinguished from truth or reality. Belief is a mental and emotional condition that orients us to a view of reality. When that belief has sufficient correspondence with what is out there then it becomes a powerful coping mechanism to deal more easily with the world. It also serves to align people in a common cause and in concerted action. Belief is also the stories we tell ourselves about what is going on; these stories easily subside into the subconscious and are assumed to be reality.

Beliefs are hard to change because they carry a weight of emotional and cultural investment. Indeed, humans are the only species on the planet to go to war over their beliefs. Yet shared beliefs are also a source of shared meaning that enables communities, families, corporations to act reasonably coherently. So there is an inherent ambiguity in a belief system. On the one hand, it is an essential condition of shared aligned action vital for successful implementation. On the other hand, it is a constraint on truth and reality which can render us blind to the wider environment and its changes. When belief systems come into conflict with reality, reality eventually prevails. Most strategic shocks to corporations and governments are through the mismatch between their belief systems and reality. Beliefs lock down the appreciative system and prevent learning.

The tendency to run after 'me too' fashions in business or policy is an example of a belief trap. In essence, the core of Wack's 'gentle art of re-perceiving' (Selin, Chapter 2) is the way out of this trap.

Sequence of information

How we interpret information is through pattern recognition of meaning. The information may show conditions, trends and changes in the current situation. It may also contain extrapolations and assumptions of continuity or discontinuity. This mass or mess of information can be arranged in many different ways, each of which may lead to a different interpretation. The brain is very prone to arrive at an arrangement or pattern which is determined by the sequence in which it encounters the information. If we are bombarded with rectangular objects we begin to piece them together in a rectangular way. A 'rectangle' hypothesis forms and becomes through repetition 'hard wired' in the brain. Emotional energy forms around the pattern which becomes its meaning. Exploration invisibly changes into dogma. This makes change of mind or entertainment of other interpretations difficult. If anomalous information (e.g., circles) comes along it is rejected as not fitting or even simply not noticed. Since in scenario thinking we need to be able to create multiple interpretations of the same data, it is critical to get out of the sequence trap. Caught in it we pursue our first understanding, leaving no room for second and third thoughts that may be better. Pride in quick decision making can be a danger.

This is perhaps the most serious limitation of analytical method in a complex and changing world. Sequencing methods drive towards an inevitable pattern which can totally miss the point. Edward De Bono (1992) has pointed out the neurobiological inevitability of this trap in a pattern forming brain. Lateral thinking is a way to avoid the trap.

Single-loop learning

Behind every current strategy there is a set of assumptions. We can call this the 'business as usual' mindset. Any action that is taken to achieve intended results is embedded in this assumption set. As action proceeds, performance may confirm the assumptions but deviations will occur that do not. The response is then to make corrections while remaining within the assumption set; tactical changes are made to get back on track, to make a 'work around'.

The assumption set, remaining unquestioned, will sooner or later reveal itself through unbending commitment to the strategy and the pressure to prove 'we are right', in spite of increasing underperformance. However, if the assumptions themselves are incorrect, then momentum builds up until a crash or a bubble burst occurs demonstrating that deviation correction learning was not sufficient. A second loop of learning is necessary to reframe and revise initial assumptions (Figure 11.2). This requires some form of reflective inquiry, a pause to stand back.

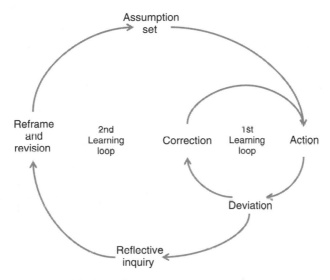

Figure 11.2 Double-loop learning

Examples of this are where increasing resources are applied to fix a problem when the assumptions behind the problem are the real problem. In this trap great energy is put into single-loop learning which is doomed to failure without the second loop. Argyris (1993) has pointed this out in depth with his analysis of defensive routines and professional incompetence. Carrying out reflective learning in parallel with operational learning is a way out of this trap.

Time horizon extrapolation

Part of the assumption set is the view of time and change held by the strategy owners. Consider the example of a strategy based on an analysis of trends, and aiming to reach a certain goal over a time span in which the trend is still valid. Two ways of looking at this can be called the *linear* and the *sophisticated*. The linear is most common and relates to the cognitive difficulty people have in visualizing trend bends driven by non-linear dynamics, for example exponential curves. The sophisticated version takes into account non-linear trends but still places them within the same shape of environment or context. If a new business ecology emerges or there is a paradigm shift (Kuhn, 1996) then this continuous view of time leads to conclusions that are far off the mark. This is because of the misfit between a discontinuity of pattern and longer range strategy simply collapsed into short-range strategy extended in linear time.

This is seen most clearly where players are competing on the basis of their previous winning strategies without noticing that the game has changed. This shows up strongly in the innovator's dilemma described by Christensen (1997). The three-horizon method is a way out of this trap (Sharpe and Hodgson, 2005, see Chapter 5).

Intolerance of ambiguity

It will now be clear that all the above thinking issues share the common characteristic that a single standpoint – however effective it might seem to be in the immediate and short term – carries the seeds of its own destruction. In a fast-changing world going through discontinuous changes, single standpoints have a very short half-life. Since many social and organizational systems are based on hierarchical authority, where leadership is expected to have the answers and know what is going on, and where the achievement and retention of power depends on this, the intolerance of ambiguity is both a cognitive condition and also a political necessity. The group equivalent of this state is intolerance of alternative or deviant views arising within a group. This is, perhaps, the strongest reason why scenario thinking is hard for the mainstream. The pressure to be decisive, clear and not change your mind is often too great to leave space for strategy work as defined here.

This shows in the intolerance of thinking in the margin in many businesses and institutions, hence not recognizing where renewing innovation is most likely to come from. The way out of this trap is the cultivation of curiosity and multi-track thinking in both individuals and teams to extend the range of strategic conversation.

SOME REQUISITE COGNITIVE SKILLS

A leader or facilitator skilled at strategy work will be on the watch for these tendencies and try to steer the group away from them. However, success or failure in this regard will be determined by the extent to which the individuals have the capability for double-loop learning. There are a number of cognitive skills that the facilitator can learn and impart to the team in the strategy work process. The skill areas are evidenced partly by the behaviour of the group when they are together, and partly by the behaviour of the group when they have broken up. They are essential interventions in the usual thinking process that increase the chances of a change of mental model (see Selin, Chapter 2). The conditions in which these skills can be exercised are best achieved by involving a broad spectrum of people who do not suppress dissent but treat this as evidence of uncertainty and accommodate maverick views to stretch thinking. In this way there is more chance of achieving the requisite variety in understanding the world of business.

Consider how these capabilities operate in groups rather than in individuals. In the group setting we can identify distributed cognition capabilities. If no member of a group is individually skilled, then the team is vulnerable to 'group think'. If some members have some of these cognitive skills then, in interaction with their colleagues, they can lift the level of thinking. Indeed, like skilled team players in a ball game they can pass ideas and insights around the group. In this way the performance of a team involved in strategic conversations can surpass the sum of the individual performances.

To bring this discussion down to the pragmatic level of actual strategy work in teams, and to show how facilitators can move to overcome these problems, we describe below 15 specific cognitive skills that can be applied in actual strategic conversations. Any of them may be useful at any time but they gain in effectiveness as clusters. Each trio of skills creates enabling conditions for the resolution of one of the five framework dilemmas introduced at the beginning of this book (page 58). The way these enabling skills relate to a dilemma is illustrated in Figure 11.3.

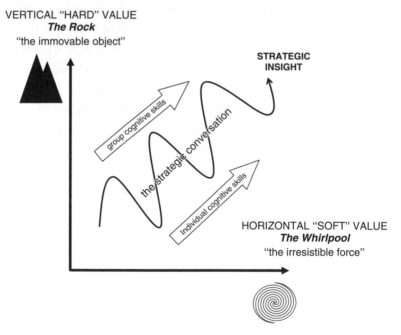

Figure 11.3 Strategic insight as dilemma resolution

The dilemma is portrayed as having a vertical 'hard' value or dimension and a lateral 'soft' value or dimension. Though usually experienced as antithetical, the dilemma approach moves from 'either/or' to 'both/and' by orienting them orthogonally. The resolution of the dilemma is then a navigated pathway of give and take between the dimensions until sufficient strategic insight is generated to achieve the 'both/and' transformation. In this context the wavy line of the pathway (likened to steering a sail boat against wind and tide) is the strategic conversation (Hampden-Turner, 1990).

AMPLIFYING TO THE DILEMMA

Simplicity/Complexity

Questioning the status quo

Strategy work is often triggered when evidence comes to light that a key assumption upon which business-as-usual depends is open to question. However, there is often inbuilt resistance to questioning the status quo because of the momentum of the current business; it may even be considered 'disloyal'. Bringing assumptions to the surface requires courageous questioning and much cross-comparison with other views, including those that are unwelcome. Strategic messengers risk being shot.

Recognition and acknowledgement of complex 'messes'

This is a well-researched factor in creative thinking dating from the post-Sputnik era of creativity research. However, it is a difficult one for the action-oriented operational mindset to practise. Fuzziness, ambiguity and paradox are inherent in the nature of complex systems of interacting problems. Ackoff (1999) calls such systems of problems messes: 'The behaviour of a mess depends more on how its parts interact than on how they act independently.' A strategy process that does not go through a period of messiness and confusion will not be creative, and be unlikely to reframe or upframe to a new level of effectiveness (Normann, 2001).

Graceful entry

This is a term used by some cognitive scientists to indicate an optimum level of challenge for learning. If the challenge is too weak, then complacency rules the mind. If the challenge is too great, then fear or panic rules the mind. In either case the challenge is suppressed or denied. However, there is an intermediate threshold, usually identified by the region in which the person will openly acknowledge doubt, where learning can take place. Finding that spot is part of the art of facilitation. John Holland and colleagues suggest 'Competition allows the system to marshal its rules as the situation demands, and it allows the system to gracefully insert new rules without disturbing established capabilities' (Holland *et al.*, 1986).

Certainty/Uncertainty

Unearthing and articulation of assumptions and beliefs

To be effective, the operational mindset has to take as given a belief structure and act on it, often rapidly and without hesitation. The strategic mind, however, is interested in its own belief system, not as dogma, but as a factor that may determine its boundaries. This is often uncomfortable even for people who have practised the skill. Collyns notes 'my memory of doing this work is of feeling ill half the time because you are hit in your gut about things you hadn't thought of before and the impact they might have' (see page 20).

Sharing current perspectives and negotiating relevance

In strategy work individuals working in a group need to challenge assumptions and negotiate the relevance of trends and facts. This can be helped by using appropriate frameworks such as, for example, the classic 'uncertainty/impact grid'. A framework becomes an effective catalyst for strategic conversation when a group works collaboratively to populate it with their knowledge and insights; it acts as an organizing principle, based on in-depth intellectual research, but used to re-pattern shared thinking and judgements rather than analyse for 'the answer'. This works only if the framework introduces an unaccustomed way of looking at the situation and stimulates the questioning and unearthing of assumptions. The right level of cognitive dissonance ensures that the participants are thinking, using their knowledge and listening to each other in the context of the framework. Mental models begin to surface and become shared.

Appreciative inquiry

This is both a cognitive skill (especially of listening) and a way of interpersonal interaction in teams and networks. It seeks deliberately to discover people's exceptionality – their knowledge and perspectives. It actively seeks out and recognizes people for their specialties – their essential contributions and achievements. Critical for strategy work, is its base on the principle of equality of voice – everyone is asked to speak their viewpoint. Appreciative inquiry builds momentum and success because it credits the decision-making constituency with the inherent capability to generate its own decisions. Its goal is to create organizations that perform at the level of people's shared potential.

Knowing/Intuiting

Reframing or re-perceiving both present and future

This perhaps is the essential core of Wack's 'gentle art of re-perceiving'. It is, as he says, changing the microcosm or mindset of the individual in order to see the big world differently. Perhaps we could also speak of re-appreciating the future in this context. The appreciative system goes through re-patterning and so sets new foundations for the three judgements of reality, options for action and value priorities. However, we must remember in this context also the point that the past has gone, the future is not yet and the only reality is the present. So re-appreciating the future is also re-appreciating the present.

Visualizing and narrating stories that reveal an unfolding logic and dynamic of strategy

When asked why scenario practice works well, Schwarz makes the point that 'storytelling is what people do' (page 14). Taking the researched and thought-out components of both scenarios and strategies and presenting them as a list or a diagram of strategy does not energize or inspire nearly as effectively as a well-crafted story based on those components. Narratives create plots, thread things together and appeal to the imagination. Many scenario and strategy efforts fail to realize their potential because they have not come alive as mental images in the minds of the decision makers and their staff. This is where strategy work is as much an art and design discipline as it is a management process.

Tolerating initially anomalous information to shift perspective

One of the reasons for emphasizing the in-depth approach originally pioneered by Pierre Wack is that unusual insight doesn't come cheap. However, it is possible that, given the right mental training, it can come quickly. A mind accustomed to dealing frequently with anomalous information (which is usually unnoticed or tuned out by the majority) develops an instinct for anomaly. As we know from creative science, paradigm shift (Kuhn, 1996) arises not from things that fit but from things that don't fit. This is reflected in business by observations such as those of Christensen (2003) regarding disruptive technology. Something that 'can't be done' or 'won't work' may prove its effectiveness all too quickly.

Reactive/Proactive

Constructive expression of doubt

In any working group there will be assertions and doubts. Doubt can be simply an inhibiting factor that saps energy and motivation, as in the case of 'idea killers'. Constructive doubt, however, is the ability to treat even certainties as provisional and is open to alternatives. This is important to build on for group cognition. For example, when experts in a room disagree about the 'facts', this can be reframed by the facilitator into an uncertainty which then feeds into the scenario thinking. In the generative stage of strategy work it can be crucial for team members to hold to 'model agnosticism'. This is also an enabling condition for avoiding the single-loop learning trap.

Assimilation of and experimentation with new frameworks of thinking

The tools of analysis are not the tools of synthesis, and strategy work requires a capability to find new patterns and connections between things. It is easy to claim that 'joined up thinking' is needed in contemporary strategy and policy, but it is hard to accomplish. Perhaps the biggest obstacle to this is the limits imposed by professionalism. A discipline will codify methods and interpretations (judgements, in Vickers's terms) based on the domainal assumptions of that discipline. But scenario thinking embraces many domains in interaction. It is essentially interdisciplinary. To support interdisciplinary work we need a rich set of frameworks that cut across the usual categories of thinking. (In the case example that completes this, over ten strategy frameworks were used as catalysts for strategic conversation in addition to the scenario techniques.)

Generating new ideas of opportunity and strategy

Idea generation is often left to chance or talent. However, it is a cognitive skill that can be called generative thinking, and can be learned. Generative thinking is at the heart of innovation. Often the components of an innovation are well known but the significant step is putting them together in novel ways that create new effects and possibilities. Scenario planning exercises are often dry because they use scenarios for testing and analysis only, and not for lateral thinking and option generation. There is a skill in applying the question 'what if?' in a way that opens up the space for new insights and options.

Planned/Emergent

Mapping complex connections that articulate strategy

In the complex fields of science and engineering, we can no longer proceed without maps and models. These are usually 3D, computer-generated. Oil and gas reservoirs are mapped and explored in virtual reality; complex buildings and objects like vehicles are constructed in CAD before they meet materials; generals no longer proceed without war rooms and simulations. Yet in strategy work we mostly rely on words and numbers on bits of paper, or we restrict strategic thinking to what can be put on a few presentation slides. Strategic conversation is the essence of strategy making but it helps if a proportion of it is conducted through visual dialogue. A scenario set of the world of business may have a hundred factors that need to be considered, and the strategic challenge of an enterprise may require a hundred factors in the world of management.

The number of possible patterns between these two is astronom-
ical. Intuition is required and needs to be supported by the power
of visualization, much neglected in management and policy circles.

Cognitive re-priming to change the pick-up of relevant information

Cognitive psychology has shown the power in our minds of cognitive priming. This happens when the ideas or world views that
we have act as a powerful filter for what we notice and what
we don't notice. One of the great benefits of multi-future thinking with scenarios is gained when, having entertained a future
we hadn't previously considered and do not believe, we subsequently find information coming to light that is consistent with,
and reinforces, that view. Scenarios that are new to us, and which
we absorb, re-prime the brain to notice new types of information. Cultivating an open mind is not simply having an empty
mind, which is impossible, but rather cultivating a mental radar
that has been extended beyond current assumptions and political
correct interpretations. Failure to re-prime in this way is perhaps the greatest cognitive failing of today's leaders (Chicoine,
2004).

Connecting ideas and analytics for testing and verification

In case the reader is now suspecting that the world of analysis has
been dismissed as irrelevant, this final point emphasizes that effective strategy work connects synthesis, in new and intelligent ways,
to the domain of analysis (economics, statistics, market research,
financial planning, etc.). Indeed, a key cognitive skill is the ability
to make new sense of information, confirm or disconfirm hypothe-
ses, and design new measurement systems or 'cockpits' to match
the reframed strategy (Heathfield, Chapter 12).

A CASE EXAMPLE OF FACILITATING STRATEGY WORK WITH SCENARIOS

What follows is an account, from the perspective of facilitating strategy work, of a designed process that took the managers of different business lines in an organization through an experience in which they learned strategic conversation while innovating a new corporate strategy. The case involves the management of a division of a major European corporation. The case history will help to show how the various components link together to form strategy work. The steps and sequences in this case were customized to start from where the managers were, meet their challenge and accelerate their development both individually and as a team. The process described below is customized and therefore not a generic method. However, it does serve to illustrate some of the important points about design and facilitation.

The division in question started as a set of functional islands each concerned with marketing and trading its own product. Although the division's performance was monitored as a whole by top management, there was no history of efforts at strategic repositioning. Indeed the financial performance was currently so good that there was no obvious reason to embark on a major exercise of strategy work. However, top management recognized that their world of business was changing and that the current business was likely to go through a discontinuity in the not too distant future. Yet in the face of unavoidable uncertainty, it was not clear what to do.

A new Division Head was appointed with the mandate to explore strategic options. He recognized that the best chance was to adopt a participative approach involving all unit heads and senior planning staff, and that it would require a designed and facilitated process of strategy work. This was underpinned by a strong sense that, in the absence of off-the-shelf answers, a 'strategy as learning' approach was most likely to develop competitive advantage through releasing the creative potential of the individuals and developing them into a strategic team. All the individuals in the group were experienced, of mixed age and gender, and operationally very successful.

As he summarized his position:

> "The method of linear analysis/deconstruction goes well with change processes which are 'political' or in need of close control. That is understandable, but one then runs the risk of giving a controlled, but inferior or even wrong answer to problems which in their nature are discontinuous and unpredictable. Adopting a method focusing on real learning, systems thinking, allowing for ambiguity includes real risk for the decision makers as the outcome of learning cannot be predicted. However, it is necessary to take this risk precisely in order to address the ambiguity, long-term uncertainty and discontinuity."

Through a series of five two-day workshops over a period of just over three months, the team were taken through a process that stimulated them to look more widely into the business and geopolitical environment; to re-examine their business areas through unfamiliar frameworks that reshaped their mental models; to change their culture from a functional structure with stove-pipe reporting to a team culture with strategic conversation; and finally to arrive at a concerted integration of the different business lines into an overarching strategy based on a newly evolving business model. In this process the availability in the company of deeply researched scenarios developed over two years was significant, in that the wider economic and geopolitical environment had been well studied by a corporate strategy group. The facilitator had been the consultant project leader for this global scenario work.

What follows is a more detailed description of the process in relation to the way the facilitation and practice methods helped to navigate the team's thinking through the five dilemmas described in the Introduction to this book (page 58) and avoiding as far as possible the mental traps. The role of the cognitive frameworks, the practical exercises to internalize them, and the changes of perception, evaluation and motivation they brought will be characterized. The section headings refer back to the original dilemmas that set the scene, and the accompanying diagram indicates the cognitive skills that received most emphasis in this stage of the process. Of course, any of these skills may come in handy at any point in a strategy work process if the symptoms warrant it. The sequence of working through the dilemmas is shown in Figure 11.4.

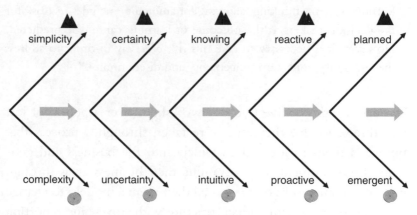

Figure 11.4 Sequence of working through the dilemmas

The challenge facing the team leader was how to refresh a high-performing unit probably based on an economic bubble that was unlikely to last more than three to five years, and hence liable to be caught out when the bubble burts. However, because of current excellent performance, there were no operational reasons for engaging in a major revision of strategy. This starting point made them vulnerable to Trap 1 – being caught in fixed strategic beliefs. Further, the team leader was new to the unit and had only partial expertise in the range of businesses in the unit. He needed, therefore, a highly participative approach that would stimulate the creativity of the group.

Dilemma: simplicity/complexity

The first dilemma resolution task was to dislocate constructively the current business model and place it into a new context for strategy work, thereby opening up the scenario space (Figure 11.5). This meant loosening the certainty in their current operation and plans. Using a scenario approach immediately would have been premature. The preparation was to have each business leader present his or her picture of the next 10 years of performance but have the team raise any questions about those plans. The sequence of information trap tends to confine thinking to a fixed pattern corresponding to the way the plans are presented; so this cross-questioning was deliberately not answered immediately but recorded and clustered to give a shared 'map of doubts'.

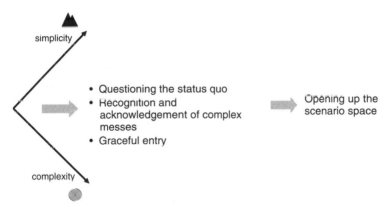

simplicity

complexity

- Questioning the status quo
- Recognition and acknowledgement of complex messes
- Graceful entry

Opening up the scenario space

Figure 11.5   The simplicity/complexity resolution

This provided a loosening up of the thinking of the group which was self-generated, drawing on the inherent diversity of the group. Many of the questions raised related to assumptions about the future, thus providing an antidote for the single-loop learning trap by shifting the thinking towards the second learning loop of reworking

assumptions. This provided a more responsive platform for a preliminary introduction to a set of three global scenarios that addressed
some of the trends and uncertainties, and provided the first exercise
in expanding the group's 'memory of the future'. A key framework introduced here was the distinction of levels between mission,
strategy and tactics and how to avoid confusing these levels.

Dilemma: Certainty/Uncertainty

The second dilemma resolution task was to identify predetermined
and uncertain aspects of the future more clearly than before, developing a richer picture of possible changes over different time scales
and introducing progressively greater levels of uncertainty about
the world of business (Figure 11.6). The scope of the group's own
thinking about the future was stretched so that they began to own
the future-thinking aspect of the scenario components.

Although their current business plans were cast in a 10-year horizon, it was clear that there were no discontinuities in their reading
of the business environment; they were, therefore, in danger of

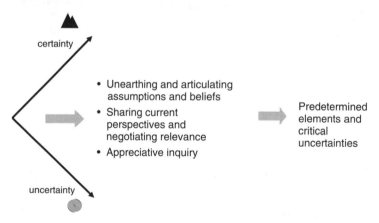

Figure 11.6 The certainty/uncertainty resolution

falling into the time horizon extrapolation trap: treating 10 years as one year 10 times over, with small changes. For this stage an approach called the 'three horizons' was used (Sharpe and Hodgson, 2005, see page 142). The gist of this approach can be described as follows. The rolling hills of the first horizon are the current business conditions known as 'business as usual'. Next, the foothills of the second horizon represent the innovations that challenge the first horizon with disruptive technologies and business models. Within the third horizon we find the higher mountains, which represent a complete change in the business ecology. The third horizon is too far away for us to predict specific technologies or societal arrangements; however, it is the domain of values and visions and hence could be the future time period in which current values might be displaced. Whether this happens depends on how far the first horizon mindset captures the innovations of the second horizon; or how far the disruptions are exploited by the longer term vision. For example, how we will make the transition from an unsustainable energy economy to a sustainable one depends on how the tension between energy security and climate change is resolved.

An important cognitive point here is that each horizon is associated with a different mindset and associated belief system. Mature strategic work is able to acknowledge all three horizons and switch between them at will. This is very hard for people not practised in taking on world views different from their own dominant belief system. It is analogous to multi-future thinking with a scenario set. However, the framework is effective in giving people permission to step outside the box of orthodox linear projection and entertain peripheral observations about what is going on and where it might lead. In this case, the exercise led a number of members of the group to recognize the bubble nature of the current business-as-usual. The motivational level of the group increased significantly at this point.

Dilemma: Knowing/Intuitive

The third dilemma resolution task was to make an experiment of stepping from the known rational to the unknown intuitive (Figure 11.7). The group first of all took the second and third horizon conditions of the business environment, as they had mapped them, as a plausible future. They then asked the question, 'What kind of a business idea (van der Heijden, 2005) would be successful in that environment?' This led to a number of ideas around opportunities, value creation and distinctive competence that were in marked contrast to their presentation of the business plans at the beginning of the process. At this stage there was little conviction that they were where the team needed to be, but they had significantly expanded the thinking; and a recognition that the current strategy was vulnerable was well established. This was particularly evident when they were asked which competitors were most likely to adopt something like the new type of business idea. Indeed, it was then recognized that some were already doing it! This further strengthened the motivation.

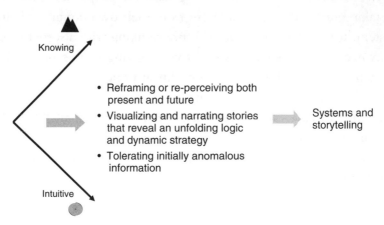

Figure 11.7   The knowing/intuitive resolution

This was now a somewhat unnerving situation for the group because they had mentally abandoned their current strategy as unsustainable, and yet had only speculated as to what the alternatives might be. Here they were most in danger from the intolerance of ambiguity trap. However, this was also a point where premature closure to get out of the tension could have shut down the process. To counteract this, a dilemma framework (Hampden–Turner, 1990) was introduced. This looked at the contrast, even incompatibility, of the first versus the third horizon and formulated them as dilemma pairs that needed resolving in the second horizon. This 'both/and' inquiry set up a strong field for creative thinking, and some initial dilemma resolution ideas began to hint at possible new strategies.

Up to this point the earlier introduction of the three global scenarios had been left hanging in the background. They were already bearing some fruit in that members were reporting current information that indicated 'pockets of the future in the present' that had previously been unnoticed. Before focusing on the development of new strategy, however, it was important to revisit the well-researched global scenarios and focus them into the transaction zone (see Figure 11.8) between the wider environment and their organization.

This began to deal with the reactive/proactive dilemma, which is the area where the scenarios shifted from the domain of 'outside our influence' to 'where we might make an impact'. The current business lines were primarily product-oriented and it was becoming clear that in the third horizon the business model would need to focus much more on the multi-product market. So four distinct market areas were designated and the team was tasked to create focused scenarios in those areas consistent with the global scenarios. The process researching the transaction zone revealed the scenarios in strong relief. By the end of this exercise they had become effectively internalized and the relevance to the business unit was incontestable. This meant that the potential for effective scenario

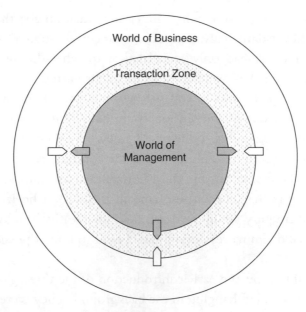

Figure 11.8 The transaction zone

impact on strategy development had been created. The group now had constructed a shared 'memory of the future' (Ingvar, 1985). But as yet there was no clearly formulated strategy for the scenarios to challenge.

Dilemma: Reactive/Proactive

The next step was to create a sketch strategy, much as an architect creates a sketch of a new building. This stepped firmly into the heart of the 'planned versus emergent' dilemma. They had firm operational plans for several years ahead with committed deliverables and yet they had, at the same time, to explore a completely different business model and a strategy to reach it. The framework used here was the strategy map (Horn, 2000). The team gathered round a long and large sheet of paper the length of a boardroom table. One end was designated the present, and the other, around three years ahead: the future. The idea was that the big changes in business model could not be conceived as discontinuous since the value generation by the current business must be sustained as long as the bubble lasted. So the strategy had to reflect the patient but urgent sowing of the seeds of strategic change. The framework here was dynamic strategy in which present and future business models have to be run in parallel and a timed transition managed. The table map was then populated with ideas for action on both business models working forwards and backwards from the future. The impression at the end of this stage was a promising but somewhat incoherent bunch of ideas which didn't seem to entirely hang together (Figure 11.9).

The next step was the introduction of strategy as storytelling. This is applying some of the same considerations that Nordfors (Chapter 8) discusses in regard to the creation of scenarios. Strategies too can be presented as stories of 'how we won', told before the battle. The team leader was challenged to place himself three years ahead and, looking back, tell the story of how the strategic transformation was now clear and well on track. As he put it, this was an act of will as well as creative synthesis. The result was a shift of energy and realization as the team saw, emerging from their ideas, a pattern of strategy that became convincing and coherent.

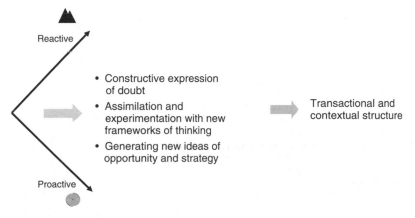

Figure 11.9   The reactive/proactive resolution

Of course, there were many rough edges, consistent with the fact that strategy work at this point is treated as a design process rather than an analytical one. The rich pictures that people had built up over the preceding stages now became a solid and arguable base for the new thinking.

Dilemma: Planned/Emergent

The strategy map was now further refined and some gaps filled in. Major threads of market position, business model and support infrastructure were clarified and these now became the strategy input for interaction with the scenarios to help to generate options (Ramirez and van der Heijden, Chapter 4). This was carried out in the three threads in each of the three focused scenarios. The thinking task was defined in three layers – testing, developing and innovating.

At the end of the process the team realized that they now had a shared strategy in a common language they had developed together; they had integrated sustaining business-as-usual with transformational activities in readiness for a changed competitive environment;

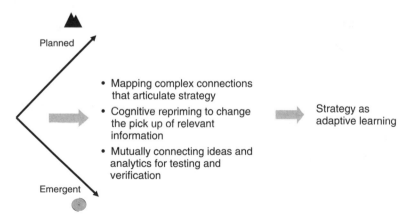

Figure 11.10 The planned/emergent resolutions

they had rehearsed the major challenges likely to be thrown at them by top management; and they had created the platform for a further six months of strategic analysis to ground the ideas in current and anticipated realities. They now had integrated the planned and the emergent (Figure 11.10).

THE EMERGENCE OF STRATEGIC CONVERSATION

Each workshop built on the new steps that had been made in the previous one. By the fifth workshop the group were standing around a huge wall-sized strategy map and engaging in animated conversations about pros, cons and possibilities. This is in marked contrast to the first workshop where there were presentations with questions, and the conversation was largely directed towards the facilitator, with people remaining glued to their chairs. However, it is important to recognize that the intervals between workshops were also very important.

After each workshop, tasks to continue consideration of aspects of strategy development were allocated by the Division Head. These deliberately involved collaboration in pairs or small groups cutting across the business lines. Workshops took place in different locations to enable people to become more acquainted with each other socially (the operations spanned South East Asia, Europe and North America). In the middle of the process people expressed difficulty in handling the cognitive challenges, especially rapidly switching from operational to strategic mindset in the midst of operations. This was demanded since work between workshops had to be slipped in wherever and whenever it could be. As things progressed, the Division Head noted how the quality of the discussion improved even in operational management meetings and, towards the end, how the team increasingly placed operational decision discussions in a strategic context. The members of the group were also seen to be exchanging intelligence about the business environment in a more comprehensive way and keeping each other informed in the context of the scenarios they had worked with. Above all, they recognized that they owned the new strategy and they could go on improving it. It was ingrained in their minds deeper than any plan.

They had all gained some experience of cognitive skills and were beginning to get the habit of consciously switching from operational to strategic mode and back again without tripping over themselves. In reviewing their original 'map of doubts' they found they had addressed them all, and noted their change in confidence. However, they also recognized that they were now in a never-ending process of strategic improvement: this was just the beginning. In a rapidly changing world they must engage the rest of the organization in ongoing strategic conversation! Their next step could include stepping into larger group exercises of the type described by Curry (Chapter 13).

IS SCENARIO PRACTICE METHOD OR MAGIC?

At the end of this chapter I would like to reflect on the never-ending story that is strategic conversation. There is a continuing debate on the relative merits of 'light' approaches and 'heavy' approaches. Schwartz (page 17) makes the point that if you can start a process from where people are, then there is a chance that they will see better what a more thorough process might give. On the other hand, Collyns (page 20) reflects on the importance for Shell in the early days working with Pierre Wack of exploratory breadth and depth. He comments, 'It's closer to magic than technique.' My own experience, leading over 50 scenario projects in the last 20 years since my initial 'apprenticeship' in the 1980s (with Kees Van der Heijden, Ged Davis and Arie de Geus), is that we need both light and heavy approaches. In fact, for me some of the magic is in having both.

From the perspective of cognitive skills, the 'light' approach begins with graceful entry. We have to delineate the arena of uncertainty with which the decision makers are willing to work openly, and explore from there. The heavy approach, however, involves being able to sit in the 'mess' for a lengthy period and accept nothing less than a cognitive repriming that gives rise to a fundamentally reframed world view. However, this is not a simple linear spectrum. As the mental traps highlight (refer to Bradfield, Chapter 10, for the many more that could be considered), progress is a step function from a base where the psychology of denial, of propaganda, of vested interests and power through commanding a dominant world view all tend to keep scenario thinking well contained within politically correct boxes. Perhaps here is the most challenging paradox of the scenario method: the very method that has been developed to move us out of limited thinking is itself prone to being captured within the thinking that needs to be changed.

There are lessons from the field of creative thinking that can offer food for reflection here. A saying by Pasteur has become a favourite among scenario planners: 'creativity favours the prepared mind'. Without technique, discipline and codification of strategy work, including scenarios, there is too much likelihood of going off down rabbit holes and losing the big picture. However, a saying attributed to Lord Byron is also worth considering: 'In order to be creative it is necessary to have read very little and thought very much.' Perhaps this describes the difference between the PhD and the entrepreneur. Without adventurous imagination we will never envision the future that is strategically game changing. In this sense the less mainstream aspects of Pierre Wack's innovations may be much more critical than has been recognized. I have no doubt my capacity to enter into this field was due to several years of intense research study with J.G. Bennett, a remarkable polymath who was a pupil of Gurdjieff, one of Wack's teachers. Gary Chicoine also developed my understanding of such factors as induction, graceful entry and deconstructing the future, drawing on his own vast explorations of western and non-western psychology.

Appreciating the future is an integration of method, technique and discipline with creative exploration, intuition and insight. Rather than being antagonistic – as they are perceived to be in everyday culture – in strategic conversation they are woven together. The quest of strategy work is to discover and create a new integrity. Its value is shown by its results, which rely on all three phases of judgement identified by Vickers, having been carried through. We are inspired by Pierre Wack's pursuit of depth and his patience in stimulating the insight of others, originating from his ability to live in the world of economic business detail and simultaneously meditate in the regions of the unknown. This is what scenario practitioners strive to sustain in their various ways of supporting and facilitating strategy work.

BUILDING A COMPREHENSIVE STRATEGIC FUTURE MANAGEMENT SYSTEM: A FUTURE MAP APPROACH

Don Heathfield

The purpose of preparing for the future is to preserve and enhance the future value of an enterprise by making the right strategic decisions. Executives everywhere are under pressure to make their companies more reactive, competitive and resilient.

The success of organizations depends on their ability to anticipate critical changes in their environment and to make people accept changes in strategy. 'If you are slow [and] unable to correctly predict the next force that's coming towards you or the force that would carry you, then you will be overwhelmed', says Lee Kuan

Scenarios for Success: Turning Insights into Action   Edited by Bill Sharpe and Kees Van der Heijden
© 2007 John Wiley & Sons, Ltd

Yew, who spearheaded Singapore's growth. According to him, for organizations to be successful in the future they must develop 'a very sensitive antenna and a good radar: an intense concentration on what will make them relevant to the outside world' (Lee Kuan Yew, 2006).

The government of Singapore is one of the organizations that, over years, has demonstrated the ability to foresee and take advantage of fundamental changes in the world. Its success is due to a large degree to the future preparedness systems – the 'antennas and radars' – that Singapore has developed. It is telling that the city-state's latest strategic initiative that focuses on keeping it 'relevant to the world' – 'World Singapore' – is coordinated by the Strategic Policy Office, the branch of the government that is also responsible for scenario planning.

From years of experience in organizational learning I have come to appreciate the role of tools and processes in driving the behaviour of people in an enterprise. The defining impact of leaders on organizations is most strongly felt through their corporate culture and systems. In the case of Singapore, the culture of continuous learning built under Lee Kuan Yew's leadership combines a long-term strategic vision with frequent and honest reassessment of rules and practices.

To improve the capacity of enterprises to deal with the future, we need to understand how strategic decisions are made, what tools enterprises use and how people come together to create systems and processes by which organizations get things done. We need to make sure that scenarios, along with other techniques, work effectively as a part of a comprehensive system that is sustainable over time.

But how good are the 'antennas and radars' of enterprises? How satisfied are corporate leaders with current systems of 'future management'? While some organizations such as Shell developed sophisticated and effective future preparedness systems, the Academy of Competitive Intelligence survey shows that the majority of businesses do not have a systematic process for dealing with risks to their strategies (Gilad, 2004, p. 56). It is clear that strategic 'future management' is yet to take its rightful place among the established organizational management processes.

The responsibility for future preparedness processes in a company lies with people directing strategy, foresight and intelligence. All three groups face a number of challenges in achieving the desired impact of future preparedness activities on strategic decision making, the most commonly reported among them being lack of commitment by senior management.

Why are corporate leaders not engaged enough in what Kees Van der Heijden calls a 'strategic conversation' about the future? How can one imagine the main beneficiaries of that strategic conversation not being committed enough to driving it throughout their organizations? What prevents decision makers from being fully and permanently engaged? It would be too easy to blame this lack of permanent commitment on short-sightedness or overconfidence. Could it be that the current future-related practices are not sufficiently connected to the management systems and tools that executives use the most?

BARRIERS TO STRATEGIC CONVERSATION

In our view, the problems in engaging organizations in a strategic conversation arise from a number of disconnects and misalignments between various future-related activities in a company, as well as between those future-related activities and the strategic decision-making processes. The internal complexity of global enterprises does not facilitate fast and coherent responses to strategic challenges. Decision makers need to reconcile multiple, frequently conflicting perspectives and priorities. They have to consider proposals derived from organizational processes that are based on different methodologies and information. Personal agendas, experiences and value judgements play an important role, while distance, cultural backgrounds and procedural differences create potential for 'blind spots'.

Insufficient executive focus on strategic future issues often reflects the disconnection between strategy development and resource allocation processes, and, broadly, the inability of many traditional management systems to link long- and short-term perspectives (Kaplan and Norton, 1996). For managers focused on delivering short-term financial results, the viability of a long-term strategy is irrelevant without the ability to manage its implementation in the immediate period. Market valuation and compensation systems encourage focus on the next quarter rather than on a strategic future.

Another disconnection is the result of divergence in priorities between the departments dealing with corporate strategy and planning, which usually are in charge of leading strategic thought, and business units responsible for implementation. For many managers at the operational level, the direction of the whole enterprise is a secondary concern. Their primary preoccupation is how to arrive at the next milestone on time and on budget. Furthermore, corporate and business unit managers are rarely located in the same building, which complicates their exchanges.

Among top managers there is an implicit judgement about what constitutes 'core' activities, essential for delivering results, and what can be defined as supporting activities. More often than not, the people running core activities (finance, operations, sales) would be part of an 'inner circle,' while those responsible for non-core departments have less influence on key decisions. Sales figures, operational results and financial data are watched daily, while other areas receive only periodic attention from corporate leaders. In many companies foresight and scenario work is done by 'supporting' departments. Unless top executives can see immediate connections between current and upcoming issues, the information coming from those departments does not receive their full attention.

Geographical distance between various locations in a global enterprise does not allow the participants in a strategic conversation to spend sufficient time together. With the growing globalization of enterprises, the ability to make well-founded decisions depends on the capacity of an enterprise to mobilize distributed knowledge and build consensus across its various parts. Communication tools cannot yet compensate for face-to-face interaction when real debates and rich exchanges of ideas take place. The power to shape organizational strategy has always been in the hands of informal networks rather than formal bodies. The geographical disconnect of like-minded individuals leads to a situation in which there are only a few occasions when they can come together as a group to form and express their vision. Enterprises need to create a virtual space where all people can have a structured, fact-supported, strategic dialogue.

Developing a long-term strategy is not the only future-oriented process in a company. People working in the domain of corporate finance, market intelligence, research and development are naturally focused on the future. They plan product roadmaps, create financial forecasts and predict competitors' moves. Some of this work, such as budgeting, focuses on the short- and medium-term future, while research usually implies a long-term strategic commitment.

Unless we develop the tools that unite all people dealing with the future, whether they are focusing on the short or long term, belong to the corporate or business units, manage 'core' or supporting departments, work at the headquarters or at remote locations, we will not achieve a true and continuous strategic conversation.

CURRENT FUTURE-RELATED PROCESSES AND TOOLS

But how well can currently used future-related tools accomplish this mission? How is the conversation about the future structured and supported? What are the strengths and weaknesses of the future-related tools and how well do they work with other management systems?

From a strategic competitive perspective, it may be more important whether an organization has the ability to continuously improve its preparedness for the future than how well it is prepared today. To achieve Chris Argyris' 'double-loop learning', we need mechanisms that make future knowledge providers and future knowledge consumers question their assumptions and strategies (Argyris, 1991).

While specific approaches and traditions differ from enterprise to enterprise, scenario development, usually integrating many other methodologies at its various stages, plays a critical role in the majority of future exploration efforts.

However, as Van der Heijden points out, despite its long acceptance as an effective method, scenario development requires a lot of persistence (Van der Heijden, 2005). Only a handful of companies have managed to make scenario thinking an effective, organization-wide process.

'Things usually start very well during scenario workshops', remarks a manager responsible for enterprise-wide scenario projects at a large American regional utility. 'We get great insights, great discussions. However, once workshops are finished, there is very little follow-up, very little tracking beyond a few newspaper clippings. It is impossible to keep people focused.'

Evidence from a number of companies in both the United States and Europe suggests that many scenario development projects are not followed by consistent efforts to monitor the indicators of change, and fail to engage top managers beyond initial workshops. Instead, the attention of executives quickly switches back to what they consider to be urgent operational concerns.

'I would not call our planning process strategic', smiles a top manager of a global communication company. 'I am not sure we are always looking at things that might be important in the future.

Do not get me wrong – of course we are working with scenario consultants. We do long-term visioning almost every year. But the culture here is very tactical. Our market is moving very fast. When a decision is made, it is not the scenarios that drive it.'

This remark is rather typical. It does not mean that executives do not want to see the 'big picture' and do not care about strategic 'blind spots'. However, to stay on top of the executives' agenda, the future-related activities must, along with raising awareness about long-term alternatives, yield immediate benefits for operational decisions. While many foresight and scenario projects pursue the exploration of long-term strategic alternatives, the majority of corporate decisions focus on a much shorter time-horizon – from a few months to three to five years. As a result, foresight projects catch decision-makers' attention too infrequently to create a permanent working engagement.

Scenario thinking gives organizations the tool for anticipation. However, scenario work is not really complete until it connects future alternatives to current reality. Quite often this part of a scenario process is either neglected or not done thoroughly enough to deliver the value it promises. Tracking changes in the business environment from one milestone to the next is a long, laborious process that requires daily commitment by many already excessively busy people and yields few immediate advantages. Corporate scenario planners, just as scenario consultants, often see themselves as artists for whom tracking is a low return work with very few available tools to make it easier.

Tracking is the part of scenario development that has the highest potential for mobilizing people across an enterprise in a continuous effort, and is the most appealing to managers concerned with short- to medium-term developments. It is unfortunate that it often is the weakest element in the whole scenario process.

Without the tracking follow-up, using scenario workshops may be compared with driving on a dark road with lights that we switch on only every few minutes. Switching the lights on from time to time may be enough to understand where we are on the road at a given moment. However, even on a straight road, driving with lights that are not permanently on makes for dangerous driving. To navigate through a rapidly changing competitive landscape we need to have organizational lights on at all times.

If the purpose of the scenario process in a company is to raise the awareness of decision makers about future alternatives, then current scenario practices generally achieve the objective. However, if we need to create a true strategic conversation we need to make the scenario process permanent.

To do so, a set of complementary, facilitating tools is needed. Tracking can only be effective if the collected information can easily and immediately find its place in the big picture of the future environment, and if this big picture can be shared, debated, and contributed to by many actors across the organization. Ideally, the shared picture of the future would be the one that top decision makers could see daily. It should be as easily available to them as the morning newspaper.

One of the main problems with making future-related work visible and useful to decision makers is that 'the methodological bridge to established business processes seems to be missing' (Neef and Daheim, 2005). Future management tools need to complement and reinforce existing systems for building and communicating corporate strategy, driving business performance and measuring implementation results. They must enable a continuous process of 'future preparedness' that links strategy, intelligence and learning.

CONNECTING TO 'CORE' PROCESSES: THE STRATEGY MAP

What are the tools that corporations use to communicate strategy and measure performance? During the last 10 years many companies have moved from tracking primarily financial outcomes to the establishment of 'the balanced scorecards' that assess the performance of organizations in a more comprehensive way, including customer focus, internal process efficiency, and learning and growth. More recently a number of businesses started building 'strategy maps' that create 'a common visual framework that embeds the items on the balanced scorecard into a cause-and-effect chain', and communicate objectives and strategies in a 'cohesive, integrated and systematic way' (Kaplan and Norton, 2000). The purpose of a strategy map is to crystallize the strategic intent of the company to ensure seamless implementation.

A strategy map is a response to the same problem that inhibits strategic conversation – the lack of alignment between various priorities, departments and processes in an enterprise. A strategy map is a reflection of a company's vision for the future. As it implies future actions, its creators are directly concerned with the environment in which those actions will take place. A change in the company's external or internal environment triggers a revision of strategy. A change on a corporate strategy map makes the new thinking 'official'.

Rethinking strategy and rebuilding strategy maps is an important exercise that usually involves key corporate executives. Tied to the budgeting cycle, this exercise is done once or twice a year, and in many cases even less frequently. Thus the strategy map often does not reflect the most recent changes in the business and its competitive environment. To manage the fast pace of change better, businesses are introducing continuous strategic decision processes, moving from a budget-driven strategy cycle towards issue-driven decision making (Mankins and Steele, 2006). The problem is that a strategy map is not dynamic, and, valuable as it is, cannot adequately support accelerated, continuous decision processes. Neither can it deal with changes in the environment in which strategy is implemented.

There is a definite need to make scorecards and strategy maps dynamic to support the new ways of making decisions. A dynamic scorecard or dynamic strategy map should be able to track the enterprise's strategy in relation to future challenges, and to compare the desirable results with those currently achieved.

COMMON FRAMEWORK FOR FUTURE SPACE

Considering these requirements, what would constitute the foundation of a comprehensive future management system that is linked to an enterprise's core processes, holds executive attention, and drives 'strategic conversation' across the company? Key to connecting all these components is a shared picture of the future.

But how can we assemble that shared picture from a multitude of diverse facts and opinions? How can we present the future in a way that facilitates decision making? How can we integrate different types of information coming from a variety of sources?

To connect scenarios, strategy and measurements we must define their common future space. We have to establish the rules for mapping the future environment, both in terms of the common denominator of the future-related information and of the structure of that space.

Common denominator of the future environment: the anticipated event

All scenarios, trigger points, objectives, decisions and milestones are expressions of the events, or combinations of events, that we anticipate in the future. Following the practice of social scientists, we define an anticipated event as *who will do what to whom/with whom, when and why.*

Using an anticipated event as the 'building block', we can recreate future business environments, both long term and short term. A coming event is something that decision makers can understand and prepare for. A response to concrete future events requires specific actions. An event implies a decision.

We believe that we need to put in front of decision makers the field of anticipated events with which the organization will have to deal in the future. This future 'event field' is the product of our collective anticipation; it is the picture that appears on our collective 'future radar screen'. A field of anticipated events can be built for any domain or entity, whether an enterprise or a country. Our goal is to create the organization's event field and then continuously question and clarify this picture using all means available.

By putting in front of managers a field of anticipated events, we are shifting the focus of discussions, as Arie de Geus proposed, from 'whether something will happen' to 'what would we do, if it happened' (de Geus, 1999). We force decision makers to 'live in the future', to go back and forth in time, to 'try on' various alternative futures, thus helping executives to make an important step from 'future awareness' to 'future appropriation'.

This process is consistent with the observations about how people unconsciously prepare for the future made by the Swedish neurobiologist David Ingvar and described in his article 'The Memory of the Future' published in 1985. According to Ingvar, a part of the human brain 'is constantly occupied with making up action plans and programs for the future', making 'alternative time paths into the future', and 'storing these alternative time paths'. This 'memory of the future' helps us to establish a 'correspondence between incoming information and one of the stored alternative time paths', perceiving its 'meaning'. It also allows us to filter out irrelevant information that has no meaning for any of the 'options for the future which we worked out' (de Geus, 1999).

Structure of the event field

Both scenarios and scorecards deal with the evolution of key driving factors of the future environment: some fairly predetermined, some highly uncertain. For a particular enterprise some of these driving factors, such as those representing its economic environment, may be generic, while others could be very specific.

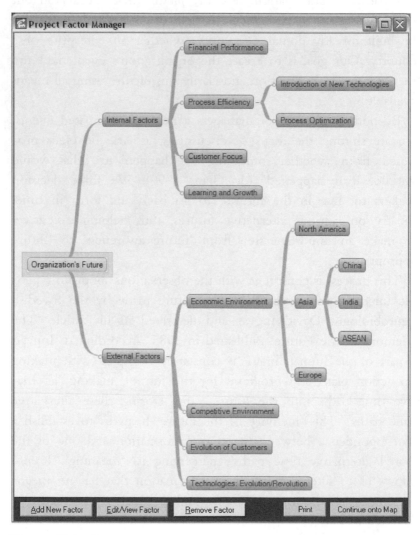

Figure 12.1 Factor map

To create a structured future space of a company we need to build a framework of factors that influence the organization's future – a 'factor map'. This factor map displays the drivers of the external environment and the internal situation of an enterprise. Each factor can be split into several levels of subfactors, down to very specific forces and actors (Figure 12.1).

Using the set of the driving factors and time as the two dimensions of the future space, we create a plane on which each event can be placed on a timeline and in the columns that represent the factors to which it relates (Figure 12.2).

The future event field starts from tomorrow and stretches as far into the future as we can reasonably project. An event field helps to create and visualize multiple tracks into the future. Various combinations of events that can be extracted from it can be tracked in the same way as scenarios.

An event field integrates into the two-dimensional 'time-factors' framework information from various sources: scenario groups, internal early warning networks, external expert communities, newswire reports, trend forecasts or automatic extraction tools.

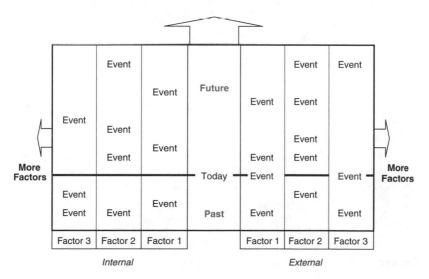

Figure 12.2   Event field

It creates a space into which the information can be continuously fed. While working with a multitude of constantly evolving events related to a large number of factors may seem exceedingly challenging, special software helps to overcome this problem (Figure 12.3).

Once the future event field for the organization has been created, we can extract from it a number of pictures of the future. These pictures, which we can call 'future maps', are the snapshots of the event field that represent the future as seen through the lens of different perspectives. Each future map can convey a particular scenario, a vision of a particular group of experts, an extract from a specific type of sources, or a view with a specific time horizon.

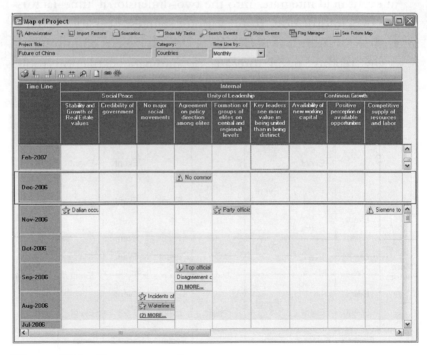

Figure 12.3 Future map software screen

BUILDING A FUTURE MAP FOR AN ORGANIZATION

The future map methodology establishes the step-by-step process of constructing the event field for an enterprise and continuously re-examining this picture of the future to factor in the latest knowledge. The development of a future map for an organization can start either from a focus on its expected future environment (strategy process) or from a focus on its desirable future (measurement process) (Figure 12.4).

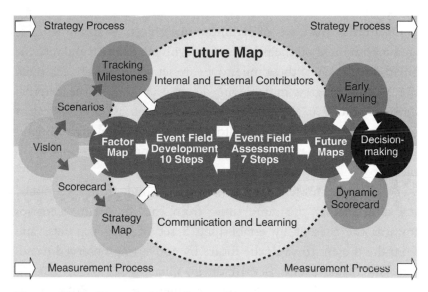

Figure 12.4   Future map deployment process

Scenario technique plays an essential role in the construction of a future map. The analysis of uncertainties and 'predetermined' elements that are at the heart of scenario thinking produces multiple futures. Each alternative future is a set of events which, taken together, would constitute a scenario narrative. However, having placed these sets in an event field, we can also imagine such combinations of those events that none of the original scenarios envisioned. In the spirit of scenarios, we can put on a map hypothetical events of high significance – the 'wild cards'. We can also establish visual connections between some events, such as scenario trigger points and their implications that span across time and factors.

The same analysis of environmental forces at play contributes to the identification of measurable driving factors that define the structure of the event field. For the purpose of tracking, on an event field each 'uncertain' factor can be split into several columns that represent various alternatives in its development.

On a future map, sets of organizational objectives and milestones are superimposed on the picture of an evolving external and internal environment. Once these milestones are set, an enterprise can track the internal progress in achieving its goals as well as the external developments that affect its performance, such as early indicators of emerging trends in its regulatory and competitive environment. Events that represent the future of its customers also appear on the map.

To ensure consistency, an event field is built from two opposite directions at the same time: from the long-term scenarios towards the present by establishing a set of trigger points, and from the present towards the future by converting observed trends into anticipated events (see Bradfield, Chapter 10, page 270). As the forecasts made using different independent methodologies are translated into anticipated events, we can cross-check and refine our assumptions and expectations. By having the capacity to show a variety of visions of the future side-by-side, a future map helps to evaluate scenarios, reconcile conflicting information, understand alternative perspectives, identify discontinuities and examine gaps in knowledge.

Inasmuch as scenarios are the tools for engaging decision makers, a future map is the tool for keeping their continuous attention. It bridges the gap between short-term trend extrapolations and long-term scenarios, helping decision makers to deal with the time period within which the majority of decisions need to deliver results – from a few months to a few years.

BENEFITS OF THE FUTURE MAP APPROACH

Why would companies use future maps? What benefits do future maps bring to existing corporate systems? One of the biggest problems with the introduction of new tools is the 'tool overload' that managers face. Tools proliferate in enterprises. Corporate departments, divisions and country organizations create systems that compete for the time of managers. Each tool has its reason, its followers and its own political support. This 'tool fatigue' leads to rejection of new tools, and the only way to win managers' attention is to 'upgrade' a tool that is already widely accepted.

During the last decade corporations invested a lot of resources in building internal buy-in for their strategies. They developed effective communication channels around strategy deployment and performance measurement. Most of the Fortune 500 companies have rolled out the balanced scorecard processes. We believe that companies can use future maps to 'upgrade' those systems to support the strategic conversation. As an extension of a familiar strategy map, the introduction of the future map is less likely to create objections.

A future map can actually reduce the number of tools that managers need to deal with by integrating strategy, measurements and business intelligence on the same inter-enterprise communication platform. Nor is there a need to create multiple future maps for each country or department, because each unit can work with different parts of a common map.

The most important benefit of a future map is its capacity to establish a connection between strategy development and strategy implementation. The information put on a future map by competitive intelligence groups, business units, departments or external consultants is immediately available to top decision makers. In return, the 'front line' business units see how their information contributes to corporate decisions and how their progress fits into the company's overall strategy.

As market and competitor intelligence is critical for implementation, such information is always in demand if offered in a convenient, accessible form, while marketing and competitive intelligence professionals crave tools that can bring the fruits of their work to a wider management audience. Executives will increasingly rely on future maps to incorporate business intelligence into their short- to medium-term decisions. Once familiar with the tool, they will start using it to track strategic alternatives.

The map's potential as a sharing tool, an integration tool, a learning tool, a strategy development tool, and a progress-tracking tool is greatest when it is used as an open system that leverages collaboration from all contributors. The future map approach delivers best results when supported by appropriate visualization and collaboration software. Such software helps to create a networked expert community around the organization and thus greatly expands the organization's capacity to foresee and meet its future challenges.

FUTURE MAP AS THE FOUNDATION OF A STRATEGIC FUTURE MANAGEMENT SYSTEM

A future map creates a shared, holistic picture of the future environment, enabling real-time global collaboration with a highly visual interface that quickly conveys both pure data and strategic analyses.

A map can become a foundation of a common knowledge management system that integrates scenario thinking, tracking of performance, early warning, global communication and continuous learning (Figure 12.5).

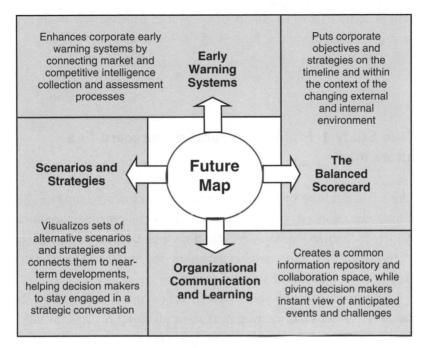

Figure 12.5   Future management system

A future map bridges the methodological gap between future-related techniques and core management tools, linking future management to strategy and measurement processes. It allows enterprises to take a decisive step from relying on only the 'components of systematic processes' (Gilad, 2004), to building comprehensive, organization-wide future management systems.

IMPLEMENTING THE FUTURE MAP APPROACH: CASE STUDIES

The following two short case studies demonstrate how a future map methodology can be used in organizations. The first case describes an approach adopted by a global consumer electronics company, while the second deals with its application in research practices at a

School of International Affairs of a major US university. Both case descriptions focus on the process of deployment.

Case Study 1: From the balanced scorecard to a future map

The US subsidiary of a global consumer electronics company has a long tradition of using scorecards for managing performance. Widely recognized for its successful implementation of the balanced scorecard, it has also used scenarios in its strategy development process for a number of years.

The introduction of the balanced scorecard was prompted by the need to focus the existing mid-term planning process on high-level strategy, and to close strategic knowledge gaps resulting from management rotation. Its pilot introduction started first in a few relatively small units. After positive results, more and more units joined and currently the majority of the company is involved in the scorecard effort.

A corporate strategy map, developed by the strategic planning department, was introduced specifically to address a wider audience beyond senior management, and to align its subsidiaries with the parent company's plans and targets (Johnson, 2005).

The company's senior management has been stressing the need to mobilize employee support to develop a culture of self-reformation and self-improvement. Considering the alignment of employee behaviour with the strategy of the company to be one of their key priorities, corporate leaders survey and track employee attitudes that affect productivity, satisfaction and turnover rates.

The company wants to manage the evolution of the organization's 'social system' in the same manner in which it manages its 'technical systems'. The implementation of a future map establishes a baseline for the internal situation and allows tracking of its evolution in view of market and competitive environments. A common 'big picture' of future challenges will help the enterprise to adapt to its changing environment and to build the 'buy-in' for the strategy across its business units.

As a senior executive responsible for corporate strategic planning remarked:

> We really did not have a process for looking at how the changes in our business environment affect the validity and effectiveness of the balanced scorecard. Previously, if the top management believed it was valid, we continued using the scorecard as before. Using a future map would make our scorecard dynamic. There is less fear to be wrong with our strategy if we have a process of reviewing and adjusting the scorecard.

Initiated by the planning department as a part of the yearly strategy process, the work first involved a small corporate strategy group that, together with representatives of business units, outlined various scenarios of the business environment and their implications for the company's strategy. Together with scenarios, the future map incorporates the information related to competitor intelligence and technology developments.

Bringing a new tool into an established corporate culture is always a delicate endeavour. Securing stakeholder support takes time and requires ongoing negotiation, before the map gains wider buy-in and credibility. The company plans to extend gradually the number of participants to include business unit managers, whose support is considered essential. They will be presented with a future map during regular executive meetings as a part of the process of 'getting everyone on the scorecard'. We estimate that full deployment of a future map will take up to two years.

By linking its successful balanced scorecard process with its scenario process via a future map, the company is moving towards the development of a comprehensive strategic management system that connects planning for the future with operational management. Its introduction can be seen as another step in building a participative decision culture in the enterprise. A map serves as the tool for channelling the enterprise's 'bottom-up' feedback on corporate strategies while bringing the scenarios (and thus uncertainty management perspective) into the strategy communication process.

Case Study 2: From scenarios to a future map

The second case study involves a group of graduate students at the Elliott School of International Affairs at George Washington University working under the guidance of Leon Fuerth, a research professor and former National Security Advisor to Vice President Gore. The concept of 'Forward Engagement' put forward by Professor Fuerth focuses on identifying major future contingencies that are likely to affect the long-term future of the United States. Those contingencies, from the ageing of the US population to catastrophic terrorist acts, have important implications across multiple domains, from environment and energy to international relations. Dealing with those contingencies will require a proactive forward engagement by the US government. In order to make legislators aware of the implications of these major societal developments and to build the momentum for appropriate decisions among the public, a 'big picture' of future challenges must be constructed first.

The factor map of the project follows the STEEP (Societal, Technological, Economic, Environmental, Political) framework with the key factors broken into several levels down to specific forces in play. A special website is set up for the group through which the students can access the software and work in a wiki-like virtual environment, allowing several people to build a future map simultaneously.

First, the students outlined a number of scenarios with several major anticipated events that represent current trends in the development of the driving factors, and a number of 'wild cards' with extreme or catastrophic consequences for the country.

The next step involved the analysis of the implications of the mapped events across economic, environmental, security and other domains, as well as their significance for the future of the United States.

The final goal of the project is to propose an appropriate Component Level Implementation Process (CLIP). It is a process of breaking down a policy which seeks to achieve a long-term objective into a set of legislative proposals. Each milestone, while furthering a longer term agenda, represents a viable stand-alone policy with immediate positive impact. Students put these CLIP milestones on the map and develop ways to track the anticipated impacts of the proposed policies on the management of future contingencies.

The leaders of the project expect that a big picture of the anticipated future of the country would help drive the debate among the concerned public and build a nationwide community in support of policy changes. Future maps help to connect the discussion about the future of a country with the development of a specific legislative agenda.

In our view, the value of the future map approach for the stakeholders of the project is in its capacity to give a concurrent view of the developments about which the public policy community used to think sequentially, and thus help to manage the complexity of the environment. It opens the debate about the implications of policy decisions across factors and the need for inter-agency cooperation. A future map can be seen as a tool for supporting distributed, networked decision-making processes that become an imperative in many public policy domains such as national security.

CONCLUSION

Future preparedness is increasingly important to enterprises; however, only a handful of companies have managed to build effective future management systems. In many instances future-related efforts fail to engage decision makers. To maintain the commitment of senior management to the 'strategic conversation', companies need comprehensive future management systems linked to wider, established core business processes that bring tangible and immediate benefits to a large number of stakeholders across the enterprise.

In order to develop and implement successful strategies, managers rely on systems and processes that help to bring together various perspectives that exist within the enterprise. The complexity of global companies makes comparing and reconciling those perspectives extremely difficult.

To secure the interest of various actors in a 'strategic conversation' we need a shared 'big picture' of the future that not only drives the discussion about strategic alternatives, but also links future-related tools with the company's core goal-setting and measurement systems, and provides real-time information about its external and internal environment. We need an appropriate conceptual framework for building such a picture.

A future map provides this framework. Based on a common denominator – an anticipated event – a future map can track external and internal developments, offer a forum for all contributors, and effectively communicate the picture of the future to executives to drive timely decisions.

CHAPTER 13

ACTING ON THE FUTURE

Andrew Curry

The world everyone sees is not *the* world but *a* world which we bring
forth with others.

Humberto Maturana and Francisco Varela

Some of the best-known quotations in the futures and scenarios
literature are about the need for futures work to influence the
present. One thinks of Gaston Berger's remark that 'looking at
the future should disturb the present', and of Peter Schwartz's
observation that 'The test of good scenarios is not getting the
future right... The real test of a good scenario is: Did I make better
choices as a result of having looked at and understood both my
own environment better and the consequences of my actions?'

The intention of this chapter is to understand better how this
happens in human activity systems. It will argue that scenario processes enable participants both to structure their understanding of
their external environment, and allow them to test their understanding against shared culture and values, which can be thought of

Scenarios for Success: Turning Insights into Action   Edited by Bill Sharpe and Kees Van der Heijden
© 2007 John Wiley & Sons, Ltd

as the 'internal' environment. Language is central to this process, for language creates new knowledge and new meaning. Scenarios workshops, if well run, create a safe forum in which such knowledge and meaning can be generated and tested. Increasingly the participants in such conversations come from different communities of practice, or different disciplines, or have competing political or organizational views of the future. The role of the scenario set is to create 'boundary objects' that permit such groups first to engage with each other, and then, through shared stories, find sufficient common meaning to serve as a frame for action. This enables them, in Geoffrey Vickers's phrase, to make instrumental judgements.

The chapter will draw on my experience (and those of colleagues at Henley Centre HeadlightVision [HCHLV]) of working with clients on scenarios and futures projects. This includes work in both the public and private sector mostly in the UK, and with both single organizations and multi-stakeholder groups. Embedded in this will be a view of how our approach, as it has evolved over time, differs from the North American scenario-planning approach discussed elsewhere in this book. I will also argue that the depth of such processes comes from their alignment with what we now know about how groups learn, and how knowledge is created in such environments.

COMPARING SCENARIOS PROCESSES

The classic drivers-based scenarios process was developed by SRI, and later adapted by the Global Business Network. SRI describes a six-stage process (Wilson, 1997). Step 1 is to identify and analyse the organizational issues that provide the 'decision focus': 'which strategic decision (and the issues surrounding it) should provide the focus for the scenarios'. Step 2 specifies the key decision factors; Step 3 is the identification and analysis of the key environmental forces, which are then assessed for importance and uncertainty. From this follows Step 4, in which the scenarios 'logics' are established; Step 5 involves the selection and elaboration of the scenarios; while in Step 6 the scenarios are interpreted for their decision implications.

Global Business Network's eight-stage approach, which is broadly similar, is outlined in Peter Schwarz's book *The Art of the Long View*. Like SRI, GBN's process starts from the identification of a 'focal issue or decision'. GBN identifies as a separate stage the assessment of importance and uncertainty, and adds a final stage in which indicators and signposts of subsequent change are identified.

Although these approaches have the merit of transparency, they have also been the subject of criticism from the 'critical futures school', most explicitly by the Australian futurist Richard Slaughter. He argues that because mainstream approaches to scenario building emphasize the empirical and external, they therefore tend to objectify existing power relationships. 'This means', he writes, 'that scenarios are readily assimilated into existing power structures, with all their inequities and dysfunctions, without anyone being aware of the fact' (Slaughter, 2004). In contrast, critical futures studies

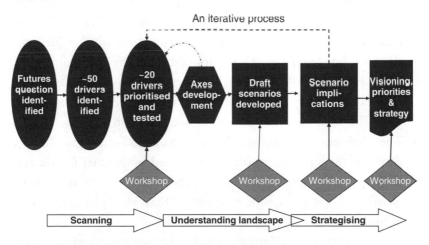

Figure 13.1 Schematic of typical scenarios process
Source: Henley Centre HeadlightVision.

emphasize the importance of 'inner' meanings in understanding the 'outer' world, and focus on 'the renegotiation of meanings'.

In its overall shape (Figure 13.1), the process discussed in this chapter has similarities with the process-based approach of SRI and GBN. It is a drivers-led process which then seeks to identify important and uncertain drivers. These are used to develop axes of uncertainty from which scenarios are constructed. Following this, implications of the scenarios for strategy or policy (in the case of public sector clients) are identified, along with the scope for strategic choice.

But there are also significant differences that give space within the process for greater interpretive reflection. These will be explored more fully later in the chapter, but it is worth summarizing them here:

- The initial scenarios question is not about the 'decision' that is to be made, but instead acts to define the 'system under scrutiny' that will contain the eventual decision. This system – rightly – can be a subject of controversy among stakeholders at the start of the project.
- The analysis of drivers draws not only on 'external' factors that may influence the organization, but also on the 'internal'. This includes drivers that emerge from shifts in individual values and attitudes ('micro' level drivers) and also shifts in community and social behaviour ('meso' level drivers). These have some correspondence with the importance placed by integrative futures analysis on the 'interior' as well as the 'exterior'.
- The tools used to validate the important and uncertain drivers draw on the structural analysis developed by Michel Godet and others of the French prospective school, and therefore link to causal and systems approaches, rather than the 'planning' focus of SRI.
- The uncertainties identified within the scenario logics, which structure the scenarios, are therefore typically fairly complex,

because of the analysis of the drivers, and lead to the development of rich and reasonably complex worlds.

- The workshops, which are spread through the process, are attended not just by decision makers but by people from across the organization or the stakeholder network who are likely to have a broad range of views about the working of the system and the significant drivers within it.

I will argue in this chapter that these differences are more than technical differences about practice. Instead, they represent a clear difference in philosophy about how change occurs in the contemporary organization. They attempt to combine the interpretive aspects, which are underlined by the critical futures school, with the benefits of transparent process offered by the 'North American' practitioners, in such a way that the futures work and outcomes go beyond 'flatland'. I will return to this argument after the case studies.

CASE STUDY 1: SWITCHCO

SwitchCo was a telecoms systems manufacturer with a predominantly European customer base. It had mostly recovered from misreading the internet market during the late-90s 'bubble', but faced significant challenges: liberalization and privatization of national telecoms markets had weakened traditional connections between national telecoms companies and their suppliers, and a low-cost Chinese supplier had changed customer expectations about price and performance. The senior management team was working on a conventional 'bottom-up' strategic review by region and product area. The Marketing Director, with the support of his Chief Executive, decided to conduct a scenarios process in parallel with the strategic review, as well as engage a wider group in thinking about the challenges faced by the company.

The scoping question asked, 'What could the European telecoms network be in 2012?' (then eight years hence). The scenario set that emerged was based on axes (Figure 13.2) that captured, on one hand, the rate of change of rigid markets (from slower to faster) and, on the other, the range of customer demands: complex, high-involvement customers were contrasted with those seeking standardized solutions.

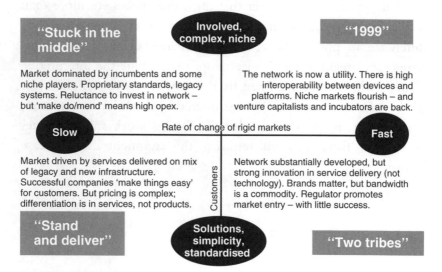

Figure 13.2 'SwitchCo' scenarios
Source: Henley Centre/'SwitchCo'.

As the scenarios were developed, a set of 'dimensions' was also developed, as an analytical tool to add an additional descriptive layer to the scenarios, to help to understand the differences between them at a strategic, marketing and operating level. These included headings such as 'market structure', 'adjacent markets', 'regulation', 'standards', 'sources of innovation', 'role of brand' and 'structure of network'.

Because the working group was internal, there was fairly consistent attendance across the three workshops, at the stage of drivers, scenario building, and implications. Many participants had worked together during their time at the company. By the third workshop, the discussion about the company and its prospects was candid. In all the scenarios there is persistent downward pressure on costs. The national telecoms companies (PTTs) buy less in all scenarios, although they do still buy. There is significant market fragmentation. The company's markets are unstable and unpredictable. Large and small companies seem to fare better than medium-sized vendors such as SwitchCo. New alliances and partnerships emerge in all scenarios, and the market remains tough for SwitchCo in all of the scenarios. But there are still opportunities. Some of its technology is world class, and its problem-solving culture is valued by customers. Even if its partnership skills need developing, it has a brand and skills that will attract partners.

It is conventional, in cases such as this, to report that the futures process generated new energy in the business, the managers focused on those things that could make a difference, and the company was transformed. Sadly, this wasn't the case. An aggressive round of cost-cutting by one of its biggest customers – a feature of several of the scenario narratives – saw it lose some substantial contracts, and it needed to align itself with a partner far more rapidly than it had expected. It appeared that it left its futures work too late.

But even in the organizational crisis that followed the end of the contracts, the futures work proved valuable. The Board, which had not been involved in the scenario development process, was more sceptical about the benefit than the participants. However, the learning from the scenarios was decisive. 'Because of the scenarios, we understood that this wasn't just a blip, but a seismic shift in the industry', one of the participants told me later. 'It was a sign of serious price erosion in the market, and it meant that consolidation among suppliers would follow. So we acted very quickly. And that was valuable because it meant that we were among the first to act, so we had a choice of partners.'

The conventional 'bottom-up' strategy review would not have produced the same understanding.

Box 13.1   Developing axes

Some futurists are sceptical about the value of the 'two-by-two' matrix as a basis for scenario development. They argue that it tends to produce at least one scenario which is 'too good to be true', and one which is clearly to be avoided. Peter Schwartz suggests that two or three scenarios are preferable. In its public policy scenarios, Shell has sometimes presented only two scenarios, although there are three in its latest set (which it describes as 'trilemmas'). However, the matrix has some significant benefits in creating the ability of the organization to act. The scenarios effectively represent the 'corners' of the futures space (where the uncertainties combine in the most extreme fashion), so the classic matrix effectively reveals most of the futures space to participants in a more transparent fashion.

But although the topic of the development of axes is one in which there is much practitioners' lore, it seems to be relatively absent from the literature. It is obvious that rigour is required if they are to be effective in creating scenarios which carry within them the potential for action. Equally obviously, the axes need to be 'orthogonal' (they must represent distinctively different uncertainties which do not collapse onto each other). They also need to create space in the scenario quadrants – in a comprehensive manner – for *all* of the drivers which have been identified as both important and uncertain. This leads to a preference for 'rich' axes, which have some complexity embedded in the uncertainties, and which sometimes require a degree of explanation, rather than simpler ones. But it also seems to help fulfil the third criterion, which is that each of the scenarios needs to include elements that are regarded as both positive and negative, certainly over the life of the scenario narrative. One reason for this is that trends are never inexorable; sooner or later they prompt a reaction.

A useful evaluative technique to test the overall credibility and viability of a set of scenarios, especially for private sector work, is to ask whether it is possible for a company with the right set of capabilities to make money in each one of the scenario quadrants.

The final requirement is that the scenarios that are generated by the axes need to be strategically interesting in addressing the scoping question. There is usually more than one set of axes that fulfils the first three criteria. The final selection is a matter of judgement; art as much as science.

CASE STUDY 2: WALES TOURIST BOARD

The Wales Tourist Board (WTB), as it was then called, was asked in 2003 by the Welsh Assembly to review its strategy to justify continued funding. As part of its strategic review process it commissioned a scenarios project that was designed to engage its stakeholders in the review. Wales is blessed with some strengths in tourism: the mountains of Snowdonia, for example, the beaches of west Wales, UNESCO world heritage sites in the castles of north Wales, and, since regeneration, Cardiff and Cardiff Bay. But it also had weaknesses, including limited airport access, poor north–south transport links, a wet climate, and a legacy of underinvestment in its tourism sector. It attracted a disproportionate share of low value visitors, and its holiday season was concentrated into the high summer. Once they have tried Wales, visitors return, but there were not enough first-time visitors.

The scenarios that were developed are in the public domain downloadable as of July 2007 from http://cycling.visitwales.com/upload/pdf/ Futures_eng.pdf, and for that reason it is necessary only to summarize the main points here before reviewing issues that emerged for WTB from the process. From the start, the project question underlined the strategic focus of the work: 'What do the Wales Tourist Board and its stakeholders need to do to optimize sustainable economic and social benefits to Wales through tourism growth, by the year 2010?' Initial research identified significant issues, including poor visitor profile, underinvestment, patchy quality of provision, lack of capability in online booking, poor gateway infrastructure, and fragmentation across agencies and providers.

However, because tourism is driven by individual and cultural meanings at least as much as by external factors, many of the critical drivers of change proved not to be these structural factors but instead changes in values and attitudes towards tourism and the purpose of holidays. Indeed, following a drivers' analysis workshop, one of the axes identified was about the type of holiday that people would seek: from 'slow' (or immersive) to 'fast' (or multi-activity). The other was about attitudes towards, and relationships with, suppliers (from predominantly independent, or individualized, to more standardized or branded) which effectively encompassed attitudes about personal identity and trust. The scenarios are shown in Figure 13.3. The role and value of such 'micro' and 'meso' level drivers are explored later in the chapter.

This framework proved to be a powerful tool. In a scenarios workshop we developed these worlds with stakeholders, then tested them using Colin Eden's 'Power and Interest' grid, which captures the interests of stakeholders in particular outcomes. Because of the relatively short timeframe (2010 was only seven years away) the scenarios did not represent alternative futures but parallel futures. (This distinction is developed later.) It became quickly clear, as one tested for capability, that the 'Rough Guide' scenario, which was closest to the present offer, was also the one that was best aligned to capability. But on its own, this was not enough to address the

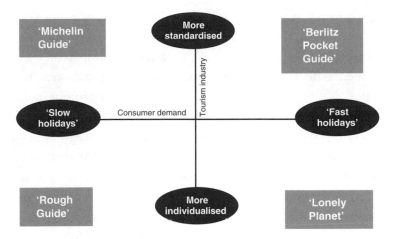

Figure 13.3   Wales Tourist Board scenarios
Source: Henley Centre/Wales Tourist Board.

industry's problems, nor the spatial issues of tourism throughout Wales.

A successful strategy based on 'Rough Guide' needed support from tourism activity captured in the adjacent scenarios, driven by different dynamics. Aspects of 'Michelin Guide', with its highly branded quality, were needed to improve the reputation and image of the industry, and to create an international profile. Celtic Manor, near Newport, which will host the Ryder Cup in 2010, was already an example of such a location. And because this was a spatial strategy, which therefore had to have regard to those areas not blessed with strong tourism resources, parts of the 'Lonely Planet' scenario, with its focus on generating activity, were also essential to success. Events and festivals spread tourism demand away from high-profile 'honey pot areas' such as the Snowdonia, National Park. Both were likely to attract different types of visitors, with different social and cultural values.

However, it also became clear very quickly that the 'Berlitz Pocket Guide' scenario, a world of short breaks, was not viable for Wales. This had had advocates before the scenarios process started, partly because of the rapid growth in the short-break market within Europe. It was hampered by a lack of airports close to the best destinations, but the scenarios process also showed that the investment required to attract new package operators would divert investment and support away from the existing industry. It was therefore both risky, and was likely to have enormous political repercussions.

This may seem to imply that the existing strategy was good enough, but the scenarios process demonstrated that it wasn't. By going through a process that identified common 'dimensions' across the scenarios, we were able to construct a bridge from the narratives represented by the scenarios to the more analytical framework required by strategy development (see Table 13.1). On its own, the 'Rough Guide' strategy would fail to attract international visitors, or enough first-time visitors.

Analysis of the dimensions, again in a workshop setting, identified critical issues that the strategy needed to address. A detailed process that used the scenarios to understand the 'customer journey' in

Table 13.1 Wales Tourist Board dimensions

Dimension	Content
Customers	Who goes to Wales, at what time of year, and for how long?
Offer and operators	What do tourists do in Wales, and what sort of operators deliver it?
Channels and marketing	How do consumers find out about offers, and book holidays?
Brand	What type of branding is deployed?
Skills base	Skills needed, specialists, gaps, and training requirements
Spatial	Which parts of Wales benefit, and which not, and how?
Organisation	Who is collaborating, with whom, and to what end?

Source: Henley Centre/Wales Tourist Board.

finding Wales as a destination produced four big strategic challenges. These were: visibility and awareness of Wales as a destination; the need to be 'distinctive'; the need to improve booking capability; and the need to improve quality. All of these were issues that the Wales Tourist Board could influence.

The strategy process was successful; the Wales Tourist Board won renewed funding from the Welsh Assembly, and tourism numbers and profile have improved since. But one of the most valuable outcomes was almost invisible. The process of engaging stakeholders in full-day workshops around an open agenda for the future of their industry helped to reduce one of the issues identified at the start of the process as a central barrier to change: the fragmentation between tourism-related agencies in Wales.

SCENARIO BUILDING AND APPRECIATIVE JUDGEMENT

As Geoffrey Vickers argues in *The Art of Judgement*, the exercise of appreciative judgement has three components: the making of 'reality judgements' (what is and is not the case); the making of value judgements (what ought or ought not to be the case); and the making of instrumental judgement (the best available ways to reduce the mismatch between what is and what should be). The latter he summarized as 'know how', and the former as 'know what'. Appreciative judgement can be thought of as 'readinesses' that have to be learned. Like all learning, they enable but they also limit; but without such readinesses we would be incapable of responding 'to *anything* in *any* way'. Readinesses are integrated into a system of viewing the world in three ways: they form part of the system by which, first, the individual makes sense of the *observed* world in which he or she lives; second, interprets the *experienced* world; and third, understands the *communicated* world they share with others. Over the course of the rest of the chapter, I will use these three concepts as a framework to explore how scenarios enable us to act on the future.

The observed world

The corporation, wrote Kenichi Ohmae, 'exalts logic and rationality'; and the world of planning, and the planning department, is a world of logic, rationality, numbers and analysis. Planning is a process, certainly, but it is also a metaphor for a centralized view of organizational life and culture, which emerged in the 1950s and 1960s. Its spirit is captured in William H. White's *The Organization Man* (1956), in Igor Ansoff's early work on business strategy, and at a cultural level in films such as Walter Lang's 1957 *Desk Set*, starring Spencer Tracy and Katharine Hepburn. This tradition is best represented now by Michael Porter and McKinsey.

Within this world, the application in the corporate context of what was called 'scenario planning' was born in a moment of contradiction. For even in its genesis, scenario planning was a child whose very existence also pointed to some of the limitations of planning-based models of the organization. In particular, it identified the difficulty faced by the classic planning model under conditions of uncertainty and ambiguity.

Since then, our sense of uncertainty has been heightened by the extension of the concept of complexity into most of the models we use to understand the world. Uncertainty is at the heart of one of the profound conceptual shifts of the last 30 years. No academic discipline has been unaffected by 'the complexity turn', as the sociologist John Urry has called it. The impact of complexity theory, with its roots in post-Newtonian physics, has also reached the popular business literature, through writers such as Richard Pascale in *Surfing the Edge of Chaos* (Pascale *et al.*, 2001) and Margaret Wheatley in *Leadership and the New Science* (Wheatley,

2001). There are competing definitions of complexity, but it can be understood as a process of self-organization that is found in all open systems, leading to the emergence and development of new forms. In this world, uncertainty takes over from determinism, process becomes more important than structure, and outcomes become unpredictable and unexpected, sometimes even random. Cause and effect become interrelated, and uncertainty becomes intrinsic.

As a result, the relationship between organizations and their environments is now understood to be more difficult and more turbulent. We can see the expression of this in technology and logistics, together with cultural effects such as changing individual attitudes to trust and authority. These combine to ensure that increasingly large parts of that environment are no longer 'external'. A better understanding of the environment, therefore, becomes more critical to business and organizational outcomes. But *how* the environment is understood is also critical. Internalizing complexity requires different approaches to understanding it.

In helping to manage ambiguity, scenarios can, on one interpretation, be thought of as systems travelling in disguise. Their narrative structure, and the requirement that they are plausible and coherent, enable people from multiple disciplines who are typically untrained in systems thinking to have useful conversations about causality. Indeed, the very process of developing scenarios and validating them requires such conversations. The safe space afforded by a conversation about the future in turn enables assumptions about the present to be shared and tested. But the value of the work, in part, is that the range of assumptions that is aired is broad enough to challenge current – and usually implicit – notions of everyday reality.

To do this effectively, however, they need to escape from the culture of the planning department. I prefer to talk about 'scenario development' rather than 'scenario planning'. (ErikØverland, who ran the Norway 2030 project, used to refer to 'scenario learning' with his stakeholders.) From this perspective, one of the limitations of the SRI process is the excessive focus placed during the first two steps on the tight 'decision focus' of the work and the 'key decision factors'. Both stages appear profoundly embedded in the 'rational' reality of the organization. The notion that one already knows the decision that is to be taken appears to render the scenarios process rather less useful. The systems theorist Donald Schön observed in his book *The Reflective Practitioner* (1983), a quarter of a century ago, that this is to confuse 'problem solving' with 'problem setting':

> From the perspective of Technical Rationality, professional practice is a process of problem *solving*. Problems of choice or decision are solved through the selection, from available means, of the one best suited to established ends. But within this emphasis on problem solving, we ignore problem *setting*, the process by which we define the decision to be made, the ends to be achieved, the means which may be chosen. In real-world practice, problems do not present themselves to the practitioner as givens. They must be constructed from the materials of problematic situations which are puzzling, troubling, and uncertain. [*Emphasis in original.*]

This is partly an issue about variety. As Vickers's contemporary W.R. Ashby observed in his 'Law of Requisite Variety', 'only variety can absorb variety'. Most management processes are about simplifying the external environment (thus reducing variety) so that it can be better understood and acted upon. Indeed, scenarios are also a tool to reduce variety while also enabling the complex to be understood. But if there is too much simplification, especially at the early stages of the work, there is a significant danger that the eventual scenarios will likewise be too simple. By skipping to problem solving instead of problem setting, important aspects of the overall environment will be overlooked which might otherwise lead the organization or the network to consider the decision in a completely different light, or even conclude that a different decision is required.

The purpose of identifying an initial question that will define the relevant 'system under scrutiny', is therefore to ensure that the futures work will address the broad context within which the issue identified by the organization or network will be played out, while not prejudging the decision that is likely to emerge by the time one reaches the stage of making an instrumental judgement. At the same time, identifying the system also manages variety; it ensures that the scenario team is able to take a view on what it is able to exclude from its assessment of the internal and external environment. The second reason for identifying an initial system is that 'scenarios are structure' (see Hodgson and Sharpe, Chapter 5). Their behaviour can be understood, at least in part, in terms of reinforcing loops and balancing causal loops, and this is often a valuable tool for testing the coherence of a scenario, and the differences within a scenario set.

Because of the importance of the embedded system within the scenarios process, when reviewing drivers for their importance and uncertainty, we use a drivers' impact model derived (if streamlined) from the work of Michel Godet, which enables a structural analysis to be made of the relationships between the drivers. This then informs the uncertainties that are embedded in the scenarios axes. In contrast, the scenario–planning process used by SRI is – even at this pre-scenarios stage – already making planning assumptions based on the relationships between the drivers (Wilson, 1997). It is a rush to judgement.

The experienced world

One of the valuable contributions of the critical futures studies (CFS) school to futures practice has been its stress on the importance of cultural and personal histories in making meaning. The work of Jim Dator in Hawai'i, of Richard Slaughter, and the more recent development by Sohail Inayatullah of Causal Layered Analysis, and related techniques, all remind us that our knowledge of the world is embedded deeply in our 'taken for granted' social world; one of the purposes of futures work is to disturb this apparently objective reality. Andy Hines's paper 'Applying Integral Futures to Environmental Scanning' (*Futures Research Quarterly*, Winter 2003) is a good general introduction. This challenge comes through greater exploration of our cultural assumptions. CFS practitioners have drawn on the work of the integrative philosopher Ken Wilber, which attributes as much significance to the 'interior' worlds of personal meaning and of culture as it does to the 'exterior' worlds of action, behaviour and structure. Although scenarios are structure, they are not just structure; they are attempts to create models of future social behaviour. Johann Galtung (in Inayatullah, 2004) reminds us that

> *social = structural + cultural.* By 'structure' we simply refer to 'patterned interaction', the macro, gross, general picture of *'who relates to whom, how, when, and where'*. ...By 'culture' we mean the *what* and *why* of interaction; and the *what not/why not* important in explaining missing interaction, the structure not there, the absent link of interaction. Whereas interaction is *between* actors (and patterned interaction is the mega-version of the single inter-act), culture is *within* actors.

I would suggest that an effective scenario process needs to bring to the surface such interior and cultural meanings through its interest in the 'micro' and 'meso' drivers. As discussed earlier, the micro drivers capture shifts in values and attitudes, and the meso drivers shifts in social and group behaviour. Embedded within these is often a shift in perceived meaning. Cultural behaviour, then, is as important a part of the construction of the world as structural factors. Even though it is influenced by external or structural change, it is not merely a set of consequences of such change. Indeed, the cultural frame may precede the structural. As Slaughter (2004) notes: 'The point is that the world "out there" is framed, understood, and conditioned through the world "in here"'.

In some scenario sets, especially where values and culture are an important component of the prevailing system, such meso and micro determinants of behaviour become a significant part of the futures story. It is worth teasing this out a little further. In the case study here of the Wales Tourist Board, for example, one of the critical uncertainties was the type of holiday that consumers would choose in the future. This was expressed as an uncertainty over behaviour ('slow' or immersive holidays against 'fast' or multi-activity holidays), but within the expressed behaviour is a critical uncertainty about meaning; a conflicting story about the purpose of leisure.

Equally, shifting behaviour and expectations by individuals around the use of technology were being driven by a number of significant external drivers of change, from the falling cost of technology, to rising affluence, to the increase in individualism. But as a cultural form, the development of behaviour in the online space was not just a technical question about distribution or channels. It represented a shift in the balance of power between users and providers. Indeed, shifts in values or social behaviour are often qualitative indicators of 'emerging issues', or early changes in the external environment, before substantial quantitative evidence is available.

There is a separate point here that is also worth making. The scenarios literature often refers to scenarios as alternatives. In *The Art of the Long View*, for example, Peter Schwartz uses the metaphor of an actor who has learned parts for plays by Shakespeare, Ionesco and Eugene O'Neill – but will only know which they are to play as the curtain goes up. But in practice this is not the case. Scenario sets are not the future; they are only a model of possible and plausible futures that help us to understand how to act more effectively in the present. In practice, with a well-constructed scenario set, the combination of structural and cultural factors will mean that parts of all of the scenarios will play out, in different geographies, or among different user or customer groups, or in different markets, or at different times. They are parallel futures. Indeed, it is this texture of scenarios which, in part, gives us the ability to act on the future.

The communicated world

We make sense of the world through language. The 'communicated world' connects the world we observe with the world we experience, and bridges our interior and exterior worlds. Our construction of knowledge about the world is a social process which goes on within groups, through the agency of language. It is also an iterative process.

As Berger and Luckman (1966) put it in their pioneering book *The Social Construction of Reality*, 'the relationship between knowledge and its social base is a dialectical one, that is, knowledge is a social product and knowledge is a factor in social change'. Knowledge, therefore, is not lying around like fossils waiting to be discovered. It is created through effort and engagement. John Seely Brown and Paul Duguid observed in *The Social Life of Information* that, 'Knowledge is something we digest rather than merely

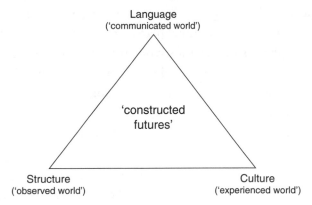

Figure 13.4   Structure, culture, and language

Source: Andrew Curry.

hold (Seely Brown and Duguid, 2002). It entails the knower's understanding and some degree of commitment.' The creation of knowledge also requires active participation by the knower. It is a social process: 'Knowledge is not a "thing" or a system, but an ephemeral, active, process of relating', said Ralph Stacey. It follows that communication is an inherent part of this process. As the phrase goes, 'How can I know what I think or feel until I hear what I say?' Berger and Luckman (1966) tease out some of the sophistication of language as a tool for sharing and creating meaning, a tool based on its reciprocity:

> I speak as I think; so does my partner in the conversation. Both of us hear what each says at virtually the same instance. ... What is more, I hear myself as I speak: my own subjective meanings are made objective and continuously available to me and ipso facto become 'more real' to me. ... As I objectivate my own being by means of language, my own being becomes massively and continuously available to myself at the same time that it is so available to him.

To summarize, then, conversation is at the heart of what we know and how we know it. It is central to both constructing the future and learning how to act on it.

The notion that language and conversation is at the heart of effective futures work is embedded in the literature. One of the best-known phrases in scenarios work is that scenarios are a 'strategic conversation' (Van der Heijden, 1996). Van der Heijden links the strategic conversation – at an organizational level – with the organization's ability to learn, partly through creating shared language and evolving new concepts to appreciate the future.

> Institutional learning requires an effective process of conversation, through which strategic cognitions can be compared, challenged and negotiated. Through this process participants learn to understand each other's world views and line of argumentation, creating a joint understanding of the situation at hand so that a collective experience results.

The role of the workshop in the scenarios process is central to the formulation of new knowledge about the future. The purpose is to surface the tacit knowledge of the participants about the system under scrutiny and their interpretations of it through the prism of the initial futures question, and make it available to all of those participating. It uses as a prompt the explicit knowledge generated at each stage through the project process. In this it draws on the work of Michael Polanyi, who captured the notion of the tacit in science discovery in a famous phrase, that 'we can know more than we can tell'. In his work in the field of knowledge management, Dave Snowden (2002) has expanded upon this. His three heuristics of knowledge (or rules of thumb) are deeply embedded in social process: 'We can always know more than we can tell, and we will always tell more than we will write down'; 'Knowledge can only be volunteered, it can never be conscripted'; and 'We can only know what we know when we need to know it.'

The number of participants in a workshop has some significance. A typical large group workshop might involve around 30 people.

In his work on group decision making, Stafford Beer argued that an 'infoset' of 30 was likely to ensure that most of the diversity of views around the topic would be present in the room. This has been my experience; one of the reasons for this is that, to paraphrase Berger and Luckman above, meaning becomes immediately and continuously open to all as participants speak. This requires the process to be open, and be seen to be open by participants, and that the facilitator protects the ability of everyone in the room to speak and be heard. Sometimes, for this reason, people from outside the organization participate. The British Army, for example, which is aware that it can be prone to 'groupthink', often invites others to join its futures processes.

Experimentation has underlined the robustness of the large group in developing knowledge. On occasion, when for reasons of time or budget it has not been possible to construct a detailed set of drivers supported by qualitative or quantitative data, we have used 'summary drivers', capturing a driver or trend with only some indicative data. In practice, this approach has proven to produce results that are as effective as the more formal version, because it invites (indeed requires) participants to suggest missing information and share it with the group. On one project, when we were working against significant time pressures, initial research had overlooked many of the drivers relating to a technical but significant area. The workshop group filled this gap from their tacit knowledge in less than half an hour. In the phrase of the late Michael Young, 'Everyone has the capacity to be remarkable.'

There is an important point here; the use of large group workshops, properly facilitated, effectively speeds up the process as it broadens it, by bringing a far greater fund of knowledge to bear, far more quickly. There is a parallel with Eric Raymond's well-known phrase about open source software development, that 'many eyes make all bugs shallow': with the right process, a large group can see gaps far more quickly than a small group. The scenario team does not, therefore, need to become subject experts; it needs to be expert at process, at listening, and at surfacing and testing assumptions.

The workshop also acts as a space where it is possible to change the frame through which groups of actors understand an issue. Sometimes this is a matter of a shift in emphasis. In the example of SwitchCo, one of the decisive conversations came when a manager suggested that its Chinese competitor, Huawei, would follow the relatively slow trajectory of the Japanese car makers in increasing quality and price. A colleague who had visited the company responded: 'In the middle of the market they are already delivering 90% of our quality for 50% of the price. I think most of our customers will settle for that.' The shift in the mood in the room was palpable.

This can also involve conflict. In another scenarios process, about economic development, there was a sharp difference of opinion about the value of diversity. A couple of traditionalist managers argued that it was a regulatory problem, and represented a business cost. Younger women retorted that diversity was a source of increased value to businesses because of the greater market understanding and potential for the innovation it created. As the facilitator, I had to stay with the argument in the room, despite the feelings of discomfort it was evidently causing to other participants. The eventual strategy included the need to improve diversity in the region's workforce – by encouraging inward migration if necessary.

The process of reframing through conversation and negotiation has parallels with the notion of 'interpretive speaking', developed in *Disclosing New Worlds* (Spinosa *et al.*, 1997). Interpretive speaking

> allows some practice, thing, or identity to appear as worthy of consideration by a mixed community – that is, a community composed of a wider range of interest than those of a group of professions

or technicians...the real work of interpretive speaking comes in making people sensitive to the experiences and practices behind them.

In an age when consultants offer workshops to clients as a matter of routine, it may seem implausible to believe that workshops could have such powerful effects. There are two reasons why they might. The first is that the scenarios process outlined here involves at least three workshops, over a period of time; participants are likely to attend at least two. This enables social relationships, and some degree of trust, to be developed. The second is that this trust can be reinforced by the facilitator. The willingness to 'disclose' is more likely to emerge if the facilitator seeks actively to ensure that the full range of meaning in the room is heard. In this, it borrows from some of the basic practices of dialogue, defined by Daniel Yankelovich (1999) as 'equality and the absence of coercive influences'; 'listening with empathy'; and 'bringing assumptions into the open'.

CROSSING BOUNDARIES

Much of my scenarios and futures work has been with multi-stakeholder groups. In such groups it has not been possible to assume that participants share a common vision or underlying set of values; indeed they are sometimes in conflict. Multiple organizations are represented in the room, as are multiple communities of practice. If it is hard to tell where an organization ends, especially in the multi-agency environment of the public sector, this is also increasingly true in the private sector. Companies are becoming far more open, and far more connected, than they used to be. Karl Weick (2001) argues that contrary to received wisdom, the notion of the boundary between the organization and its environment is itself problematic.

Organizations are more active in constructing the environments which impinge on them than is commonly recognized. That is, organizations often impose that which subsequently imposes on them.

Nor is it possible to assume, in a world of mergers and acquisitions, frequent restructuring, and global business units, that organizations even share a common culture or values. Alignment becomes a challenge, and culture is one vehicle to further this. Weick, again, argues that stories are of particular value:

When people share the same stories, those stories provide general guidelines within which they can customize diagnoses and solutions to local problems.... Stories hold the potential to enhance requisite variety among human actors, and that's why high reliability systems may handicap themselves when they become preoccupied with traditional rationality and fail to recognize the power of narrative rationality.

When dealing with multi-stakeholder groups, or even with multiple specialist groups within increasingly fragmented organizations, there are multiple views in the room, from multiple bodies of expertise and practice. A shared cultural base, or at least shared appreciation, has to be created through participation in the futures process. Fortunately, this is a virtue, since it means that differences in assumptions and values about the future are more likely to surface. The knowledge 'objects' created at each stage of the scenarios process, whether they are groups of salient drivers, or scenarios, or identified strategic areas in which action might be possible and desirable, effectively act as 'boundary objects' (a term invented by Susan Leigh Star) which enable these different groups to exchange information, and thereby to create new knowledge and understanding. They are objects which enable groups and individuals from different disciplines and bodies of practice to have a single conversation.

An example might be a dead bird, which acts as a boundary object between ornithologists and public health professionals, or a CIA plane, a boundary object for plane-spotters and human rights campaigners. Scenarios, when developed collectively, are effectively constructed from the outset as boundary objects because the process of their construction is designed to create the capacity for conversation across different groups. 'The magic of the boundary object', observes Peter Morville, 'lies in its ability to build shared understanding across social categories'.

Even in the 1960s, Berger and Luckman (1966) were able to write of the fragmentation of knowledge and therefore of knowledge-based groups. 'The increasing number and complexity of sub-universes make them increasingly inaccessible to outsiders. They become esoteric enclaves'. Since then, sub-universes have proliferated in their number and in their complexity. Technical discourse within any one such sub-universe of knowledge is specific to that discourse. Useful conversation across subjects and across professional groups becomes more difficult as a result. This is the second reason why scenarios enable the effective creation of social knowledge. they create a shared language between groups not just about the future but about the present as well. In his book *Why?* Charles Tilly (2005) explores how people give reasons for things. When offering accounts that relate cause and effect, specialized communities will give technical accounts. More popular accounts will come in the form of stories, but of a particular kind of story.

Tilly concludes that once the conversation includes practitioners from multiple disciplines, when specialist knowledge is therefore a barrier to mutual understanding, the most effective versions of cause and effect are what he calls 'the superior story':

Superior stories simplify their causes and effects. They maintain unity of time and place, deal with a limited number of actors and actions, as they concentrate on how those actions cause other actions. They omit or minimise [many] effects. But within their limited frames they *get the actors, actions, causes, and effects right.* By the standards of a relevant and credible technical account, they simplify radically, but everything they say is true.

Box 13.2   The 'Official Future'

The notion that one of the scenarios should represent the 'official future' of the organization is well-represented in the literature. It is argued that through rehearsal of the official future, by analysis or role playing, participants often come to realize that it is implausible. There are risks in this. Sometimes the 'official future' scenario is the one in which the organization has most strategic capability. In the Wales, scenarios this was the case, but achieving it nonetheless required radical improvement in implementation. In other cases the notion of the 'official future' gets in the way of understanding the overall environment.

In a set of scenarios developed on the future of intelligent infrastructure systems, for the UK government's Foresight programme, the 'official future' varied across stakeholders. Practitioners told us that each of the four scenarios reflected the official futures of different groups of experts: technologists identified 'Perpetual Motion' in which transport impacts were managed through innovation; planners and developers turned to 'Urban Colonies' where transport was designed out through management of urban space; environmentalists pointed to 'Tribal Trading', in which resource shortages caused economic downturn; transport planners identified 'Good Intentions', where technology is used to curb transport use. In contrast, a set of scenarios I was involved in developing, to understand the impact of the obesity 'crisis' on food retailers and producers, generated no scenario that corresponded to their 'official future'. This indicated that the sector was entering a period of significant turbulence, and this has since happened. SwitchCo told the same story. The concern about the 'Official Future' turns on the issue of the credibility of the scenarios with senior managers. Such credibility is also earned through participation in the process.

In short, then, they can be thought of as a causal account that gets the essence right, even while removing some of the detail that might impede broader understanding, even if a specialist would prefer to see such detail.

In fact, such 'superior stories' operate very like scenario stories.

> Stories are efficient vehicles for organizing things in our mind, relating data across a wide range of subjects. Making sense involves relating things causally, with one thing leading to another. . . . Scenarios make sense of future events in the same way as historical accounts make sense of the past.
>
> (Van der Heijden, 1996)

Scenario stories, generated in a shared space across multiple groups, enable these groups to negotiate their conflicting interpretations of the world, creating sufficient new knowledge to enable them to act.

IDENTIFYING THE ROOM TO MOVE

It is self-evident that large organizations can – and do – seek to influence their environment. They succeed in this endeavour to a greater or lesser extent. Even smaller organizations can make choices about what they should choose to do, based on their appreciative judgement of a scenario set. Equally, multi-stakeholder groups are required to formulate common views of the world if they wish to act effectively, despite differences in values, assumptions, and world view (Figure 13.5). As the futurist Wendy Schultz argues, 'While the future is uncertain and much of it is beyond our control, we can control many aspects of it. We choose our future: we create it by what we do or fail to do.' In other words, we make our own futures, but not in circumstances of our own choosing.

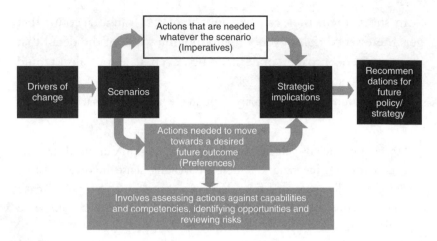

Figure 13.5   Getting to strategy
Source: Henley Centre HeadlightVision.

Nonetheless, there are practical dangers here. Scenarios work is a search for how the world could be. Strategic choice requires that you take a view of your preferred outcomes (economic, social or environmental) within the futures portrayed by the scenarios. It is a vision of where you want to go. This is an exercise that involves values, purpose and meaning, as well as an assessment of capabilities: Why do you prefer that particular strategic direction? And just as importantly: What investment is required, and what risks are involved, in getting there? Without these assessments, the preferred outcome is merely a 'wish-driven strategy', as John Kay describes it, with little chance of success.

From a practitioner's perspective, then, there are clear differences between assessing the future landscapes to create the scenarios, and making a strategic assessment. The most significant is the requirement, in working with participants, to help them in the early phases of the work to assess the drivers of change not on the basis of what they believe they can influence, but on the basis of which drivers will have the most impact (negative or positive) on the system under scrutiny.

At the same time, the notion that the work of the scenario builders and the strategic planners can be separated from one another also raises a number of theoretical issues.

A critical issue is the model of how one believes that organizations act. In the 'rational' world, strategy is formulated through formal analysis, and then implemented operationally by levers that senior managers are able to pull, and happily create intended outcomes. The flaws in this model have been evident for some time. Such deliberate strategy, according to the management theorist Henry Mintzberg, is likely to lead to 'unrealized strategy' through changes in circumstances, internal or external. Or it may not be an appropriate response to the environment. As Max Boisot wrote in *Knowledge Assets* (Boisot, 1998),

> Where the world itself is vague or uncertain, the clarity sought by managers can often be positively dysfunctional. It discourages the less codified and abstract forms of scanning . . . that might pick up hard-to detect signals of threat or opportunity.

The scenarios process creates a series of prototypes which participants can use to listen to such signals.

In addition, effective strategic innovation comes from different parts of the organization, not just the centre. While scenarios may accelerate the speed of learning, and improve the chances of innovation occurring, this remains dependent on the ability of different parts of the organization or network to internalize emerging views of change. When faced with the same stories about future worlds – the same accounts of changes in the 'observed world' – what appears to be decisive is their ability to change the meanings and cultural frames in their 'experienced world'.

Indeed, this is borne out by one of the central stories about the original Shell scenarios in which oil prices were projected, for the first time, to increase substantially. Jan Choufoer, then worldwide manufacturing coordinator, had considered upgrading his refineries so they could handle a bigger percentage of heavy crude oil in addition to higher value light crude. The high cost of such a project would be modest compared to the potential profits if the oil price increased, but the plan had previously been rejected because it did not generate a return at the current price of oil. Now he was able to use the insights from the scenarios to create the willingness in the organization to move as the crude oil price began to increase. In contrast, Shell's transport division, Marine, largely ignored the insights offered by the scenarios, and continued to interpret the oil world through a traditional set of meanings and understandings. The resulting overcapacity crippled the division financially (Van der Heijden, 1996). In the SwitchCo example above, similarly, it was the shift in meaning created by participation in the scenarios process which enabled the company to act earlier than others on the signs they saw in the market.

There is a valuable further point here. In an interesting, if dense, paper on scenarios as sense making devices, Alex Wright (2005) quotes research by Regnér which found that strategy that was developed away from the organization's centre was more likely to be based on inductive reasoning, and was more likely to lead to transformational insights. This could be because such managers were less likely to have internalized the core business assumptions that prevail in the centre, and were therefore more likely to be able to draw on competing meanings and interpretations of the world. Indeed, this may also suggest that the traditional notion, that scenarios are most effective when one can get the senior decision makers in one room, may be based on a false supposition. Unless faced by crisis or other shock, senior managers are likely to be most fully acculturated in the prevailing norms of the organization, and least likely to respond to challenges of interpretation, meaning and values.

CONCLUSION

In conclusion, then, scenarios can enable us to act on the future because they define a relevant system; they bring actors together to explore the possible futures of that system in a way that gives them an equal voice; they create fora where those actors can build new social knowledge, partly through challenges of culture and interpretation; they provide tools where individuals from different bodies of practice and knowledge can converse as equals; and they capture that knowledge in the form of stories that are meaningful to the whole group. They are, in effect, systems thinking without systems specialists. They enable the renegotiation of meaning and the reframing of understanding. They combine social exchange with knowledge and interpretation. It is all of this, together, which creates the opportunity, and the freedom, to act.

With thanks to Lloyd Burdett, Crawford Hollingworth, Rachel Kelnar, and Wendy Schultz, and my scenario-building colleagues at Henley Centre HeadlightVision.

CHAPTER 14

BACKWARDS TO THE FUTURE: SCENARIOS AS ROUTINES FOR ORGANIZATIONAL HEALTH

James Tansey

We live in societies that are populated by a vast array of organizations, from government bureaucracies to small private enterprises. When we speak about power and change in society, we are largely talking about power mediated via organizations: they are focal nodes that align and concentrate the effort of individuals towards a common cause or in a strategic direction. While a great deal has been said about the rise of individualism as a defining characteristic of modernization and democratization, it is also true that modernity relies fundamentally on the deferral of individual will and autonomy to organizations. Autonomy for individuals within this system also requires new levels of specialisation in almost every

Scenarios for Success: Turning Insights into Action Edited by Bill Sharpe and Kees Van der Heijden
© 2007 John Wiley & Sons, Ltd

aspect of life. The vast concentration of effort that has resulted from the evolution of a society of organizations has resulted in technological advances and improvements in human well-being. Moreover, it has created a kind of resilience that was lacking in pre-industrial societies. But, as Geoffrey Vickers pointed out in *The Art of Judgement*: 'Even the dogs may eat the crumbs which fall from the rich man's table; and in these days when the rich in knowledge eat such specialized food, at such separate tables, only the dogs have a chance of a balanced diet' (Vickers, 1965). The division of labour within organizations often makes managers feel like uncomfortable amateurs when it comes to saying something general about strategy. Scenario practices provide a framework for managing that discomfort.

Scenario-based approaches to strategy recognize that while organizations accumulate power to the extent that they can coordinate the effort of the individuals and routinize tasks to produce economies of scale, they must also maintain routines that enable them to adapt to changing circumstances in the wider organizational environment: the dilemma for senior managers is to strike the appropriate balance between durability and change. Strategy is the engine of renewal and may also play an important role in building solidarity within an organization, which creates the conditions for endogenous change.

While organizations maintain strong internal solidarity and are clearly demarcated by boundaries, they never operate in isolation. Organizations have very strong interdependencies and in combination they create a kind of ecosystem that has been observed by institutional theorists and complex systems researchers. Many of the most challenging problems that society now faces appear within this organizational ecosystem or at the intersection between the organizational ecosystem and the natural ecosystem. Problems falling under the broad umbrella of sustainable development, such as energy dependence, climate change, environmental pollution and resource management rarely belong to a single organization.

Instead, responsibility is shared by a multitude of organizations that must contend not only with the challenge of maintaining a robust and appropriate strategy for themselves, but also with maintaining the capacity to respond to shared challenges.

This chapter focuses on a recent Canadian effort to use a scenario tool – known as Quest – to develop a regional strategy for sustainable development. The specific method, described in greater detail below, is called backcasting. It is an explicitly normative approach to strategy that reverses the logic of most efforts to discipline the future or prospect for alternatives. Rather than beginning with the present state of affairs and projecting forwards, either through a formal predictive approach or through a less formal effort to identify alternative pathways, backcasting defines one or more normative end-points first and works backwards to identify the steps that would be necessary to achieve the end-point (see also Bradfield, Chapter 10, page 270). It is broadly similar to normative visioning exercises, although most applications have populated backcasting scenarios with quantitative data and have often used formal models to support the exercise. One of the ambitions behind this Canadian initiative was not only to sketch out desirable futures and represent them using integrated modelling frameworks, but also to provide an opportunity for participants in the exercise to modify their positions based on the interaction between discrete choices. The empirical basis for this chapter is the Georgia Basin Futures Project (GBFP), a five-year, interdisciplinary research project that considered sustainability at a bioregional scale around Vancouver on the west coast of Canada (Tansey *et al.*, 2002).

While backcasting has been applied at the level of individual projects and organizations, this project focuses on the interorganizational environment. The boundaries of this setting are primarily geographic: the study focuses on the bioregion surrounding Vancouver, including Victoria and Whistler. The region is home to around 80% of the population of the province. Most of the problems represented in the backcasting exercise are the responsibility of more than one organization and the goal was to stimulate conversation, identify key trade-offs between alternatives, and perhaps most importantly, empower users to make considered choices about the kind of future they would consider most desirable for a fast-growing region of western Canada. The audience was not limited to experts gathered from a range of partner organizations. Participants included a large number of members of the public who were engaged in a series of neighbourhood-level workshops using the backcasting methodology. Again, the normative goal was to experiment in a process of democratizing areas of decision making that have traditionally been the domain of credentialled experts.

The intent was not to forge an encompassing consensus; rather we sought to identify differences in the desirability of scenarios and to encourage debate about the basis of those differences. In addition to providing a focus for deliberations about the desirability of the scenarios generated, the backcasting process, supported by the scenario tool, made the biological and physical trade-offs between scenarios more visible and explicit. In the second phase we wanted to examine the strategies and policies that would be necessary to implement desirable futures for the region. In this phase we moved from the exploration and deliberation of the desirability of scenarios to an emphasis on evaluation and assessment of the steps that would be necessary to make them happen.

THE PROCESS OF BACKCASTING

The term 'backcasting' describes an approach used in the soft path energy studies, which emerged following the oil shocks of the 1970s. Soft path energy studies differed from traditional approaches to energy planning by focusing on demand-side management, energy efficiency, alternative non-fossil fuels and decentralized supply technologies, behavioural change, etc., rather than focusing on conventional centralized supply-side options. These studies took experts' articulation of a desirable future and analysed the feasibility of such goals. The purpose of the analyses was to shed light on the policy and resource implications of different sectoral end-points, by describing the trajectories required to connect the current state-of-play with the desired future.

The conceptual basis of backcasting lies in the recognition that the distant future is inherently unknowable, specifically in problem contexts like sustainability (refer to the third horizon in Chapter 5). Human choice and behavioural change can shape a desirable future, which is not necessarily the most probable as it is based on past and present conditions (Robinson, 2003). Policy choices in such contexts are oriented by goals that require substantive change from current trends. These discontinuities are not typically resolved by forecasting approaches that are concerned with extrapolating from the past (Morgan et al., 1999). Rather than focusing on the likelihood of probable futures, backcasting explores the feasibility of desirable futures. From the perspective of organizational renewal and change, this distinction is fundamentally important. The characteristics that make organizations durable tend to reinforce groupthink and create the impression that there is only one official organizational future. Organizations can frame problems or challenges conservatively to such an extent that they see the status quo as inevitable, and it is at this point that they can begin to stagnate. A less generous aphorism for organizations with a singular view of the future is that, 'If all you have is a hammer, everything looks like a nail.' Backcasting forces a plurality of futures into the organizational frame by asking 'what would it take to make this happen?' (Robinson, 1988; Dreborg, 1996).

Backcasting applications share the methodological steps represented in Figure 14.1, which draws on a summary paper by Quist (2003). Backcasting comprises four principal steps:

- strategic problem orientation
- articulation of values and generation of desirable future(s)

- backcasting of trajectories
- identification of interventions to implement or initiate backcast trajectories (see Figure 14.1).

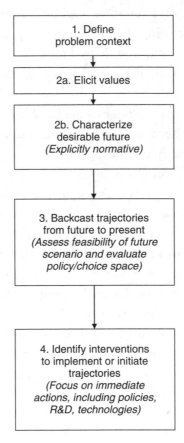

Figure 14.1 General steps in backcasting

Strategic problem orientation involves bounding the problem context, setting normative assumptions, identifying stakeholders, considering scale issues and so on (Step 1). This first step is time-consuming and resource-intensive. It requires the initiators of a backcasting process to build a constituency that is willing and committed both to engage with the exercise, but, more importantly, to integrate the process into their strategic plans. In Vickers's terms (page 67), Step 1 involves an instrumental judgement about the appropriate boundaries between the contextual and transactional environments (Ramírez and Van der Heijden, Chapter 4). The strategy employed in our regional scenario-building exercise was to secure funding commitments in advance that were matched by funding from the Social Science Research Council of Canada. This ensured that partners had resources at stake, which provided an ongoing incentive for them to be engaged. Decisions about scale are also challenging. Few problems in the interorganizational environment are neatly geographically bounded, although decision making is still largely limited to specific localities. The challenge was to find a scale for this project that was sufficiently encompassing but did not make any one of the partners a more important player. It is partly for this reason that a bioregion was chosen as the boundary: the project focused on the watershed surrounding Vancouver, known as the Georgia Basin.

The next step in backcasting is to construct a future vision or solution(s) to the problem in hand (Step 2). The future vision is a characterization of what is desirable. Consequently it reflects the values of the participants involved in the process. Once defined, trajectories are backcast from the future vision (Step 3). Trajectories refer to the development pathways from the present system state to the desired future. Whether these pathways are genuinely worked back from the future, or outlined from the present with the end-point in mind, depends on the details of the methodology employed. Backcast trajectories are typically described in terms of first-order economic, social, technological and institutional milestones and changes. First-order changes are significant structural changes – for instance, the balance between services and manufacturing in the economy. These in turn inform the types of policy measures and behavioural shifts upon which the trajectories would be founded. Backcasting provides a framework for identifying the interventions or actions required to implement, or more modestly, to initiate the trajectories which would lead to the desired future (Step 4). Steps 3 and 4 of the backcasting methodology are thus closely interrelated. Interventions are often discussed as part of the trajectory backcasting step, for example, by identifying targets or obstacles to be overcome. A supplementary final step involves embedding and implementing the action agenda and is germane to those backcasting applications that seek to drive (as well as understand) change (Quist, 2003).

Our project extended this framework to test what has been termed 'second generation' backcasting (see Robinson, 2003). In first-generation backcasting exercises, the future vision is set by researchers or technical experts at the outset and the exercise focuses on developing trajectories and identifying interventions. Second-generation backcasting gives additional emphasis to an explicit deliberation of the normative basis for the future vision. The articulation of the values that underpin the future vision is treated as a learning process. The definition of a desirable future is the outcome of a process in which participants make value-based choices, see the consequences of those choices in the future using the assessment tool, and iteratively revise their choices until a future scenario is achieved that reflects their preferences. In order to facilitate learning, the model presents the users with engaging representations of the trade-offs associated with their choices. Our assumption is that the unanticipated consequences of choices can lead users to modify what values are expressed through the scenarios they create (Robinson, 2003).

The modelling tool

The Quest modelling tool, developed to support the backcasting process, is composed of a series of linked sectoral sub-models. It is a linear input–output model that captures plausible representations of the major physical and social systems in the region. The interface to the model was designed with significant public input and allows users to make choices that resonate with dilemmas they encounter in their everyday lives. The inspiration for the model was the computer game 'Sim City' and our goal was to create a decision support system that users could enjoy playing with. Most of the choices offered to users are qualitative, emphasizing general increases or decreases rather than detailed numerical choices. While the sub-models are generally relatively simple, the tool as a whole is much more sophisticated because it is horizontally integrated across sub-models and is driven by a user-friendly interface. The tool was developed over three years and involved a large team of scientists and technical professionals from the private and public sector. It is described in detail in two recent papers (Tansey *et al.*, 2002; Carmichael *et al.*, 2004).

APPLICATIONS

The Georgia Basin Futures Project, which embeds a model in a deliberative process, was tested in the following contexts:

- In stand-alone public consultation exercises about the future of the region, involving self-selected participants for up to a day. Consultations were professionally facilitated and the goal was to use the tool iteratively in order to develop a desirable scenario for the region.
- In support of consultation processes for strategic planning pur-poses within a defined jurisdiction within the Georgia Basin as a whole. In this case, the tool was used to help to bring the val-ues of the various stakeholders to the surface; the tool provided a realistic context around which participants could engage in a debate.
- In support of consultation processes around specific planning decisions. In this case the tool was used to identify the

underlying values that might inform the positions of the actors involved in deliberations about a specific planning decision, for instance, the location and form of a new road through a village centre.

- Scenarios were generated which represented the general policy commitments of a number of federal and provincial agencies. Initial scenarios were generated in consultation with senior staff prior to the event and were refined by the participants. The objective was to reveal some of the wider impacts of departmental policy choices in the bioregion and, more importantly, to backcast from the scenario end-point, through the policy steps that would be necessary to achieve them.

Results and findings from these various applications are discussed in a number of papers including a recent special issue in the *Integrated Assessment Journal* (this can be viewed at www.iajonline.org). In the remainder of this chapter I discuss some of the more general findings from this attempt at public and stakeholder engagement.

DISCUSSION

One of the most obvious successes of the project was that we were able to navigate through a complex interorganizational environment in order to build both a robust and informed decision support tool and to retain the commitment of organizations to make use of the process when it was finished. The product remained independently owned by the research team, which was important for the credibility of the initiative. Many hundreds of members of the public used the tool in a series of workshops in the region and generated a database of scenarios evaluated according to their desirability. We also learned that it is often easier for people to state what they don't want than for them to state what they most actively desire: dystopic scenarios were as important as utopic scenarios.

The strongest outcomes of this backcasting application were that we were able to identify strategies that connect the present to normatively desirable outcomes in the future. We were also able to complete the more complex second-generation backcasting approach that encourages users to re-evaluate their preferences in response to information about trade-offs. We engaged senior officials from many of the key governmental organizations in the region in a series of eight workshops to identify coherent strategies for realizing their chosen scenarios. As suggested above, the goal was not to create a single new official version of the future, but to highlight the view that the future is malleable. Evaluations of the process through a post engagement survey revealed that it was regarded very positively by almost all participants.

Challenges: future searching as prediction

The tool primarily represents resource flows associated with different development choices in the region. In the simplest terms it represents a possibility space, bounded by material constraints. The model was designed to allow users to explore this possibility space and to assess some of the impacts of major disjunctures in the development pathways of the region.

In practice, many users could only think about the future in terms of predictions. Moreover, despite lots of input from the facilitators who consistently emphasized scenarios and 'not implausible' futures, they saw the model as a 'truth-machine' that produced predictions. The more benign response that this stimulated was to see the model outputs as inevitable, rather than contingent. In the worse case, users took issue with the model outputs and raised concerns about the quality of the scientific knowledge embodied in the Quest assessment tool. Even if challenging the scientific basis leads to developing the knowledge base underlying the model, both responses defeat the basic object of the exercise, which is first and foremost to identify endpoints that are considered desirable rather than inevitable. The embodied expertise in the tool then allows users to see some of the high-level unintended consequences of their choices.

There are at least two explanations for these responses; one cultural and one cognitive. The first is that the notion that the future is predetermined is heavily culturally entrenched. Users expect science to mediate and represent futures to which they are then able to respond. In this case, users cast themselves as passive observers with respect to the future and this is probably a reasonable rationalization of their daily experience in rapidly changing technologically oriented societies. Backcasting recognizes that, given a long enough timescale, a number of alternative futures are possible through intentional policy intervention and design. For instance, one could develop a scenario end-point where there is large-scale penetration of renewable energy into the energy supply system, and then identify the series of policy changes that would be necessary to achieve this outcome. Very few individuals could claim to have sufficient power to actually determine this kind of outcome and generally these large-scale systems are thought of as the evolutionary product of competition among a number of organizational interests. It requires a kind of benign megalomania for a user to imagine how aggregate human choices could create this kind of disjuncture.

The second explanation is that users may not have explicit preferences about the future they would like to see. Traditionally, consultation exercises focus on incremental changes from a 'business-as-usual' trajectory. In this case they have a benchmark against which they can evaluate incremental changes. Backcasting asks users to forget about the present and focus on a distinct future: a significant cognitive leap. Despite what some economists and psychologists suggest, individuals don't carry around ordered and explicit preference lists that can inform their choices.

Interactive social science, client considerations

In designing the project as a whole, the team developed strong interactive working relationships with a number of governmental and non-governmental agencies in the region. A condition of the original funding was that the project be made accessible to a range of organizational 'clients'. These included the federal environment ministry, the regional district for Greater Vancouver, a number of provincial ministries and major NGOs in the region. The goal had been to integrate the Quest tool into real regional consultation processes. Consistent with the broader advice of scenario practitioners, our goal was to identify a real client for the exercises in the region. Having a client means that the scenario exercise is tethered at one end and has a greater degree of credibility than would have been feasible with a stand-alone academic consultation process.

The tool was used by a number of smaller municipalities in the region to support long-range planning processes and was generally well received. As well as the logistical challenges of seeking to coordinate the development of a technical tool with a number of formal consultation processes in the region, we encountered a number of other challenges in the course of the project. First, we invited technical and professional staff from the agencies to be involved in the design of the underlying models and the interface. Their engagement was generally productive and useful and procedurally it helped to create buy-in for the final product. One of the challenges we encountered was that many of the professional staff who were responsible for the formal consultation processes of their agencies were dubious about the level of sophistication of the public at large. Typically they saw consultation as either a 'rubber stamping' process or as a public education process. We were advised to 'keep the choices simple' and 'write text for a Grade 8 education level'.

It became clear that it would be very difficult to integrate the tool meaningfully into formal consultation processes that typically lasted between a few hours and a day. As a team, we became obsessed with the problem of fitting a full iterative scenario process for the entire bioregion into a one-day workshop. The priority was to maintain the integrity of the relationship with the clients we had engaged in the project in order to maintain relevance. In retrospect, the needs and expectations of many of the clients were inconsistent with the requirements of a good process for an exercise on this scale. It became clear that if consultation processes were to produce good substantive outcomes then we would need to invest much more time in developing a skills base among the users. If consultation processes are treated as fleeting encounters to create an illusion of legitimacy, then users are bound to respond accordingly. Until consultation processes on this scale are given the social significance of activities like jury duty, they are unlikely to produce outcomes of any merit. While a commitment to an interactive approach to social science was central to the process, being over-responsive to the client really limited the scope of the exercise. The conclusion is that while the mantra of scenarios methods is always to identify a client, this may be difficult for consultation projects on this scale. Ultimately, there is no single client that has jurisdiction over the bioregion within which we worked. While it could be argued that it is foolish to talk about the future without a client and a jurisdiction, many of the issues – such as the interactions between transportation and land use – are only evident on this temporal or spatial scale.

Future processes

From a purely academic perspective some of the problems encountered in these exercises were constructive failures. While some were foreseeable, many aspects of this project were unique, and the ambition to create a vibrant debate about regional sustainability was grand. Despite the problems described above, we were able to engage a large number of people in a constructive dialogue about the kind of future they would like to see for a region. The key lessons from this work are:

- Good process takes time and should be treated as a serious substantive activity.
- Scenario thinking is unusual and unfamiliar; users need practice and coaching to see alternatives to the official future.
- Expressed preferences about the future are often inevitably anchored in the political struggles of the present. In some cases, the participants projected the political struggles of the present onto the blank tapestries of the future and fought battles in defence of their official version of the future. This also makes scenarios subversive. The notion that there is more than one official future may threaten the status quo. One expert participant suggested at the end of a scenario exercise that it would be 'dangerous' to allow the public or other stakeholders to see the resulting scenario.

CONCLUSION

The aims of this chapter were to consider the merits of using scenarios as a way of approaching strategy and to identify ways of linking organizational decision making to action. Secondary goals were to consider a proactive context for the use of scenarios, to provide a focus on prototyping and to indicate how scenarios could be embedded in a learning process.

In this chapter I have elaborated one of many scenario methods: backcasting. Conceptually, the benefits of this approach are that it encourages participants to detach their preferences from the dominant organizational setting in which they are embedded and to create one or more desirable alternatives to the status quo. In practice, this proved difficult, although not impossible. Experts in workshops found it difficult to make this separation because so much of their day-job requires them to make their organization stable and durable. Not surprisingly, they were aware of the tension between durability and change. We would expect to see this tension in the organizational setting as well as in the interorganizational setting of this study. While I have talked about organizations almost as though they were single personalities, that is really a convenience. Organizations almost always display a kind of schizophrenia, an internal struggle between competing interests. Arguably, one of the most powerful uses of backcasting is that participants can identify alternative futures and start to work out what it would take to achieve that future, before declaring a preference. Instead of asking which option is best, backcasting asks 'What would it take to make this happen?'

The theme of linking intent to action is a greater challenge for an interorganizational project, because it is difficult to create binding commitments in this domain. While in some cases the process and tool were used within an official decision-making process, generally there was no direct connection to an action agenda. While the absence of a clear client violated one of the golden rules of scenario planning, I would argue that this made it easier to set the official future aside. As a general rule, however, if linking intent to action is one of the primary goals of a project, then it is essential to engage the client throughout the process.

The future for these approaches depends on the willingness of decision makers and managers to take risks with ideas. Some of the healthiest organizations cultivate a culture of internal deliberation, although most organizations need to bracket the absolute minimum set of assumptions about the future necessary to develop a strategy around the Business Idea (Van der Heijden, 2005). Building scenario processes into the organizational routine is a powerful way to maintain a healthy and essential balance between durability and change in a world that shows no signs of slowing down.

CONCLUDING REMARKS

We have reached the end of this fascinating trip through scenario land. What can we take with us from this adventure for our own practice as managers or practitioners? We will all have been struck by different aspects, depending on the mental models that we bring to our perceiving. The following is what the editors make of it. The reader may want to reflect on his or her own conclusions against what we saw.

The first overwhelming impression is the vibrancy of the field of scenarios. This is not an area stuck in orthodoxy. It seems obvious that scenario work still is overwhelmingly a practitioner's art. While in some academic circles there are attempts to develop conceptual frameworks and theories of scenario planning it is out in the field that demand is racing ahead and new thinking is developing. Most practitioners are not just 'doing it'; they are involved in progressing the state of the art. We see many new aspects.

There are attempts to get on top of the field by mapping out the territory with new conceptual frameworks: the five dilemmas of scenario planning; the world of business versus the world of

Scenarios for Success: Turning Insights into Action   Edited by Bill Sharpe and Kees Van der Heijden
© 2007 John Wiley & Sons, Ltd

management; the threefold judgement involved in strategy; the three horizons of decision making; the contextual versus the transactional environment; inductive versus deductive processes; the taxonomy of 'thinking traps'; the strategic conversation; and so on. These attempts to delineate the field prove powerful in gaining an overview of what it is about.

The field of scenario work is no longer satisfied with 'making sense' of the environment as a goal in itself, leaving it to managers to think about what this means for them. Practitioners are increasingly considering strategic implications as an intrinsic part of the process. We see this as part of the general shift in the field of strategy, from 'business-as-usual' to 'game changing', from 'adapting' to 'shaping', from 'inside the box' to 'outside the box' innovation, from 'managing' to 'leading'.

Gaining a new deep understanding of the strategic situation, now and in the future, remains one of the key objectives of the scenario practice. Without this there can be no 'seeing the situation in a new way' and therefore no strategic insight and renewal. The awareness is growing of the overlap between scenarios and systems approaches. We see fascinating attempts to use concepts from systems theory, such as dominant loops, to help scenario thinkers distil the essence of the situation they are describing. Some go so far as to describe scenarios as 'systems in disguise' and scenario building as systems analysis 'without the need for specialists'. In this connection practitioners emphasize that good scenarios must be plausible, internally consistent and based on a causal structure. In addition, they see the power of the narrative in terms of efficiency of expression and weight in the battle for attention. It seems obvious that we can expect further major developments in this general direction.

It is fascinating to see how the field is starting to come up with new links to entrepreneurial invention. Even if the strategic invention will always remain a highly personal moment, scenario practitioners are finding ways to prepare the ground for the 'moment of magic' when things fall into place; when you feel you now understand the basic forces driving value in the situation and what you need to do is staring you in the face. While scenario practitioners on the whole do not see themselves in the business of making strategic decisions, they do increasingly subscribe to Pasteur's dictum that 'luck favours the prepared mind'.

The strategic moment of truth is when one discovers a way to be distinctive in an area of value (i.e. a scarcity) in the world. To be successful you have to do two things: understand where the bottlenecks will be developing in the new world, and discover how to develop a distinctive capability in some of these areas. We are starting to see how scenarios can contribute in both tasks.

Another area under development is the psychological perspective on scenario thinking. Here it is suggested that the big payout of scenario work is in the avoidance of thinking traps and flaws that condition the human mind. Scenario practitioners are becoming increasingly interested in the psychology of scenario thinking to improve their facilitation effectiveness in general. This is related to the increased interest in scenarios as tools in the world of management. While in the past the world of management was associated with 'implementation' of strategy thought out in the top of the organization, modern practice recognizes the social nature of knowledge and the need to harness the thinking capability of the whole organization in developing superior strategy. We have discoved scenarios as the ideal tool to turn the power of social networking into the effectiveness of the 'strategic conversation'. This is where facilitation skills and knowledge infrastructure are becoming increasingly important.

However, some people see danger signals ahead and warn us of negative developments. The main one concerns superficial work by practitioners who find it difficult to stand up to clients' demands for standardized processes, fixed budgets and deadlines. New clients do not always clearly understand that this is not another version of the mechanistic forecasting we did in the past, but about new and original ways of strategic thinking. This is a big dilemma for most practitioners. At what point are you constrained to such a degree that it becomes highly unlikely that any sort of 'magic' arrives, leading to a dissatisfied client and making the whole thing counter-productive? There are too many reports of projects that ended in a big 'so what' question for the client because the conditions for creating original insights and turning them into effective action were ignored.

You cannot legislate for invention. It will take its own sweet time to arrive. But the good news is that it will always come if you prepare the ground and give it enough time.

REFERENCES

Ackoff, R.L. (1999) *Re-Creating the Corporation: A Design of Organizations for the 21st Century.* Oxford: Oxford University Press.

Amado, G. and Ambrose, A. (eds) (2001) *The Transitional Approach to Change.* London: Karnak Books.

Argyris, C. (1991) Teaching smart people how to learn, *Harvard Business Review*, May-June.

Argyris, C. (1993) *Knowledge for Action.* San Francisco: Jossey-Bass.

Bates, C. (2000) What is the future of the Tobacco Industry? *Tobacco Control*, **9**, 237–238.

Berger, P. and Luckman, T. (1966) *The Social Construction of Reality.* London: Penguin.

Boisot, M. (1998) *Knowledge Assets: Securing Competitive Advantage in the Information Economy.* Oxford: Oxford University Press.

Buchanan, L. (2006) A brief history of decision making, *Harvard Business Review*, January.

Bunn, D.W. and Salo, A.A. (1993) Forecasting with scenarios, *European Journal of Operational Research*, **68**, 291–303.

Carmichael, J., Tansey, J. and Robinson, J. (2004) An integrated assessment modelling tool, *Global Environmental Change*, **14**, 171–183.

Chesbrough, H.W. (2003) *Open Innovation: The New Imperative for Creating and Profiting from Technology.* Boston, USA: Harvard Business School Press.

Chicoine, G. (2004) *Deconstructing the Future – The Case for Scenario Planning.* http://www.greaterviability.com/articles/deconstructing.htm.

Christensen, C.M. (1997) *The Innovator's Dilemma.* Boston, USA: Harvard Business School Press.

Christensen, C.M. and Raynor, M.E. (2003) *The Innovator's Solution: Creating and Sustaining Successful Growth*. Boston, USA: Harvard Business School Press.

Christensen, C.M., Anthony, S.D. and Roth, E.A. (2004) *Seeing What's Next – Using the Theories of Innovation to Predict Industry Change*. Boston, USA: Harvard Business School Press.

Collins, J. (2001) *Good to Great*. New York: Random House.

Curry, A., Hodgson, A., Kelnar, R. and Wilson, A. (2006) *Intelligent Infrastructure Futures: The Scenarios – Towards 2055*. London: Foresight Directorate.

Damasio, A. (2000) *The Feeling of What Happens: Body, Emotion, and the Making of Consciousness*. New York: Vintage Books.

De Bono, E. (1992) *Serious Creativity: Using the Power of Lateral Thinking to Create New Ideas*. London: HarperBusiness.

de Geus, A. (1997) *The Living Company: Habits for Survival in a Turbulent Business Environment*. Boston, USA: Harvard Business School Press.

Denning, S. (2005) *The Leader's Guide to Storytelling: Mastering the Art of the Business Narrative*. San Francisco: Jossey-Bass.

Dreborg, K. (1996) Essence of backcasting, *Futures*, **28**(9), 813–828.

Dumez, H. and Jeunmaitre, A. (2006) Reviving narratives in economics and management: Towards an integrated perspective of modelling, statistical inference and narratives, *European Management Review*, **3**, 32–43.

Einhorn, H.J. and Hogarth, R.M. (1981) Behavioral decision theory: processes of judgement and choice, *Annual Review of Psychology*, **32**, 53–88.

Emery, F.E. and Trist, E.L. (1965) The causal texture of organizational environments, *Human Relations*, **18**, 21–32.

Emery, F.E. and Trist, E.L. (1972) *Towards a Social Ecology: Contextual Appreciations of the Future in the Present*. New York: Plenum/Rosetta.

Ertel, C. (1998) *Research in Scenario Planning at GBN*. Emeryville, CA: Global Business Network (4 May).

Fink, A. and Siebe, A. (2006) *Handbuch Zukunftsmanagement* (Handbook Future Management). Campus.

Fink, A., Siebe, A. and Kuhle, J.-P. (2004) How scenarios support strategic early warning processes, *Foresight*, **6**(3).

Fink, A., Marr, B., Siebe, A. and Kuhle, J.-P. (2005) The future scorecard: Combining external and internal scenarios to create strategic foresight, *Management Decisions*, **43**(3).

Friedman, T. (1999) *The Lexus and the Olive Tree: Understanding Globalization*. New York: Farrar, Straus & Giroux.

Gersick, C.J.G. (1988) Time and transition in work teams: Towards a new model of group development, *Academy of Management Journal*, **31**, 9–41.

Gilad, B. (2004) *Early Warning*. New York, USA: AMACOM.

Gloor, P.A. (2006) *Swarm Creativity: Competitive advantage through collaborative innovation networks*, pp. 4–12. Oxford: Oxford University Press.

Gosselink, J.W. (2002) Pathways to a more sustainable production of energy: Sustainable hydrogen – a research objective for Shell. *International Journal of Hydrogen Energy*, **27**, 1125–1129.

Grant, R.M. (2003). Strategic planning in a turbulent environment: Evidence from the oil majors, *Strategic Management Journal*, **24**, 491–517.

Hampden-Turner, C. (1990) *Charting the Corporate Mind – From Dilemma to Strategy*, Oxford: Basil Blackwell.

Heckscher, C., Maccoby, M., Ramírez, R. and Tixier, P.-E. (2003) *Agents of Change: Crossing the Post-Industrial Divide*. Oxford: Oxford University Press.

Hines, A. (2003) Applying integral futures to environmental scanning, Futures Research Quarterley, Winter.

Hmimda, N. and Hultén, S. (2005) *Social Construction of Technology: Verification, Certification, Social Cognition, Adoption and Diffusion*. Paper presented to 4th EMAEE conference, Utrecht.

Holland, J.H., Holyoak, K.J., Nisbett, R.E. and Thagard, P.R. (1986) *Induction – Processes of Inference, Learning and Discovery*. Cambridge: MIT Press.

Horn, R. (2000) *Apparent Strategy of Genetically Modified Food Companies*. http://www.macrovu.com/GMProStrategy.html.

Hufbauer, G.C. and Mitrokostas, N.K. (2003) *The Awakening Monster: The Alien Tort Statute of 1789*. Institute for International Economics. Washington DC: USA

Hutchins, E. (1995) *Cognition in the Wild*. Cambridge, USA: MIT Press.

Hutzchenreuter, T. and Kleindienst, I. (2006) Strategy-process research: What we have learned and what is still to be explored, *Journal of Management*, **32**(5), 673–720.

Iansiti, M. and Levien, R. (2004) Strategy as ecology. *Harvard Business Review*, **82**(3), 68–77.

Idenburg, P.J. (2005) *Oog voor de toekomst; Over marketing en consumenten in een veranderende samenleving* (Viewing Futures, on marketing and consumers in a changing society), Scriptum.

Inayatullah, S. (ed.) (2004) *The Causal Layered Analysis*. (CLA) Reader. Tamkung: Tamkang University.

Ingvar, D. (1985) Memory of the future: An essay on the temporal organization of conscious awareness, *Human Neurobiology*, **4**(3), 127–136.

Janis, I. and Mann, L. (1977) *Decision-making, a Psychological Analysis of Conflict, Choice and Commitment*. New York: Free Press.

Johnson, L.K. (2005) Sharpening Strategic Focus, *Balanced Scorecard Report*, **7**(4), 7.

Jungermann, H. (1985a) Inferential processes in the construction of scenarios, *Journal of Forecasting*, **4**, 321–327.

Jungermann, H. (1985b) The psychological aspects of scenarios. In Covello, V.T., Mumpower, J.L., Stallen, P.J.M. and Uppuluri, V.R.R. (eds) *Environmental Impact Assessment, Technology Assessment and Risk Analysis*. Berlin: Springer-Verlag.

Kaplan, R. and Norton, D. (1996) Using the balanced scorecard as a strategic management system, *Harvard Business Review*, January-February.

Kaplan, R. and Norton, D. (2000) Having trouble with your strategy? Then map it, *Harvard Business Review*, September-October.

Khakee, A. (1991) Scenario Construction for Urban Planning, *International Journal of Management Science*, **19**(5), 459–469.

Kleiner, A. (1990) Consequential heresies: How 'thinking the unthinkable' changed Royal/Dutch Shell. *Global Business Network Training Manual*. Emeryville, CA: Global Business Network.

Kuhn, T. (1996) *The Structure of Scientific Revolutions*. Chicago: University of Chicago Press.

Lee Kuan Yew (2006) Speech at the World Leadership Summit, *The Straits Times*, 22 November, p. 19.

Leonard, D. and Swap, W. (2004) Deep smarts, *Harvard Business Review*, **82**(9), 88–98.

Lesourne, J. and Stoffaes, C. (eds) (2001) *La prospective straté gique d'entreprise: De la réflexionà l'action*. Paris: Dunod.

Levin, B. and Nordfors, L. (1999) *Vem tar Makten?* Stockholm: Ekerlids förlag.

Mankins, M. (2004) Stop wasting valuable time, *Harvard Business Review*, **82**(9), 58–66.

Mankins, M.C. and Steele, R. (2006) Stop making plans: Start making decisions, *Harvard Business Review*, January, p. 83.

Medjad, K. (2006) *In search of the hard law: Judicial activism and international corporate social responsibility.* In Allouche, J. (eds) *Corporate Social Responsibility*, pp. 181–204. London: Palgrave McMillan.

Moore, G.A. (1999) *Crossing the Chasm: Marketing and Selling High-Tech Products to Mainstream Customers*. London: HarperBusiness.

Morgan, G., Kandlikar, M., Risbey, J. and Dowlatabadi, H. (1999) Why conventional tools for policy analysis are often inadequate for problems of global change, *Climatic Change*, **41**, 271–281.

Moss Kanter, R. (2002) Strategy as improvisational theater. *MIT Sloan Management Review*, Winter, 76–81.

Neef, A. and Daheim, C. (2005) Corporate foresight. The European experience, *Foresight, Innovation and Strategy*. World Future Society. Bethesda, Maryland, USA.

Normann, R. (2001) *Reframing Business – When the Map Changes the Landscape*. Chichester: John Wiley & Sons Ltd.

Normann, R. and Ramírez, R. (1993) From value chain to value constellation: Designing interactive strategy, *Harvard Business Review*, July–August, 65–77.

Nye, J.S. (2004) *Soft Power: The Means to Success in World Politics*. Cambridge, MA: Public Books.

Ogilvy, J. and Schwartz, P. (2004) *Plotting Your Scenarios*. Emeryville, CA: Global Business Network.

Pascale, R.T., Milleman, M. and Goija, L. (2001) *Surfing the Edge of Chaos: The Laws of Nature and the New Laws of Business*. New York: Three Rivers Press.

Porter, M.E. (1998) *On Competition*. Boston, USA: Harvard Business School Press.

Porter, M.E. (2004) *Competitive Advantage*. New York: The Free Press.

Quist, J.N. (2003) Greening foresighting through backcasting: more than looking back from the future. *Greener Management International*.

Rabobank (2002) Economic Trends, Political Trends, Societal Trends, Technological Trends, Ecological Trends (five trend reports were published internally).

Rabobank (2003) *Rentescenario's 'the price of money'*, September (external thematic publication).

Ramírez, R. (1996) Reinventing Italy: Methodological Challenges, *Futures*, April.

Ramírez, R. and Wallin, J. (2000) *Prime Movers*. Chichester: John Wiley & Sons.

Ringland, G. (2006) *Scenario Planning*. Chichester: John Wiley & Sons Ltd.

Ringland, G. and Young, L. (eds) (2006) *Scenarios in Marketing*. Chichester: John Wiley & Sons Ltd.

Ringland, G., Edwards, M., Hammond, L., Heinzen, B., Rendell, A., Sparrow, O. and White, E. (1999) Shocks and paradigm busters, *Long Range Planning*, October.

Robinson, J. (1988) Unlearning and backcasting: Rethinking some of the questions we ask about the future, *Technological Forecasting and Social Change*, **33**, 325–338.

Robinson, J. (2003) Future subjunctive: Backcasting as social learning, *Futures*, **35**, 839–856.

Schön, D.A. (1983) *The Reflective Practitioner: How Professionals Think in Action*. New York: Basic Books.

Schwartz, P. (1991/1996) *The Art of the Long View: Planning for the Future in an Uncertain World*. New York: DoubleDay.

Seely Brown, J. and Duguid, P. (2002) *The Social Life of Information*. Boston, USA: Harvard Business School Press.

Selin, C. (2006) Time matters: Temporal harmony and dissonance in nanotechnology networks, *Time and Society* **5**(1), 121–139.

Sharpe, W. and Hodgson, A. (2005) *Intelligent Infrastructure Futures Technology Forward Look – Towards A Cyber-Urban Ecology*. London: Foresight Directorate, UK Government.

Shell (2005) *Shell Global Scenarios to 2025 – The Future Business Environment: Trends, Trade-offs and Choices*. Shell: London and The Hague.

Slaughter, R. (1999) A new framework for environmental scanning, *Foresight (Camford Publishing)*, **1**(5).

Slaughter, R. (2004) *Futures Beyond Dystopia*. London: RoutledgeFalmer.

Smith, E.A and Malone, R.E. (2003) Thinking the 'unthinkable': Why Philip Morris considered quitting, *Tobacco Control*, **12**, 208–213.

Snowden, D. (2002) Complex acts of knowing: Paradox and descriptive self awareness, *Journal of Knowledge Management*, **6**(2).

Spinosa, C., Flores, F. and Dreyfus, H. (1997) *Disclosing New Worlds*. Cambridge, MA: MIT Press.

Tansey, J. (2006) Interactive sustainability, *Special Issue: Integrated Assessment Journal*, **6**(4). www.iajonline.org.

Tansey, J., Carmichael, J., Van Wynsberghe, R. and Robinson, J. (2002) The future is not what it used to be: Participatory integrated assessment in the Georgia Basin, *Global Environmental Change*, **12**(2), 97–104.

Tibbs, H. (1998) In memory of Pierre Wack, *Netview*. Emeryville, CA: Global Business Network.

Tilly, C. (2005) *Why?* Princeton, NJ: Princeton University Press.

Trist, E.L., Emery, F.E. and Murray, H. (eds) (1997) *The Social Engagement of Social Science Vol. III: The Socio-Ecological Perspective*. Philadelphia: University of Pennsylvania Press.

Tversky, A. and Kahneman, D. (1982) Judgements under uncertainty: Heuristics and Biases. In Kahneman, D., Slovic, P. and Tversky, A. (eds) *Judgements Under Uncertainty: Heuristics and Biases*. Cambridge: Cambridge University Press.

UN (1999) *Global Compact*. United Nations Organization. http://www.unglobalcompact.org.

Van der Heijden, K. (1996) *Scenarios: The Art of Strategic Conversation*. Chichester: John Wiley & Sons Ltd.

Van der Heijden, K. (2005) *Scenarios: The Art of Strategic Conversation*, 2nd Edition. Chichester: John Wiley & Sons Ltd.

Verloop, J. (2004) *Insight in Innovation*. Amsterdam: Elsevier.

Vickers, G. (1965) *The Art of Judgement*. London: Harper and Row.

Vygotsky, L.S. (1986) *Thought and Language*. Cambridge, MA: MIT Press.

Wack, E. (1998) *Pierreve: 1977–1997* Curemonte, France, 15 April (unpublished).

Wack, P. (1984a) *Scenarios: The Gentle Art of Re-perceiving, A Thing or Two Learned while Developing Planning Scenarios for Royal Dutch/Shell*, Harvard Business School Working Paper, pp. 1–77.

Wack, P. (1984b) Scenarios: Uncharted waters ahead, *Harvard Business Review*, **63**(5), 73–89.

Wack, P. (1984c) Scenarios: Shooting the rapids, *Harvard Business Review*, **63**(6), 139–150.

Wack, P. (1993) *Scenario Planning Seminar*. Presentation at Global Business Network (19 April).

Wack, P. (1995) *Planning in Turbulent Times*. Presentation at Global Business Network.

Wales Tourist Board Scenarios Report (2007) Wales Tourist Board website (now VisitWales) no longer includes the report; available at http://cycling.visitwales.com/upload/pdf/Futures_eng.pdf.

Weick, K. (2001) *Making Sense of the Organization*. Malden, MA: Blackwell.

Weisbord, M. and Janoff, S. (2000) *Future Search: An Action Guide to Finding Common Ground in Organizations and Societies*. San Francisco: Berrett-Koehler.

Wheatley, M.J. (2001) *Leadership and the New Science: Discovery Order in a Chaotic World Revised*. San Francisco Berrett-Koehler Publisher.

White, W.H. (1956) *The Organizational Man*. New York: Doubleday.

WHO (2002) *The Tobacco Atlas*. World Health Organization. http://www.who.int/tobacco/statistics/tobacco_atlas/en/.

Wilson, I. (1997) Mental maps of the future: An intuitive logics approach to scenarios. In Fahey, L. and Randall, R. (eds) *Learning from the Future*. New York: John Wiley & Sons.

Wilson, I. (1998) An Obituary for Pierre Wack, *Planning Review*, **31**(1), iii.

Winnicott, D.E. (1965) *The Maturational Process and the Facilitating Environment*. London: Hogarth Books.

Wright, A. (2005) The role of scenarios as prospective sensemaking devices, *Management Decision*, **43**(1). www.transhumanism.org.

Yankelovich, D. (1999) *The Magic of Dialogue*. New York: Touchstone.

Zentner, R.D. (1975) Scenarios in forecasting, *Chemical and Engineering News*, **October**(6), 22–34.

INDEX

Scenarios for Success: Turning Insights into Action   Edited by Bill Sharpe and Kees Van der Heijden
© 2007 John Wiley & Sons, Ltd

Index compiled by Annette Musker